IMAGES
of America

RAYNE

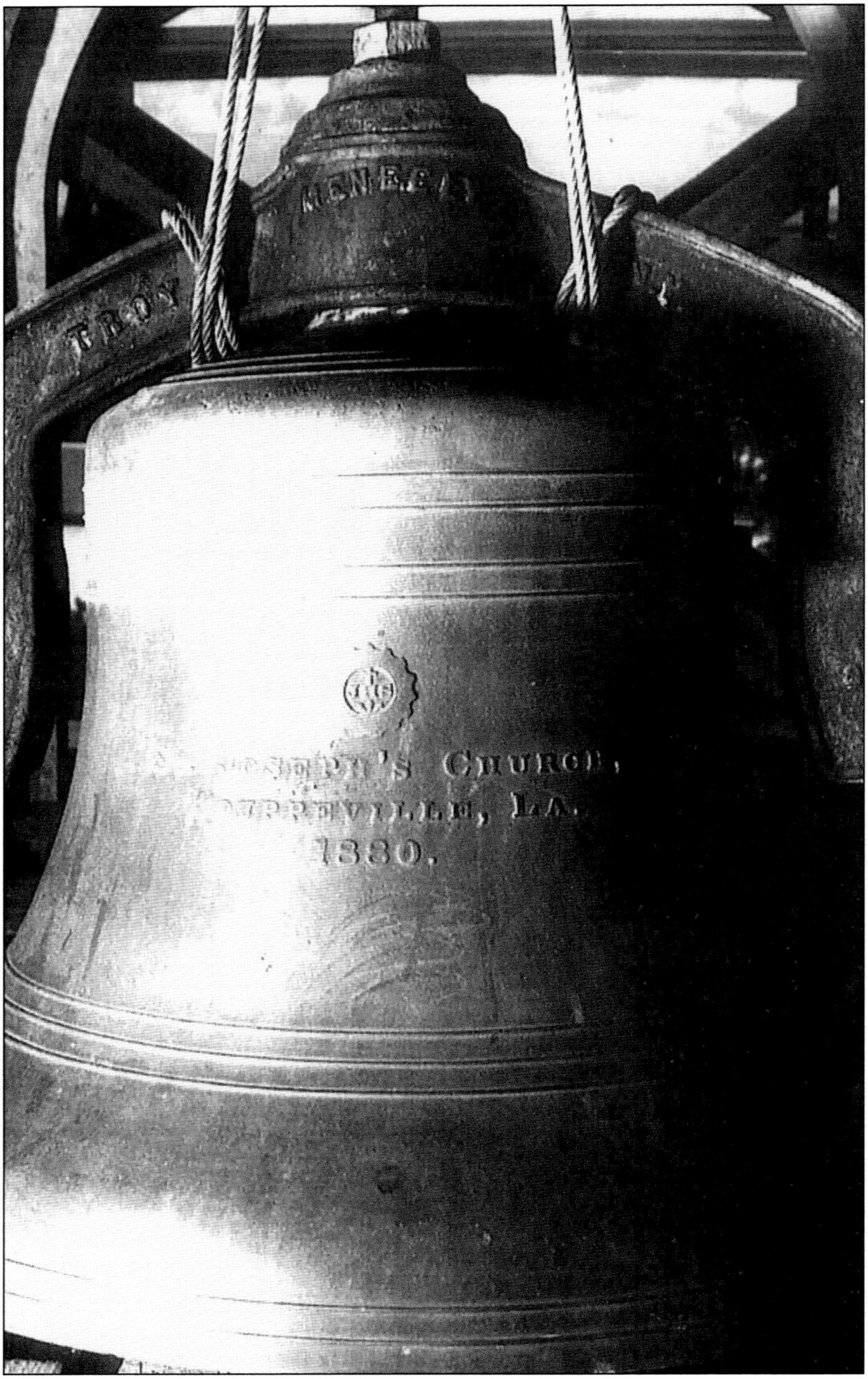

The original church bell from St. Joseph's Catholic Church in Poupeville, dated 1880, is in the current St. Joseph's Church. The bell was originally in the first church in Poupeville, which was moved by ox to Rayne. When the old Poupeville church was moved to Mire in 1960, the bell was placed in the second church, then in the third church, where it rings today. (Courtesy Charles S. Stutes.)

IMAGES of America

RAYNE

Cheryl McCarty and Tony Olinger

ARCADIA PUBLISHING

ISBN 978-0-7385-1471-0

Published by Arcadia Publishing
Charleston, South Carolina

Printed in the United States of America

Library of Congress Catalog Card Number: 2002108732

For all general information contact Arcadia Publishing at:
Telephone 843-853-2070
Fax 843-853-0044
E-Mail sales@arcadiapublishing.com
For customer service and orders:
Toll-Free 1-888-313-2665

Visit us on the Internet at www.arcadiapublishing.com

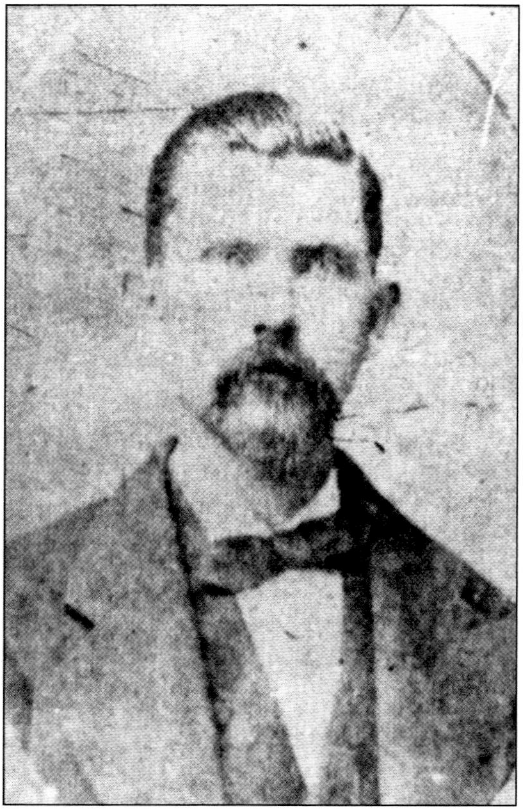

Dr. William Harris Cunningham is considered the founder of Rayne. He purchased 1,157 acres around Rayne Station from the heirs of Antoine Mouton in 1880. He had the land surveyed into town lots and sold them for $5 per lot and sometimes less. He gave lots to both the church and school. The remaining lots were sold at public auction of his estate after his death in 1881. (Courtesy Charles S. Stutes.)

Contents

Acknowledgments		6
Introduction		7
1.	A City Emerges	9
2.	City Commerce	23
3.	Educational Foundation	61
4.	Fabulous Frogs	69
5.	Streetscapes	79
6.	Planes, Trains, and Automobiles	85
7.	Building Blocks	93
8.	Famous Faces	105
9.	Events and Cultural Celebrations	115

ACKNOWLEDGMENTS

At the very beginning of this project, we wondered how the people of Rayne would react to our request to share their family pictures with the rest of the world. In the beginning it was a slow process, but it soon picked up to a feverish pace. With the help of our two newspapers, *The Rayne Independent* and *The Rayne-Acadian Tribune* running photos of yesterday, the word soon got out and we had calls from people who live in the New Orleans area all the way to Tulsa, Oklahoma—people who get the local papers and wanted to contribute to the book.

To tackle a project as large as this, one must know the history of Rayne and where the pictures will fit. We would like to thank Mary Alice Fontenot and Rev. Paul Freeland for their previous works on the history of Acadia Parish as well as Gene Thibodeaux for his recent written history of Rayne. Their works laid down the framework of Rayne history and made our endeavor a success. We would like to thank several local historians who helped out tremendously with the book including Fair Craig Hash, who learned of Rayne's history from stories her mother, Myrta Fair Craig, told her. Her family was involved for many years with the *Tribune* and we were privileged she shared her pictures and stories with us. Known as a Rayne historian, Charles S. Stutes graciously let us go through his files and copy the pictures we needed. His zest for history was contagious and in talking to him about Rayne, it became clear why he is a favorite teacher among his students. With his retirement looming, we are sure Mr. Sidney has more projects up his sleeve.

We would like to thank Jo Cart and Becky Boudreaux of *The Rayne Independent* for sharing their resources, knowledge, and pictures for our project. Aunt Jo has always supported and helped us in our endeavors and we appreciate all she has done. Thanks to Carl Blanchard for his Mac and expertise with some of our pictures in need and Donald Petitjean for his picture collection and his good eye for faces. We appreciate the help of Paul Kedinger, Carol Stutes, and Josie Henry of *The Rayne-Acadian Tribune* who allowed us into their safe to do research. We would also like to extend our thanks to the staff of the Rayne Branch Library for their help in researching information and with the microfilm machine.

We would like to thank Hilary and Melba Olinger with their help tracking down pictures and Rose Marie "Sis" Stelly for her help with identifying people in pictures for the book. We would also like to thank the following who donated pictures: Doug Ashy Building Materials, Pete Babineaux, Lucille Barrows, Michael "Pickle" Besse, Margie Breaux, Valerie Borne, Rhonda and Tom Broussard, Jim and Mary Ann Bush, Clarence Cahanin, Josie Cook, Lucille Daigle, Raymond Domingue, Willie Etta, Joyce Faulk, Andrus Fontenot, Norma Gardiner, Margo Goertz, Annette Gossen, Jeremy Granger, Lawrence Guidry, Norman Hanks, Faye Harrington, Ray Hebert, Marguerite Kahn Hoskins, Tucker Johnston, Tom Johnson, Lafayette Clerk of Court, Nanette Leblanc, Steve Leblanc, Phyllis Leonards, Marjorie Hains McCarty, Dr. Ed Moody, Freddie and Carolyn Morgan, Julie Ousse, Albert Owers, Martin Petitjean II, Louis Plattsmier, Hazel Prevost, Louis Privat, Rayne Fire Department, Rayne State Bank, Yvette Babineaux Richard, Myrtle Servat, Virginia Soileau, Sue Babineaux Stutes, Horace Thibodeaux, Doug Vincent, and Margaret Zaunbrecher.

We would like to especially thank Verna, Nolan, and Jim for the family time they gave up for this book to become a success. Our only regret was that we could not use all the great pictures that were given to us. Thanks to all who helped make this book a reality.

INTRODUCTION

The following words were captured in a 1907 report on the prosperity and importance of Rayne in the commercial world by Emile Daboval Jr., entitled "Rayne, Louisiana: Its Products and Industries and could only surmise what lay ahead for a city in its infancy."

> A glance at the map of Southwest Louisiana will convince you that Rayne, situated 160 miles west from New Orleans, is destined to be the most important center in the Parish (County) of Acadia; being on the main line of the Atlantic System of the Southern Pacific railroad running east and west; and also on the main line of the Opelousas, Gulf & Northeastern railroad (the Gould System), running north to the Texas & Pacific and south to the Vermilion Bay, the proposed deep water terminus selected for shipping port.
>
> Messrs. J.D. Bernard, F. Crouchet and others started to build a town one and a half miles south of the present site of Rayne, called Poupeville, but in 1879, the Southern Pacific company having secured its right of way, those gentlemen, realizing the importance of locating a town at once and with the use of oxen, moved every building from Poupeville to the place where the city now stands.
>
> In 1880 the first train of the Louisiana Western (Southern Pacific) was operated through the town and in 1886, it was incorporated with the Honorable J.D. Bernard, for its first mayor.
>
> The town is one and a half miles square and is beautifully situated between the rivers Wikoff and Queue de Tortue, with an elevation above the sea level of thirty-six feet.
>
> It has two well attended churches, three school houses, two banks, two rice mills, three cotton gins, one brick-making plant with a capacity of 100,000 bricks per day, one cotton seed oil mill of forty tons capacity, two lumber yards, two pop factories, three bakeries, ice factory, four butcher shops, opera house, newspaper and other industries too numerous to mention, including one of the most modern machine shops, a system of electric lights and water works, of which larger cities might be proud.
>
> The hotel accommodations are first-class in every respect. The Commercial Hotel, a modern two-story building, is owned and managed by Miss Nellie Clark
>
> The town has very wide streets, with eight and ten feet sidewalks, along which a number of shade trees have been planted, giving the city a typical southern appearance.
>
> The cane, cotton, corn and rice crops cultivated in the country tributary to Rayne, make it the largest shipping center west of Lafayette. The land being so well adapted for the cultivation of these four products, insures the town of Rayne a continued prosperity and future aggrandizement.
>
> Rayne possesses natural drainage by a system of ditches, which carry the water to the rivers on either side of the city.
>
> The climate of Rayne is by far the healthiest in Southwest Louisiana, reminding one of Southern California. In an air line we are about forty miles from the Gulf of Mexico and naturally we receive the gulf breeze during the summer, and with the magnificent

oak groves on the north we are amply protected from the winter winds.

The affairs of our town are ably administered by officers.

We are now contemplating the building of a public school house of white stone to cost in the neighborhood of $40,000, keeping this city well up with other communities in which progress for public education has made such rapid strides. This will insure those wishing to locate on this beautiful spot the intellectual development of their children; and with the churches, under the able and fatherly direction of their pastors, aid materially in developing the child to true American manhood.

If the City of Rayne has developed so wonderfully up to this writing, what will be in the near future, with two competing lines of railroad traversing its territory?"

One hundred years after the incorporation of the City of Rayne on May 2, 1883, this quaint community celebrated its centennial. Mayor Ralph Stutes, in an open letter to the citizens of Rayne, wrote the following:

One cannot peruse our past without being struck by the simple but powerful strength of the faith of our forefathers. Here they came to this locale with all the hopes and dreams that inspire people to move from one place to another. Here they settled—not in a major thoroughfare of commerce—but here in Rayne. It was here they found in each other that special quality which made them decide to call this home. And they set about immediately demonstrating their faith in their God and in each other. Here they built their churches and their schools. Here they built their homes. Here they married and reared their children, conducted their businesses, entertained themselves, and served each other. Here they lived their lives. Their community was an act of faith. The Rayne of 1983 is a gentle town—its people are gregarious, outgoing, concerned, sharing. There is a quiet reserved sense of pride in being regarded as a friendly community. Its churches are dynamic; its schools are progressive; its government is responsive. We are, in many ways, the typical American community.

For those that call Rayne home in 2002, the images in this book will bring to life a past many had forgotten and many never knew. This publication hopes to capture a past that typifies the strengths of all early families whose part is so firmly embedded in the history and building of today's Rayne—a city beginning its second 100 years of dedicated existence and looking forward to many more wonderful community contributions through the spirit of the families who will pass on the traditions of progress through time while remaining a lasting symbol of the pioneer spirit of the past.

One

A City Emerges

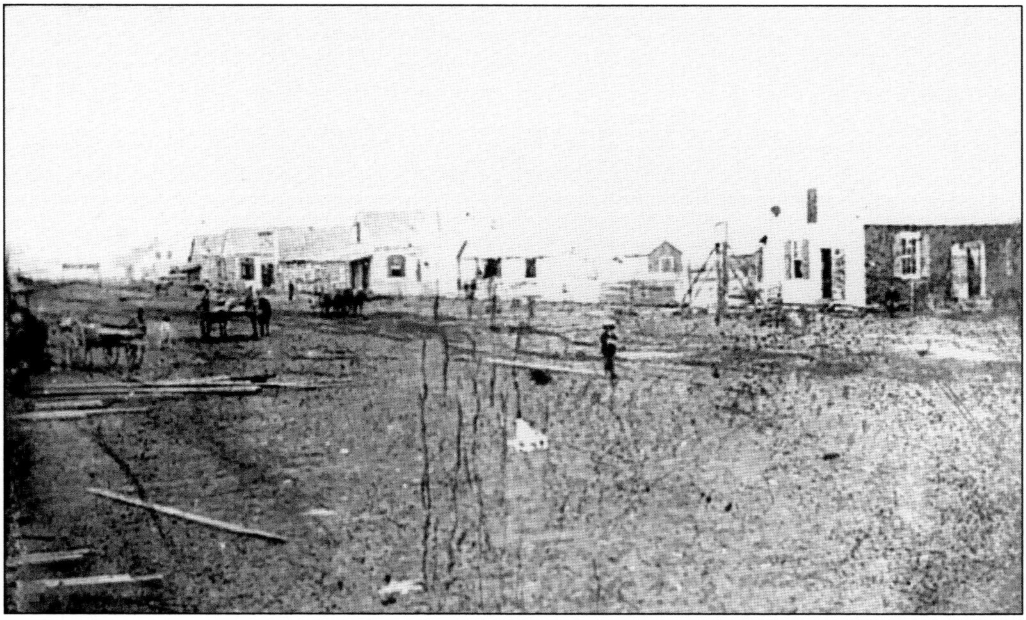

This early scene of Rayne, taken from an old tintype, shows Texas Avenue in the latter part of 1881. The buildings shown are, from left to right, Crouchet Hotel, Numa Chachere's Restaurant, J.D. Bernard's Store, Dr. Morris's Drugstore, Arenas Store, R.J.C. Bull's Office, Stranger's Hotel, and the Bourdier Home. (Courtesy Charles S. Stutes.)

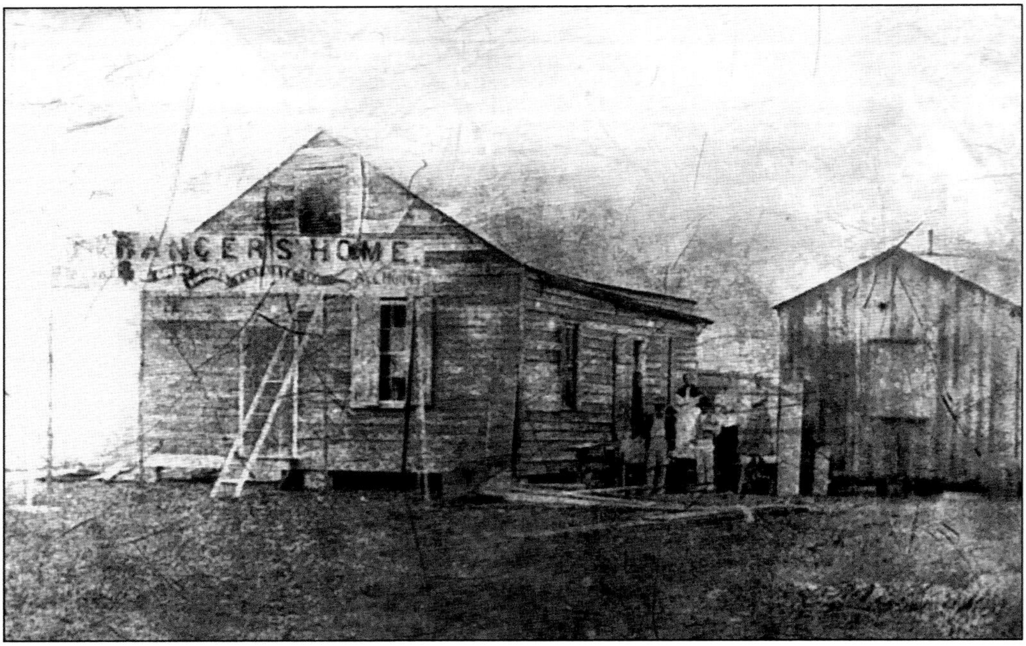

The Stranger's Home, Rayne's first hotel, was under construction in 1880–1881. It was owned by Mr. and Mrs. George Bourdier, who moved from Breaux Bridge to make their home in Rayne. (Courtesy Charles S. Stutes.)

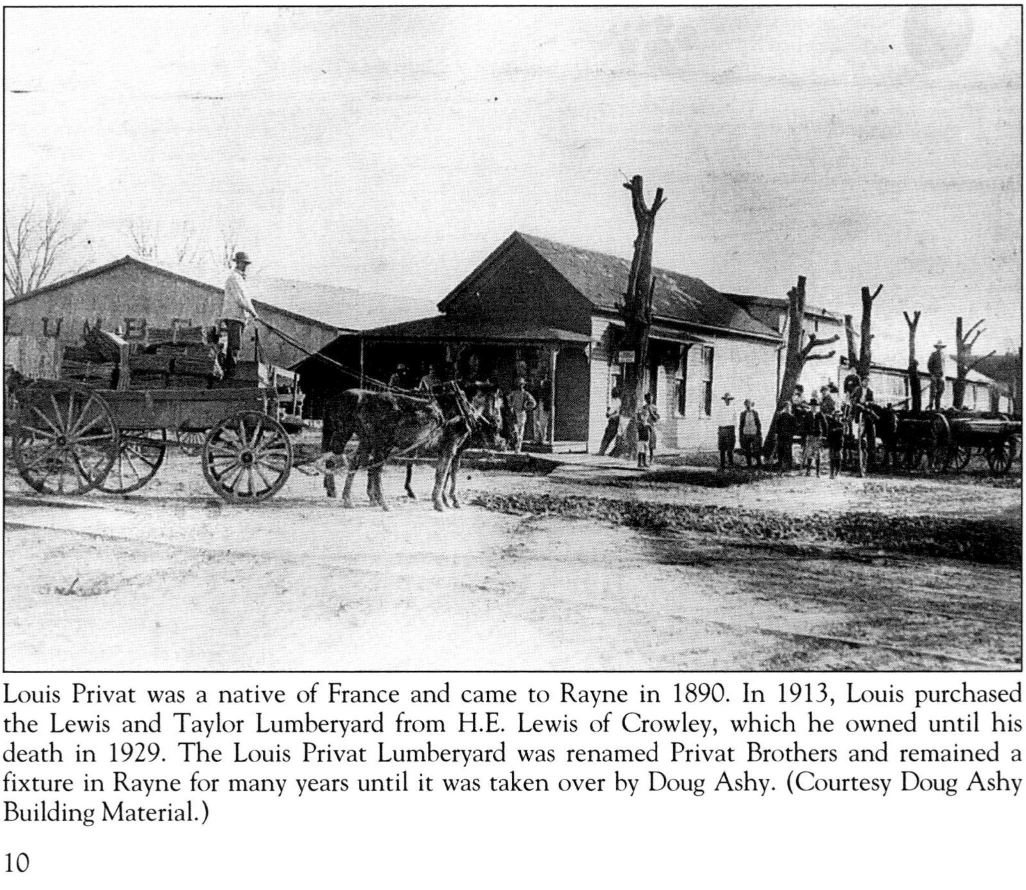

Louis Privat was a native of France and came to Rayne in 1890. In 1913, Louis purchased the Lewis and Taylor Lumberyard from H.E. Lewis of Crowley, which he owned until his death in 1929. The Louis Privat Lumberyard was renamed Privat Brothers and remained a fixture in Rayne for many years until it was taken over by Doug Ashy. (Courtesy Doug Ashy Building Material.)

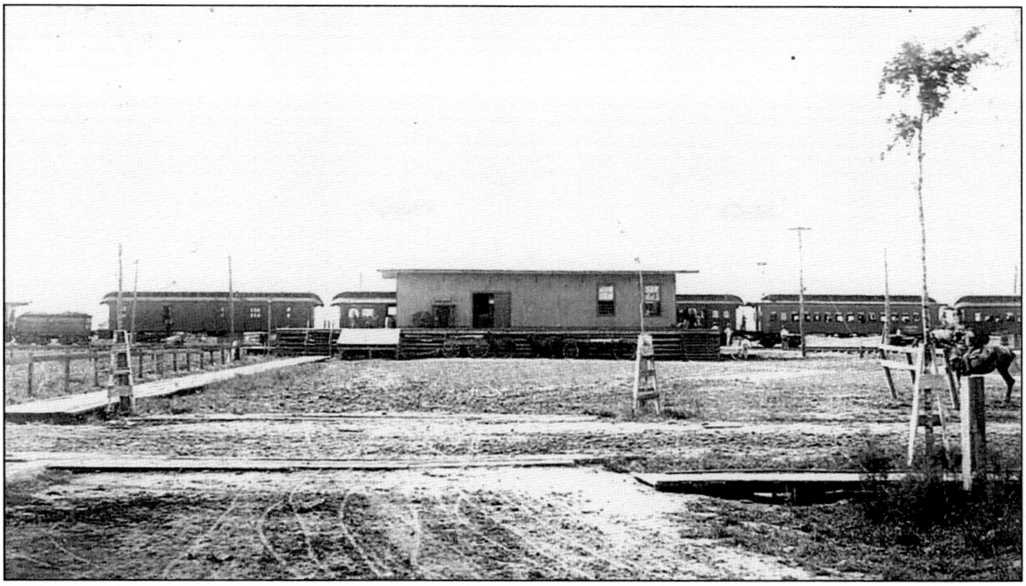

Early Cajun settlers of Southwest Louisiana, who established Poupeville, a sturdy Acadian community, demonstrated their courage and determination by moving businesses and homes one mile north and relocating on the site of the line of the Louisiana Western Railroad, the first depot serving the settlement renamed "Rayne." The coal-burning engine, coal car, and baggage and passenger cars were being serviced when this picture was taken in 1888. A.O. Boudreaux was the first telegraph operator at the Rayne Station. Facilities included a separate passenger depot, no longer on the Rayne scene. (Courtesy Fair Craig Hash.)

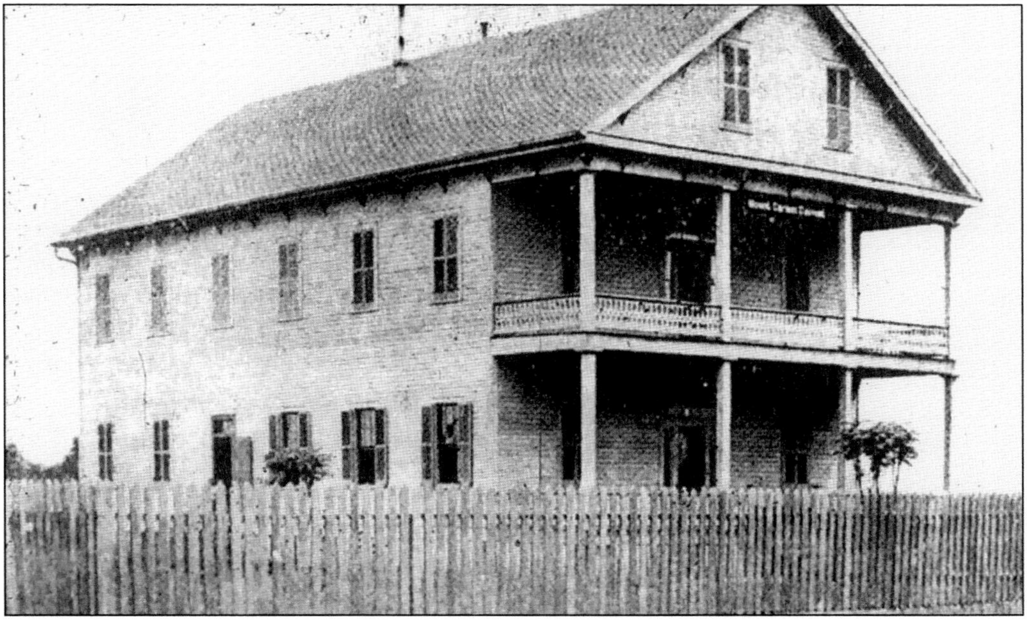

Mt. Carmel convent was constructed in 1892 after the arrival of the Sisters of Mount Carmel in 1891 and was the first catholic school in Acadia Parish. It was an all-female school and boarding house. The Mt. Carmel nuns lived on the second floor. One of the boarders at the school went on to become Sister Edith. It was located where Rayne Catholic Elementary now stands. (Courtesy Charles S. Stutes.)

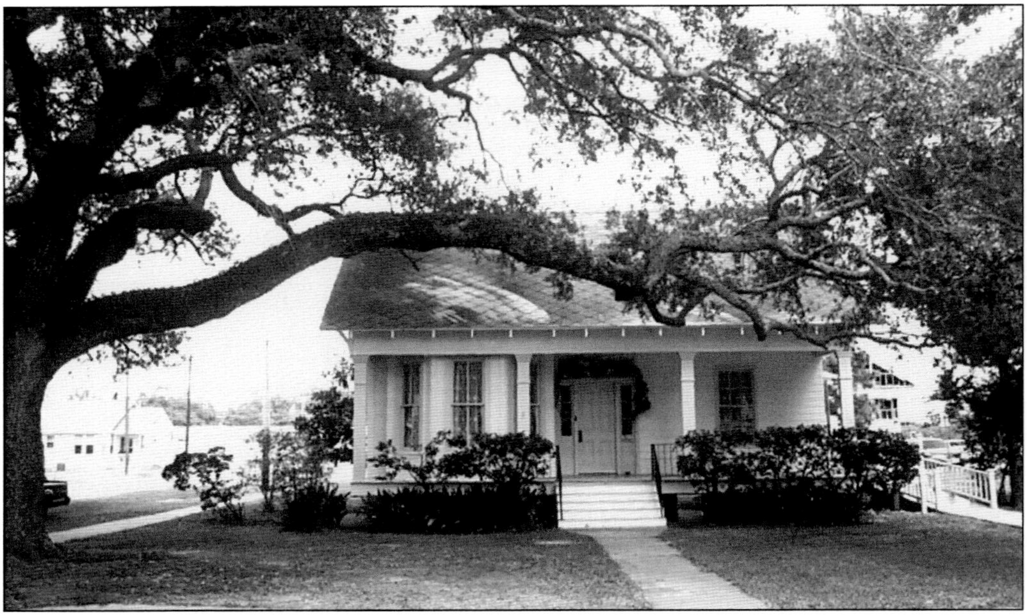

In 1883, when Rayne was still part of the old "Imperial St. Landry Parish," the Town of Rayne was incorporated and J.D. Bernard served as first mayor in recognition of his leadership in the formation of the new town. Shortly after, Bernard built the residence, which stands today as one of the few remaining early structures in Rayne. Originally, the home faced east along Devil's Alley and was bound on the south by West South First Street. It was later purchased by E.J. Bertrand, the operator of Rayne's Municipal Power Plant. The home was moved to its current location on the Boulevard to make way for the progress of growing businesses. The Bernard-Bertrand House is listed on the National Historic Registry and now serves as the City of Rayne's Cultural Center. (Courtesy Cheryl McCarty.)

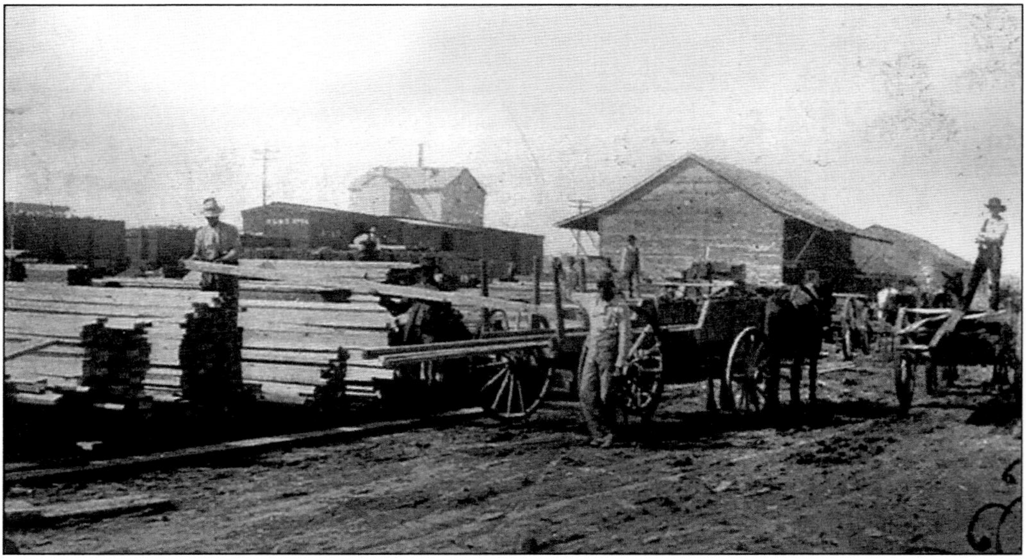

Lewis and Taylor Lumber Dealers was located on the corner of South Parkerson and East Texas Avenue in the 1880s. Like most businesses in Rayne, it was close to the railroad tracks for easy receiving of products. The business was later bought by Louis Privat in 1913. (Courtesy Charles S. Stutes.)

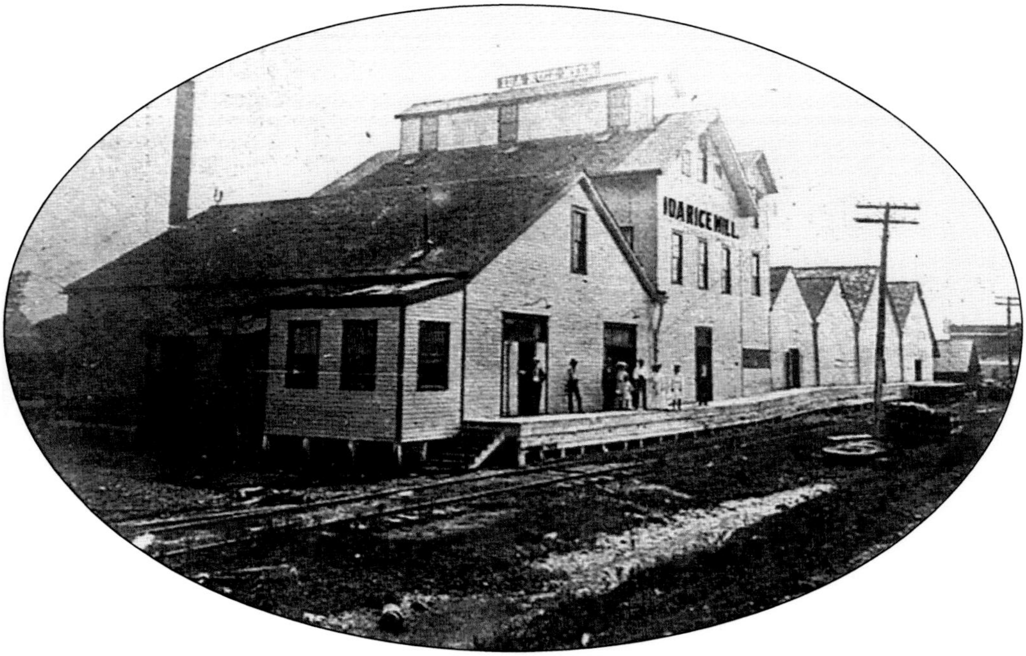

The oldest rice mill in Acadia Parish was the Acadia Rice Mill. Purchased by Jefferson Davis Marks, it was remodeled and named after his daughter Ida. The mill was totally consumed by fire in 1908. This was the first Louisiana rice mill operated outside of New Orleans and was a major step for rice production in South Louisiana. (Courtesy Charles S. Stutes.)

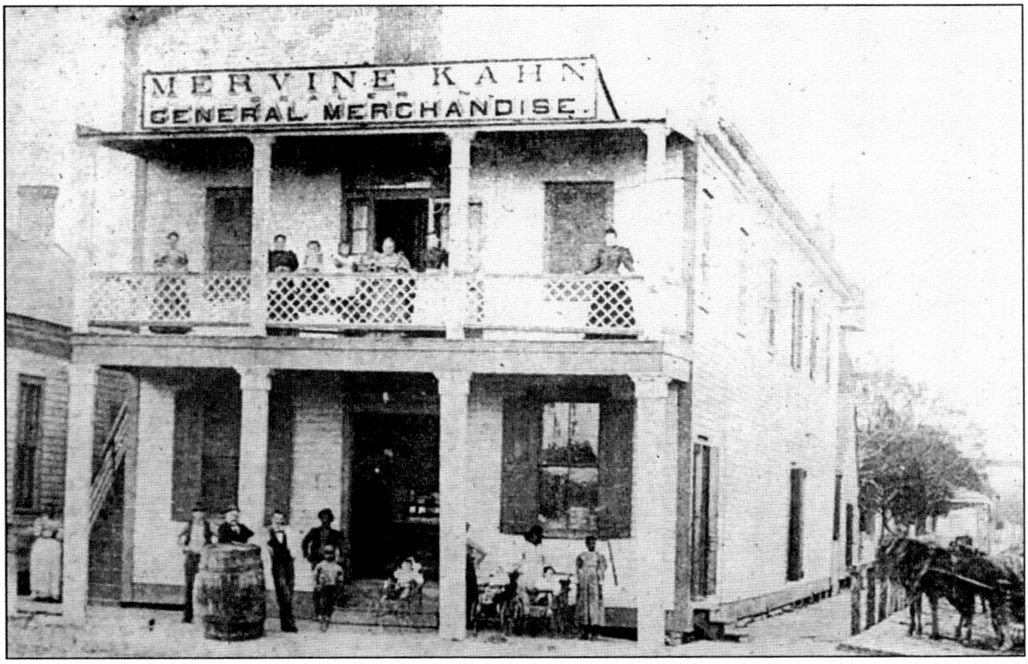

This is an exterior view of Mervine Kahn Dealer in General Merchandise taken in 1886. The family resided on the top floor until the business expanded and the upper floor was used for storage. Their motto was "money saved is money earned." They advertised selling James and Graham wagons, buggies, hacks, and agricultural implements. (Courtesy Fair Craig Hash.)

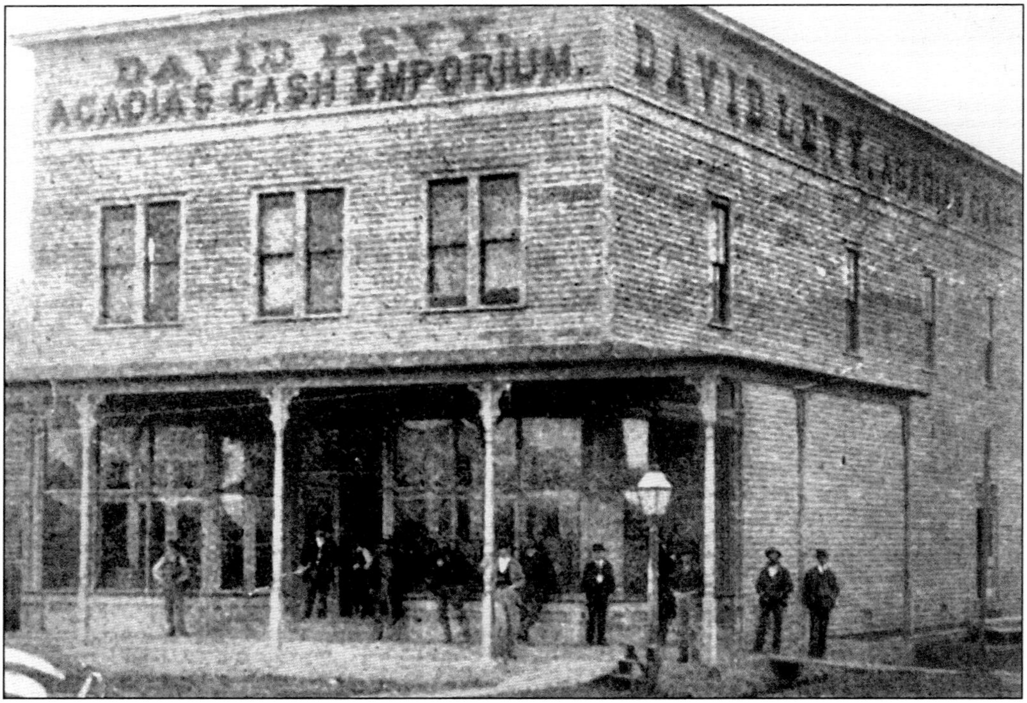

David Levy Acadia's Cash Emporium was located on the corner of Louisiana and North Adams Avenues. The wooden structure burned down in 1908 losing its entire inventory. (Courtesy Charles S. Stutes.)

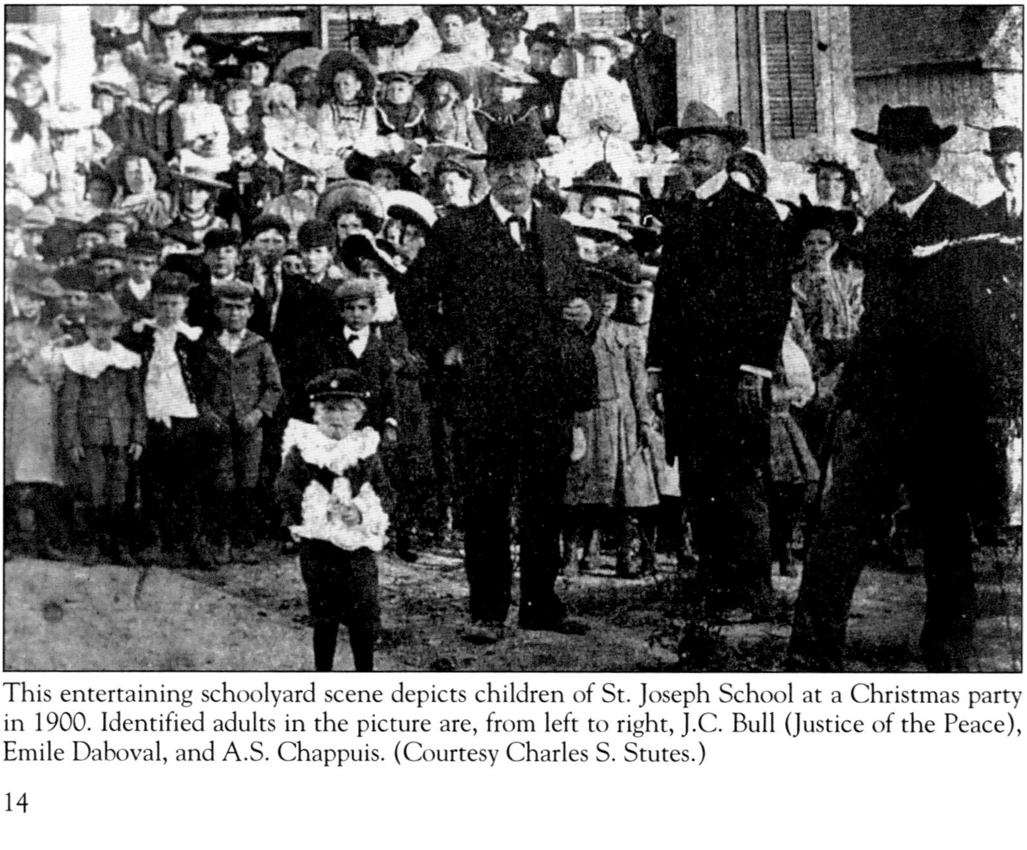
This entertaining schoolyard scene depicts children of St. Joseph School at a Christmas party in 1900. Identified adults in the picture are, from left to right, J.C. Bull (Justice of the Peace), Emile Daboval, and A.S. Chappuis. (Courtesy Charles S. Stutes.)

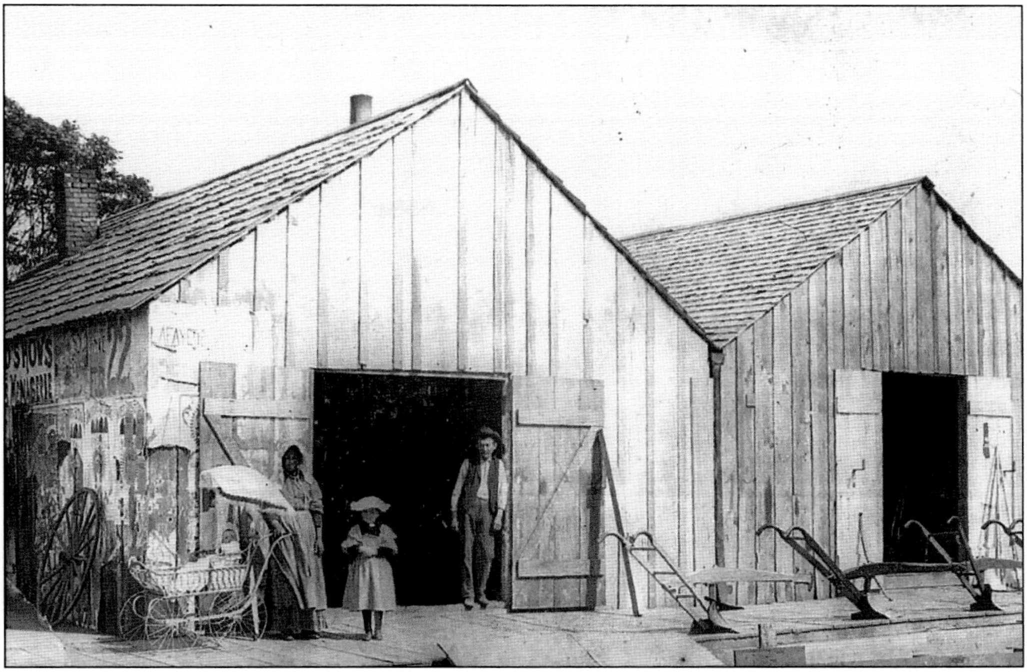

W.S. McBride, proprietor of McBride's Hardware Store, is shown standing in the doorway. Corinne Mouton, the daughter of Rayne pioneer physician Dr. G.C. Mouton, is in the baby carriage and her nursemaid keeps a watchful eye. The young girl is Ella McBride, W.S.'s daughter. (Courtesy Fair Craig Hash.)

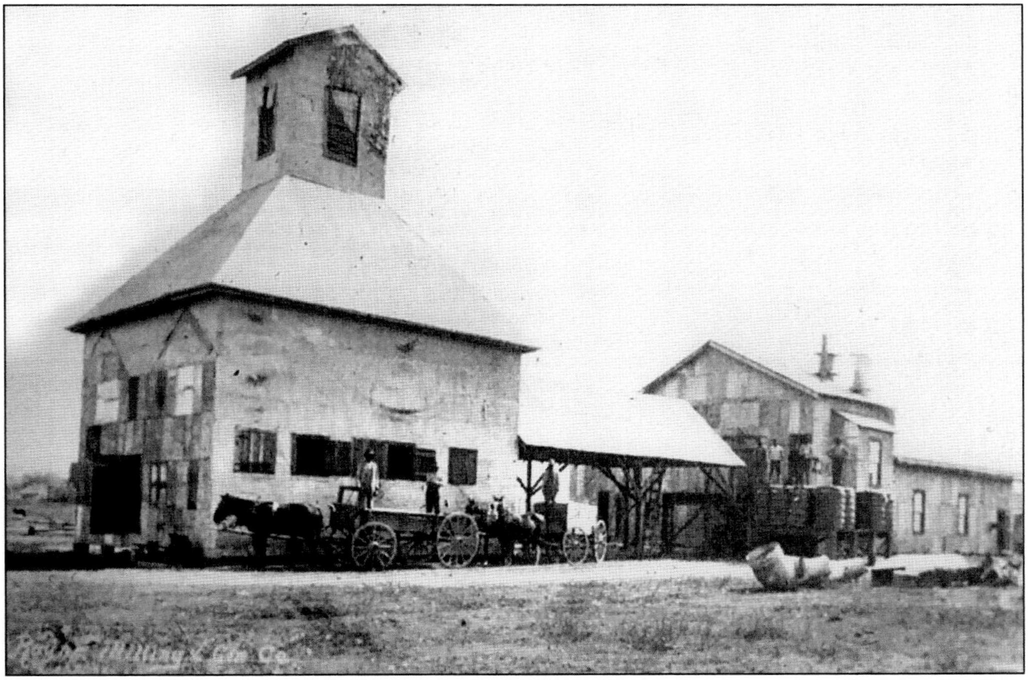

Several cotton gins served farmers of this area in the early days of Poupeville. They moved the operation to the railroad in the early 1880s as was this Acadia Cotton Gin Co. Ltd,. pictured at the peak of the season. (Courtesy Charles S. Stutes.)

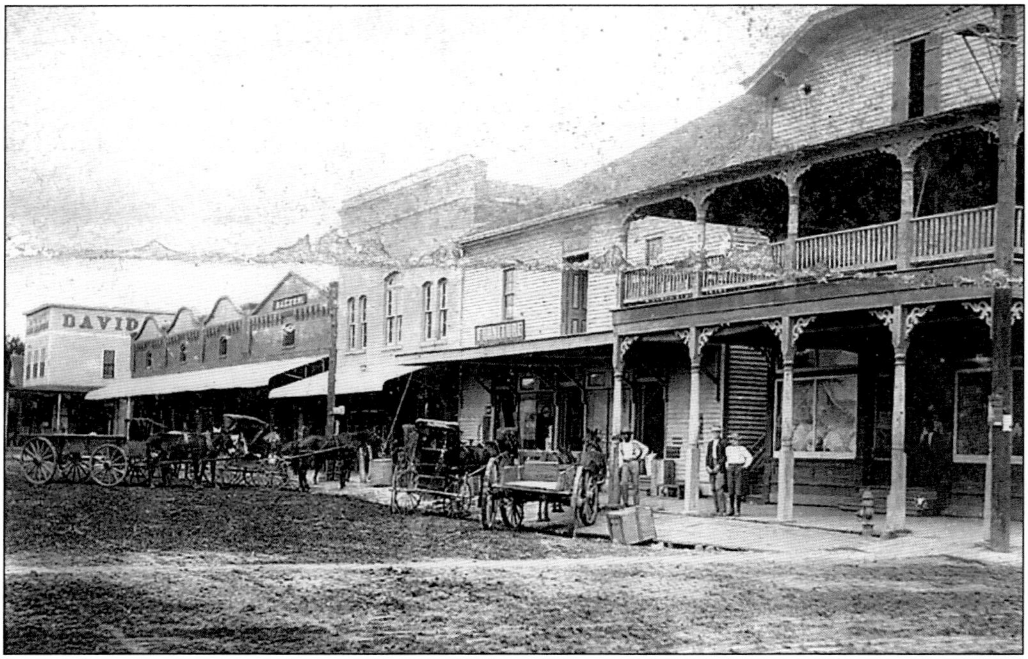

This westward view of Louisiana Avenue was taken in the 1890s and shows, from left to right, David Levy's Acadia Cash Emporium, Sol Kahn, a Restaurant and Furniture Store, and Mervine Kahn's. Notice the corner near Mervine's you can see a fire hydrant. (Courtesy Albert Owers.)

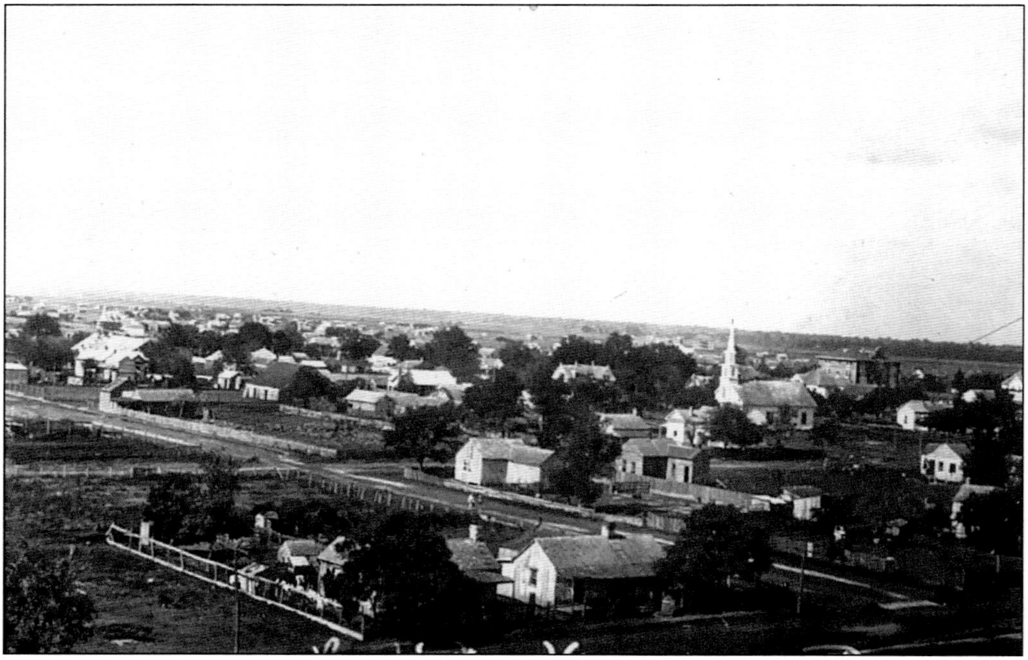

Taken from the roof of the Louisiana State Rice Mill, this bird's-eye-view looking northwest shows Rayne School (to the right of the Centenary Methodist Church, marked by the white steeple) and the Acadia Parish Training School (just to the left of the steeple of the church). (Courtesy Charles S. Stutes.)

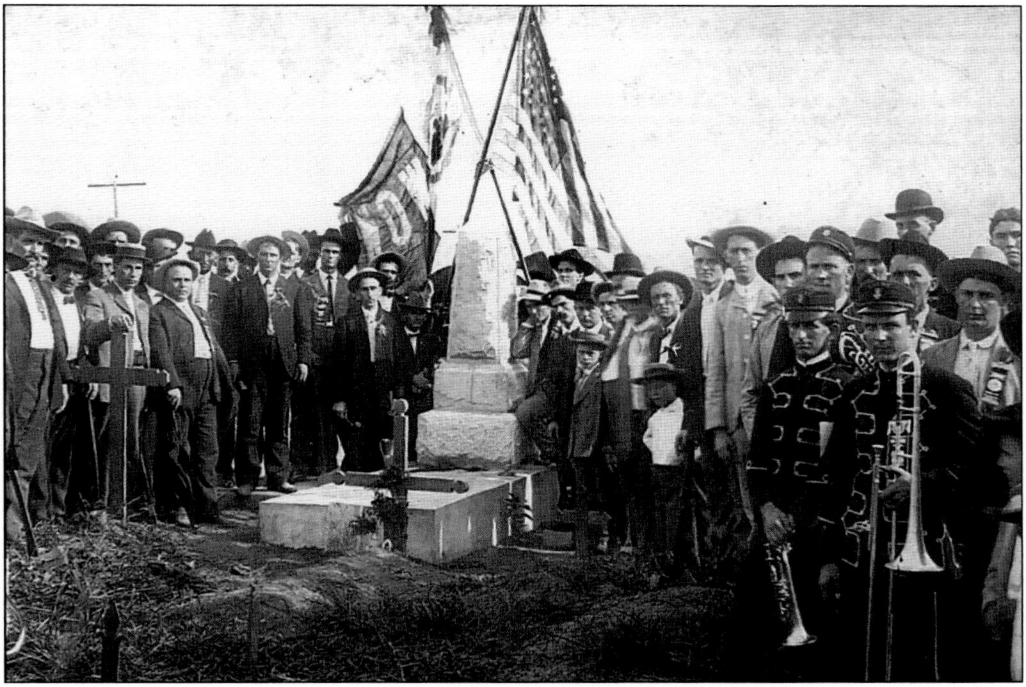

This picture was taken at the original St. Joseph's Cemetery during the unveiling of the monument for Ambrose Mallet in 1905. A member of the Old Hickory Camp #31 Woodmen of the World (WOW), Mallet's grave is marked with a brass plaque identifying his membership. (Courtesy Margo Goertz.)

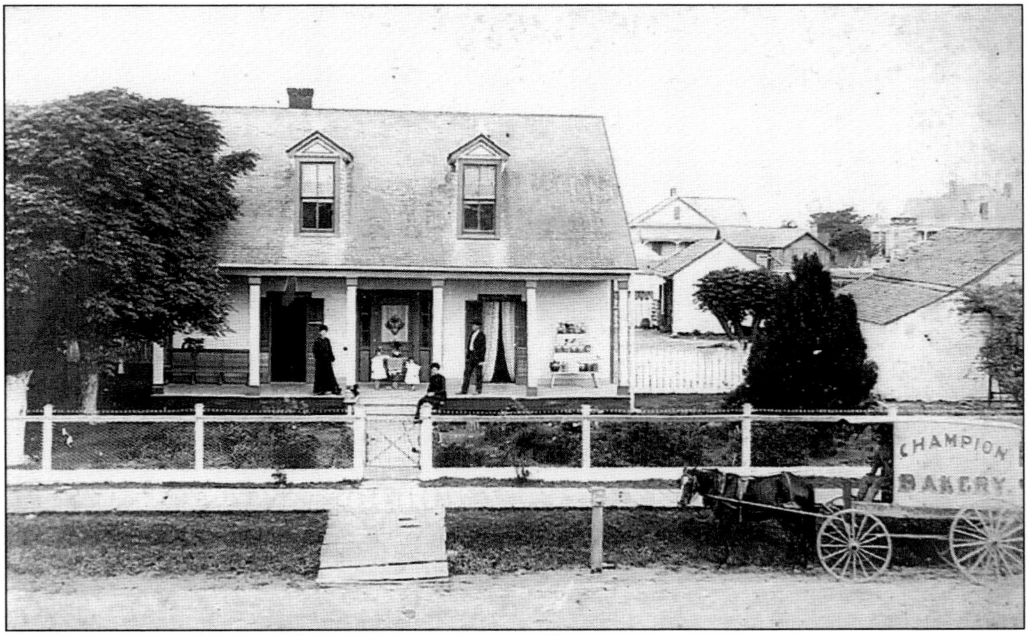

This is the residence of A. Abel Hains located across the street from the St. Joseph Catholic Church. Hains operated the Champion Bakery in his home. The property was previously owned by Louis Keller, who moved his operation to Lafayette where it became Keller's Bakery. (Courtesy Margo Goertz.)

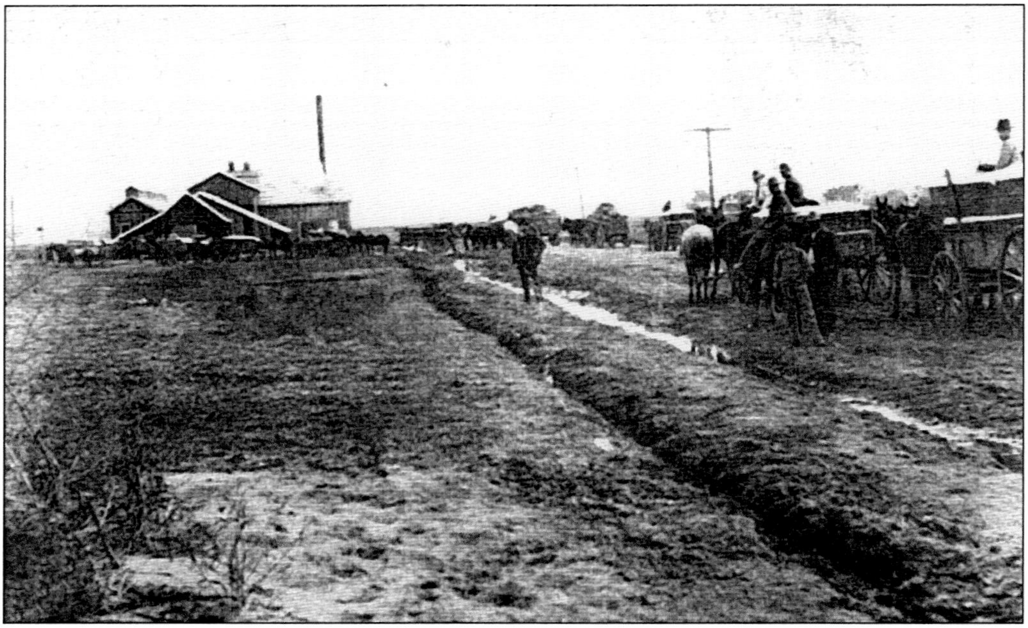

The enterprising Weil Brothers recognized an opportunity to branch out from their original frog and produce shipping business and to fill a growing need for a plant to accommodate increasing cotton acreage in the area. The Mathilde Cotton Gin was constructed and named for the wife of Jacques, one of the brothers. The old plant was located just east of Rayne and north of U.S. 90 along the railroad lines. (Courtesy Charles S. Stutes.)

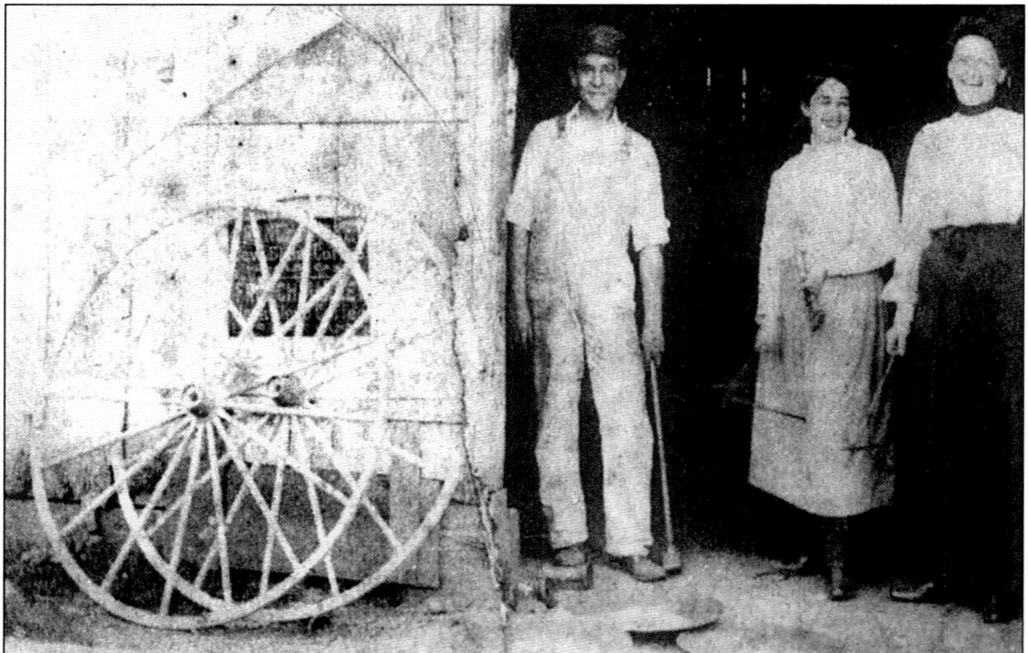

This early picture of the Felix Peres Blacksmith shop depicts Felix Peres, Lucille Peres, and Mrs. August Peres Jr. Note the wagon wheel in the picture, a prelude to their future business, the Rayne Wagon Co. (Courtesy Charles S. Stutes.)

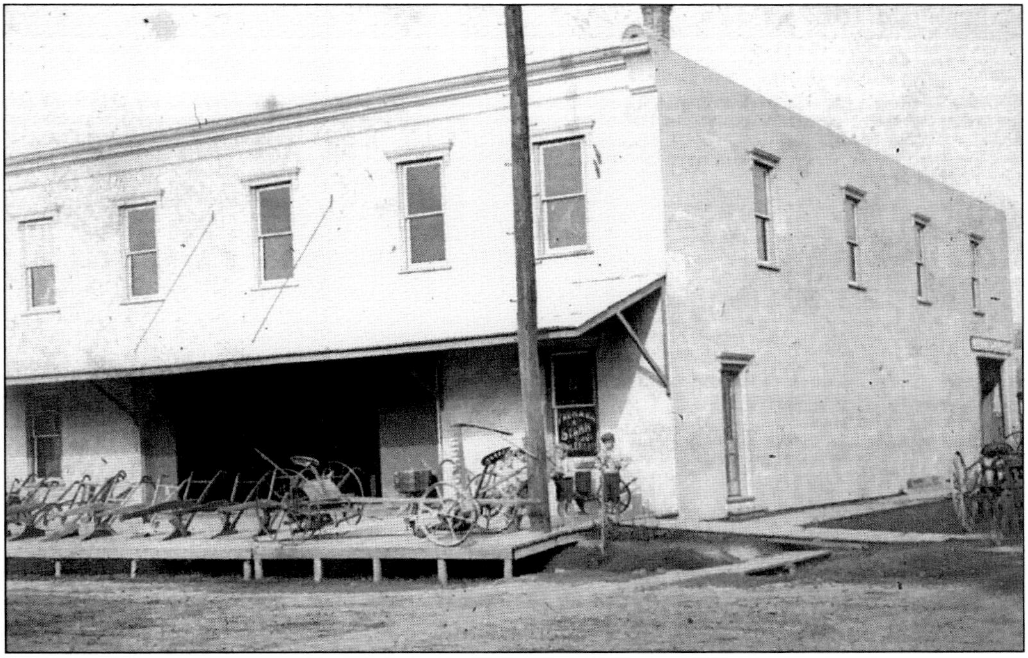

This is a great view of the frontage of Fremaux and Stamm Implement Co. The exact location of the store is unknown but the raised wooden sidewalk indicates heavy foot traffic. (Courtesy Charles S. Stutes.)

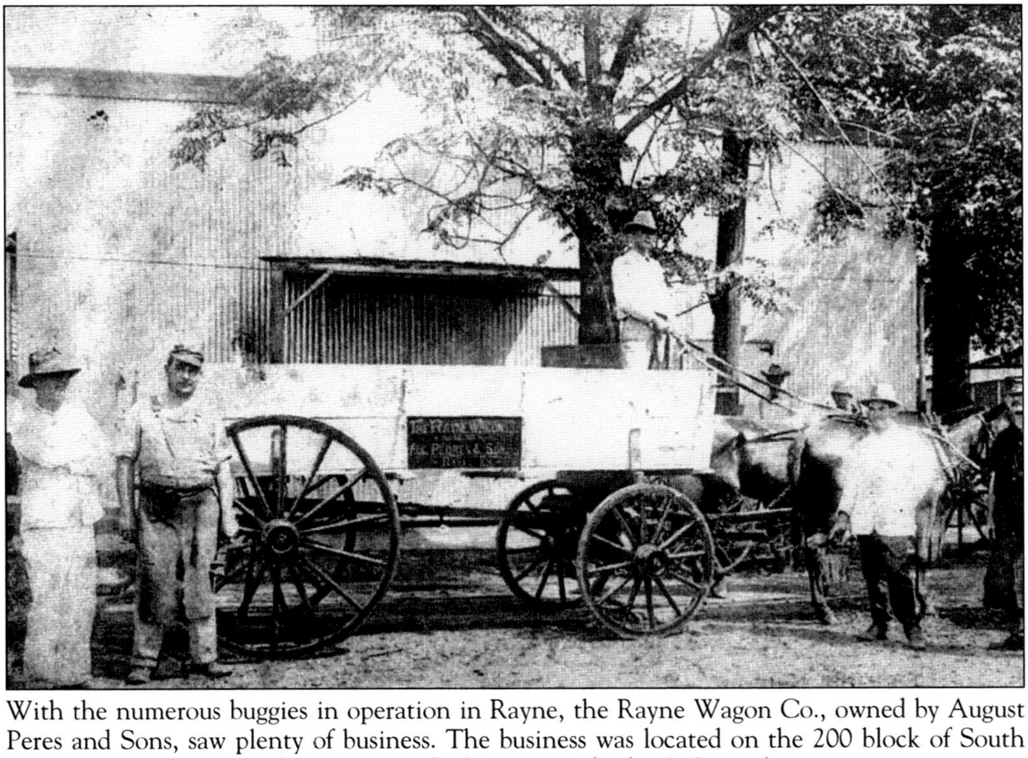

With the numerous buggies in operation in Rayne, the Rayne Wagon Co., owned by August Peres and Sons, saw plenty of business. The business was located on the 200 block of South Adams, across the street from Paco's cafe. (Courtesy Charles S. Stutes.)

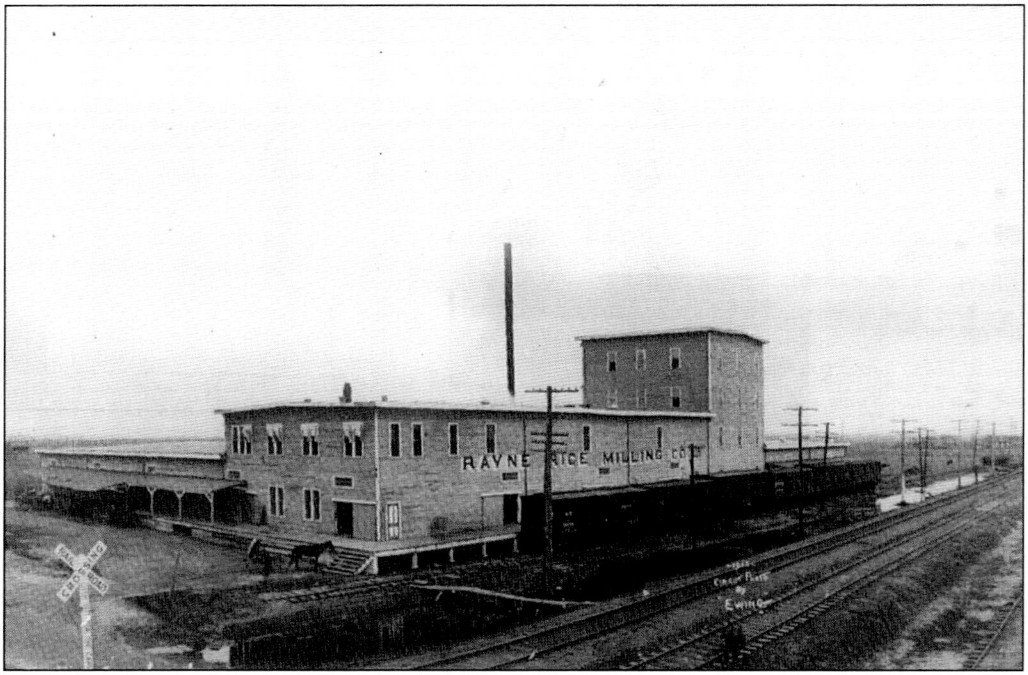

This 1910 picture shows the Rayne Rice Milling Co., which was built in 1902. It was located on North Arenas next to the railroad tracks, which allowed for easy shipping. The company was later sold to Louisiana State Rice Milling Co. (Courtesy Fair Craig Hash.)

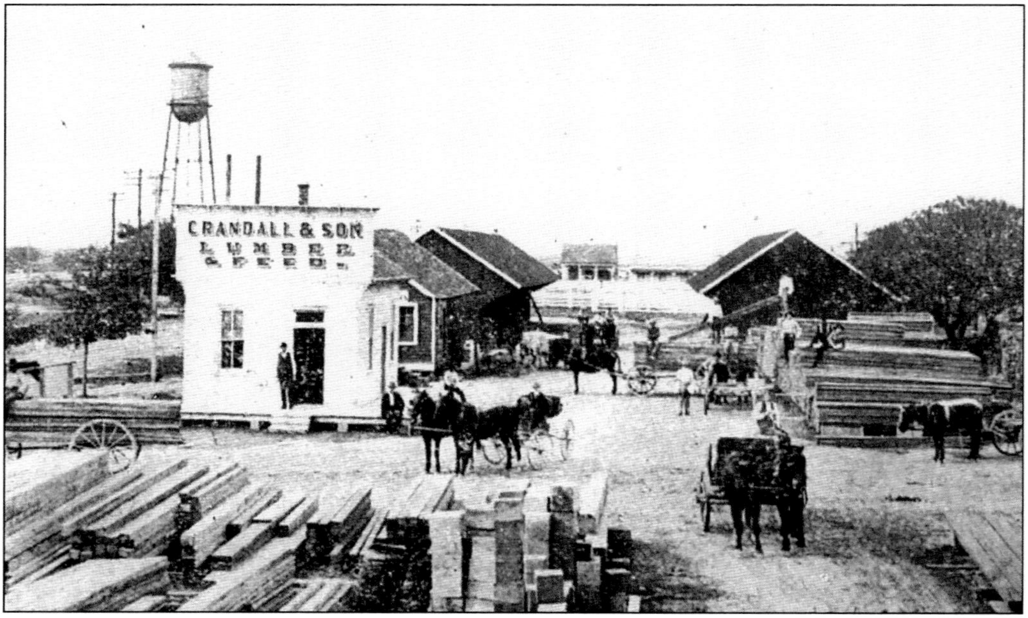

This establishment was originally owned by Charles Oudin. Oudin once told Dr. John Mauboules, who had worked for him, that he had come to Rayne by mistake, which is the way many businessmen came to Rayne, but stayed. Oudin later sold to the Crandalls and the business became Crandall and Son Lumber and Feed Co. and was located on West Texas. It was later purchased by William Joseph Gossen and became Rayne Lumber Yard. (Courtesy Charles S. Stutes.)

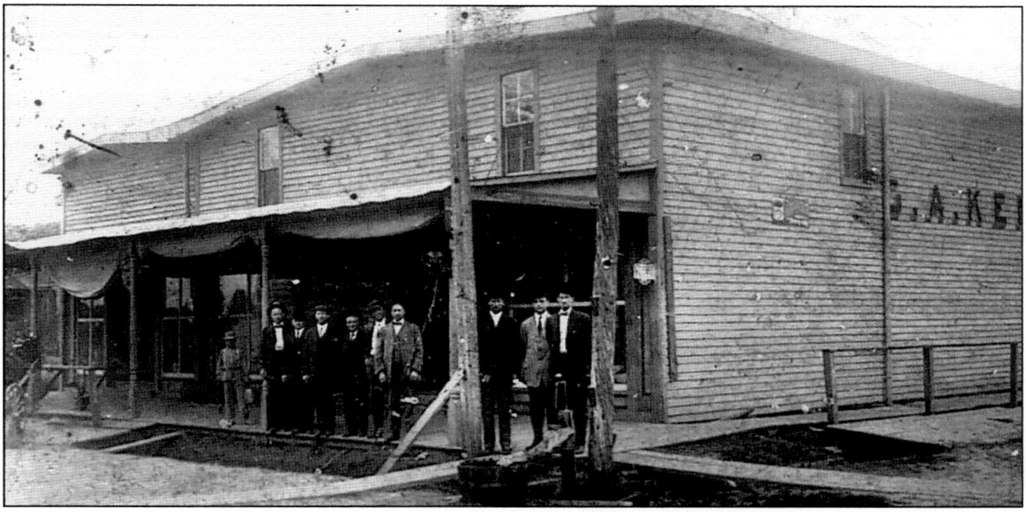

W.A. Kennedy, "The Complete Store," was founded in 1908 by G.A. Kennedy. The large attractive store offered many departments stocked with every need for the family and home. Pictured on the front porch in this 1909 photo, from left to right, are Sheriff Walter Larcade, Glady Johnson, W.A. Kennedy, Elwood Harkins, Harvey Hightower, Luther Harkins, Moise Richard, G.A. Kennedy, and others. (Courtesy Andrus Fontenot.)

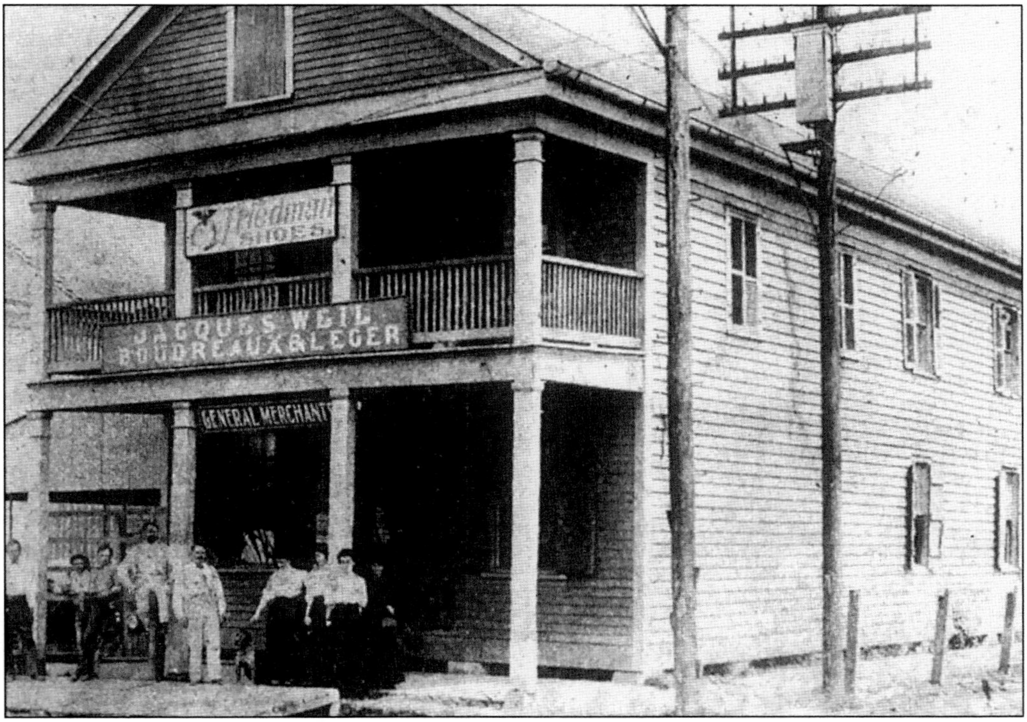

Another Weil enterprise was the Jacques Weil, Boudreaux, and Leger General Merchants store. This two-story frame building housed a general merchandise store and later was used for offices for cotton buyers and a number of other purposes. Note the familiar hitching posts along the side for shoppers arriving in wagons and by horse and buggy. It was located on the corner of Texas Avenue and South Polk, the future location of the Joy-Acadia Movie Theater. (Courtesy Charles S. Stutes.)

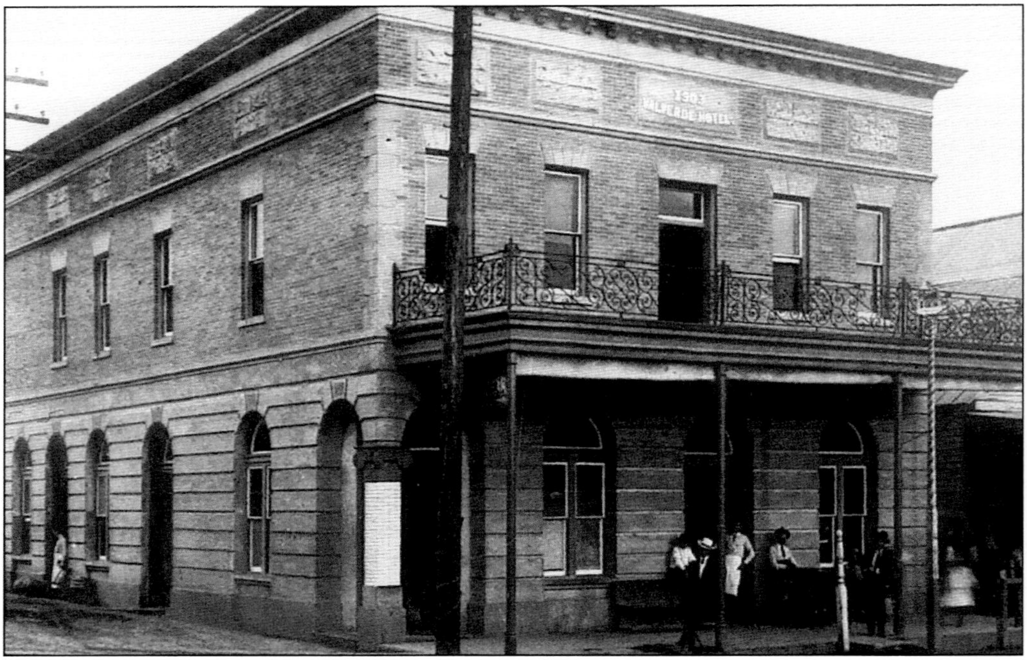

The Valverde Hotel was built in 1903 on South Polk near the railroad tracks and had 19 guest rooms, a dining room, and a bar. This building was known as one of the most elegant buildings in Rayne with its unique structure and terrazzo floor in the lobby. The hotel burned in 1916 and was later remodeled and used by many businesses including Rayne Farm Supplies. The Bruce Theater opened on the bottom floor and the second story was used as a bowling alley in the 1940s. (Courtesy Charles S. Stutes.)

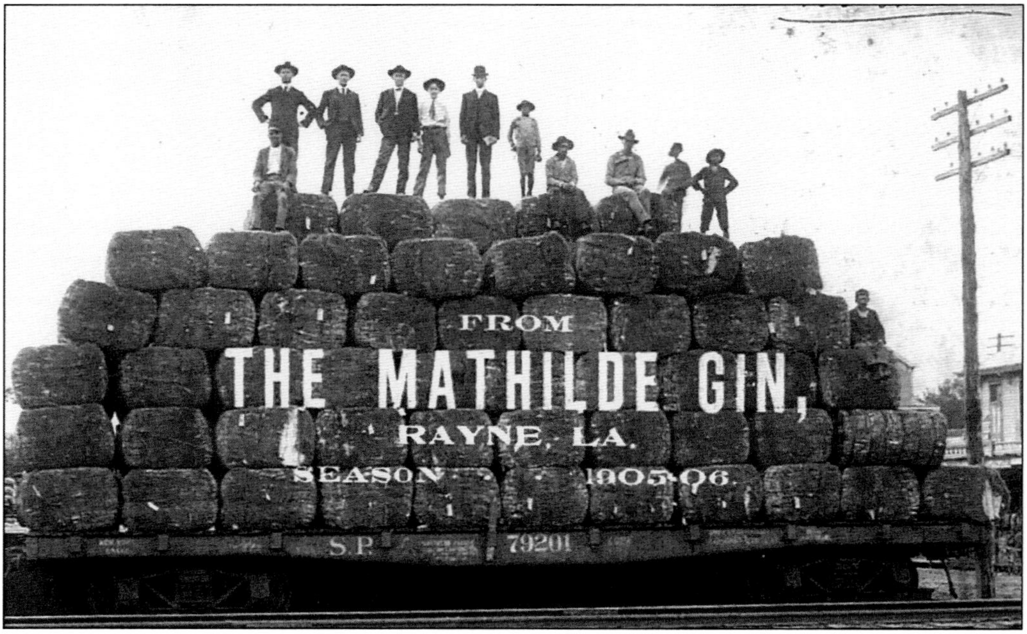

This unique picture is a train carload of 106 bales of cotton from the Mathilde Gin for the 1905–1906 cotton season probably heading for New Orleans. There were several cotton gins in the area, but the Mathilde Gin was the first to produce square bales. (Courtesy Margo Goertz.)

Two

City Commerce

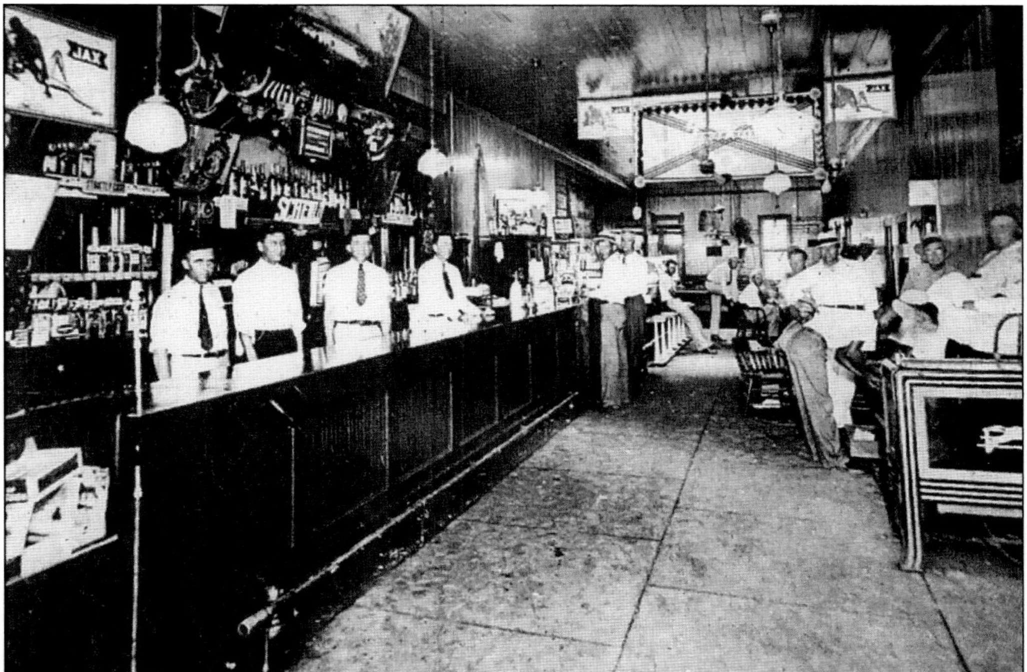

Back in 1932, long before the days of "women's lib," this was strictly "man's domain." Located somewhere along the block where Mervine Kahn's is now situated, this was T. Miers Pool Hall and Billiard Parlor. Behind the bar, from left to right, are A.J. "Gee" Herbert, Clet Dupont, D.L. "TiiTii" Boullion, and owner Theo "T" Mier. Others identified are Cy Underwood, "Chick" Hilliard, Lessin Benoit, E.J. Faulk, Joe Savoie, Clesmay Cormier, Charlie Rourke, Julian Hulin, and Waddy Arceneaux, having his shoes shined on the far right. (Courtesy Charles S. Stutes.)

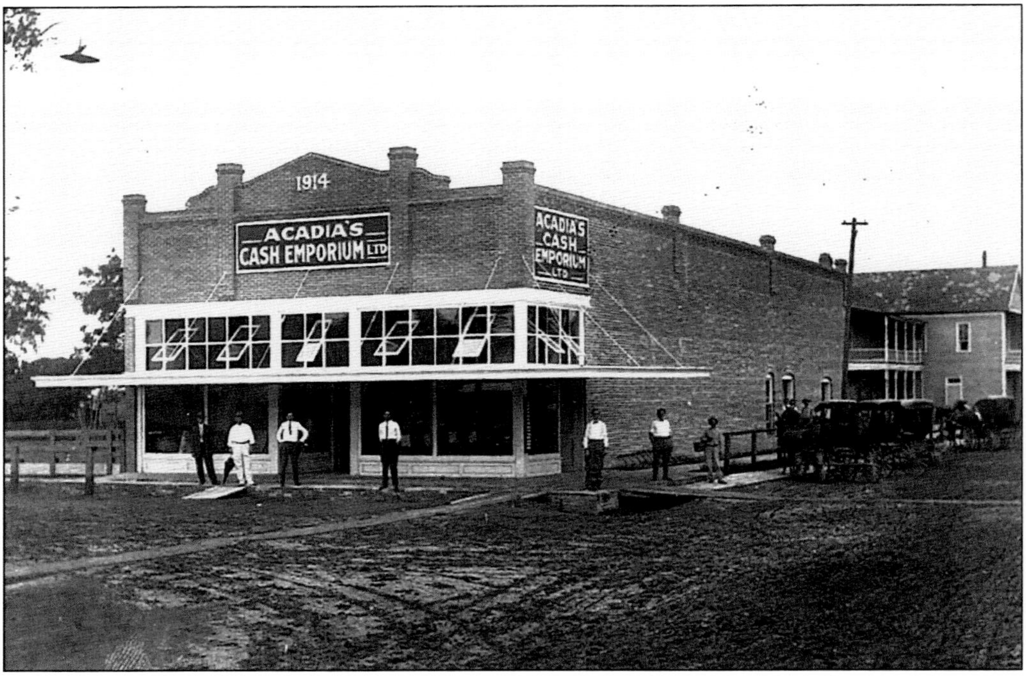

The newly built Acadia's Cash Emporium, Ltd. was rebuilt in 1914 after the wood structure burned. Note the fire hydrant and the wooden sidewalks. To the right of the building, the famous Commercial Hotel can be seen. (Courtesy Doug Vincent.)

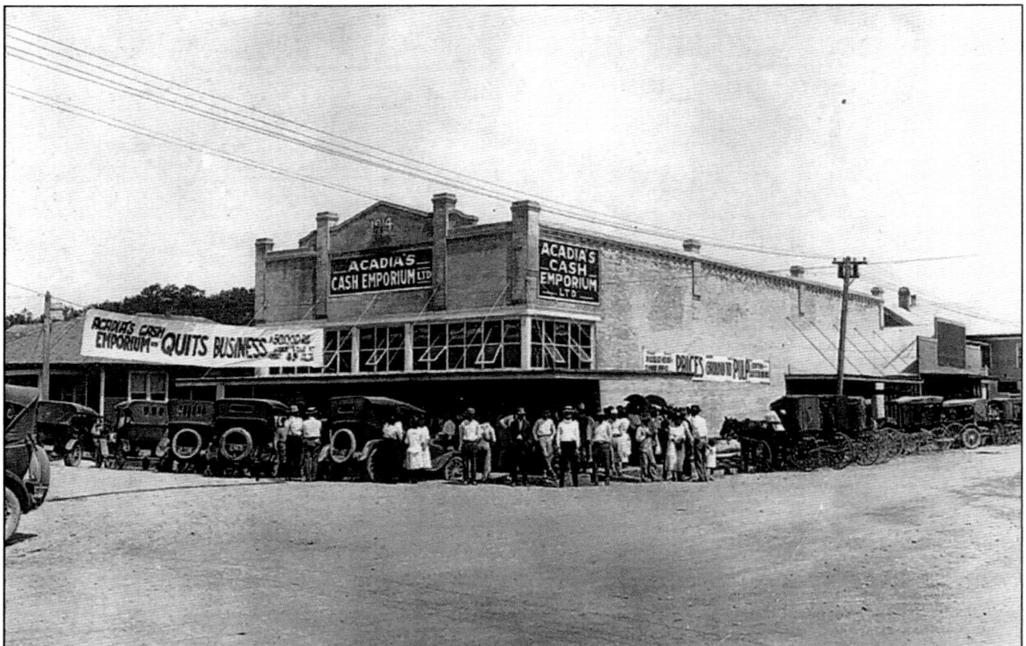

"Acadia's Cash Emporium Quits Business. Over $50,000 of Inventory needs to be liquidated. Prices ground to a pulp" is proclaimed in this *c.* 1920 picture. To the immediate right of the building is the medical office of Dr. Mike Clark. (Courtesy Willie Etta and Myrtle Servat.)

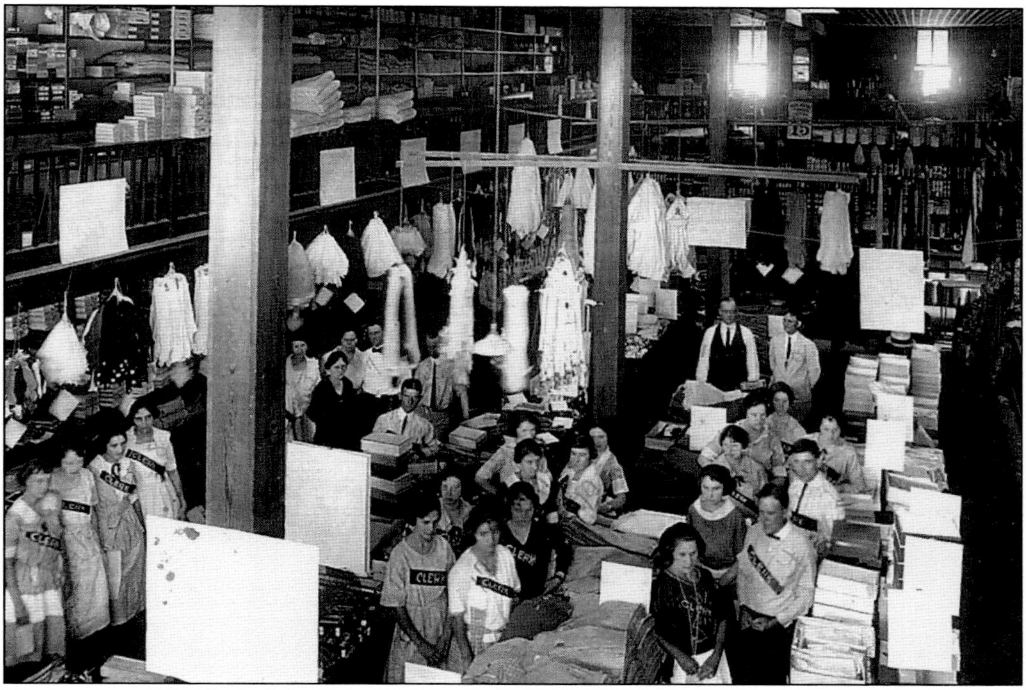

This is an inside view of the liquidation sale for Acadia's Cash Emporium. This picture shows 25 sales clerks and 2 members of management supervising the sale. (Courtesy Willie Etta and Myrtle Servat.)

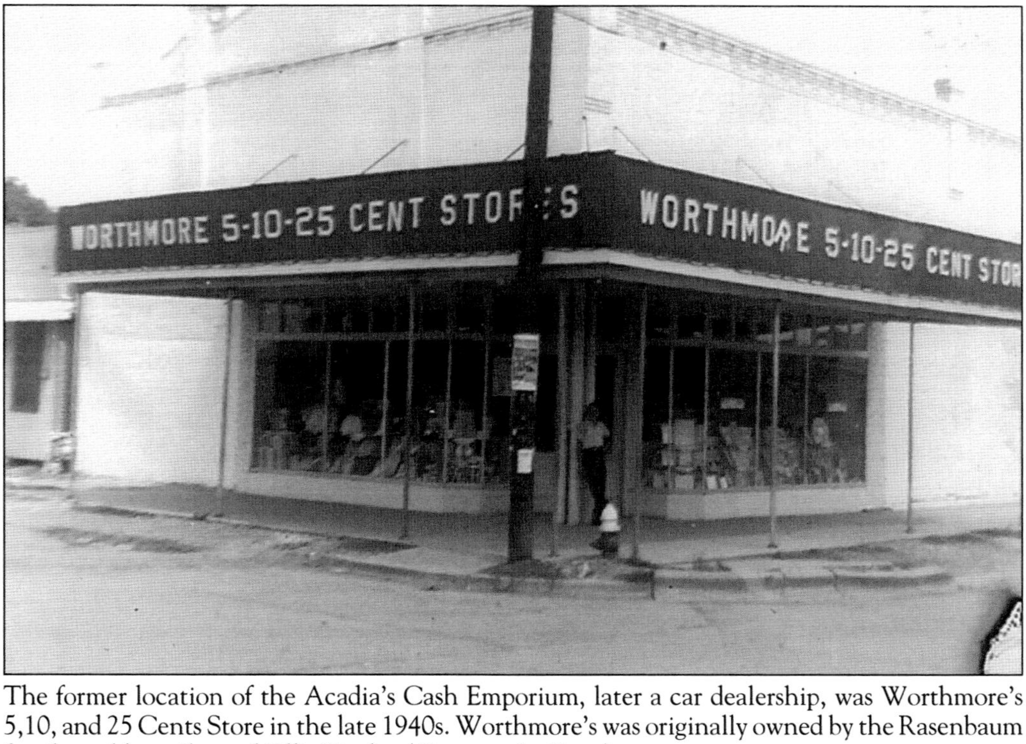

The former location of the Acadia's Cash Emporium, later a car dealership, was Worthmore's 5,10, and 25 Cents Store in the late 1940s. Worthmore's was originally owned by the Rasenbaum family and later Ike and Effie Hanks. (Courtesy Jo Cart.)

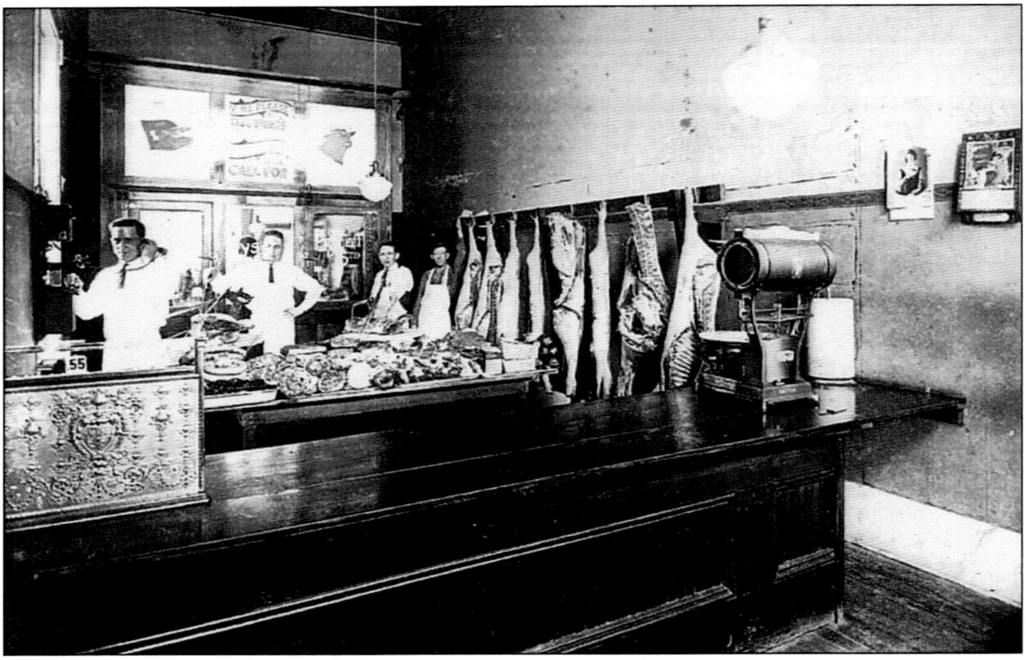

An inside picture of Robichaux's Meat Market shows second from left Wilbur Robichaux. Of special interest are the sides of meat on the wall and the sign showing the sale of pigs feet for 5¢ a pound. (Courtesy Phyllis Leonards.)

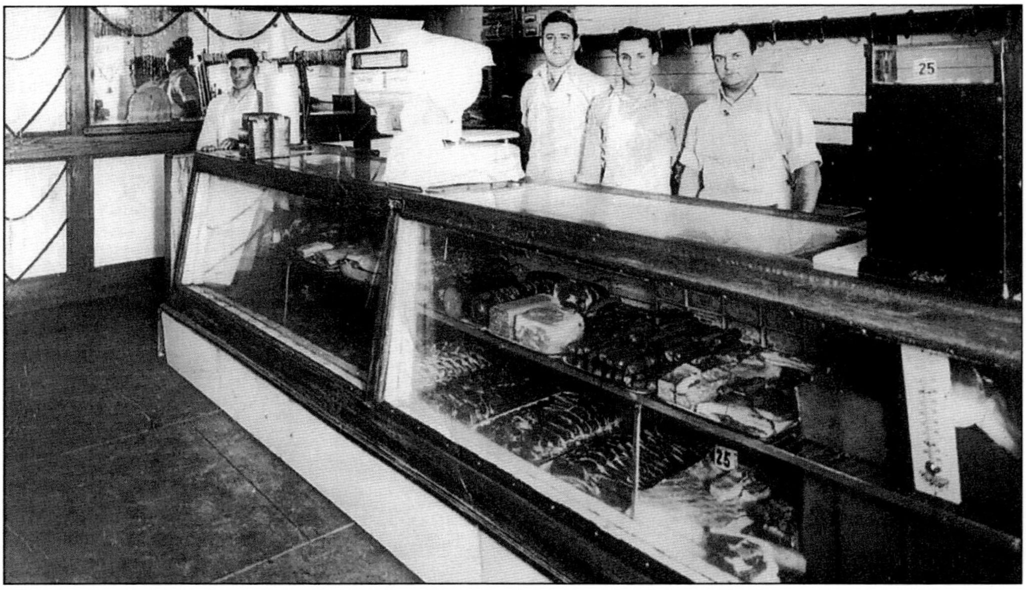

The front counter area of Robichaux's Meat Market shows Albert Primeaux, Frances Robichaux, and Lauless Robichaux. Many stories are told of parents giving their children 25¢—the cost of going to the movie, soda, and popcorn, and then stopping at Robichaux's to pick up their meat on the way home. (Courtesy Rose Marie Stelly.)

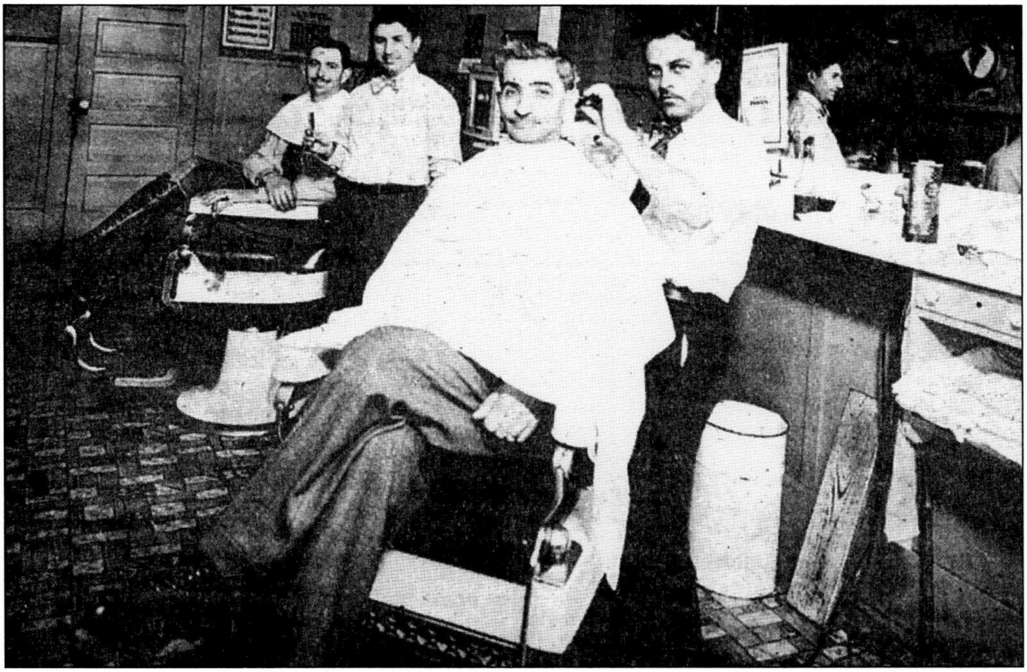

The Central Barber Shop is shown with Isadore Aube cutting the hair of Syl Sommer (front) and Lawrence "Pee Wee" Romero Jr. cutting the hair of an unidentified man in the rear. This barber shop was located across from the freight depot. (Courtesy Charles S. Stutes.)

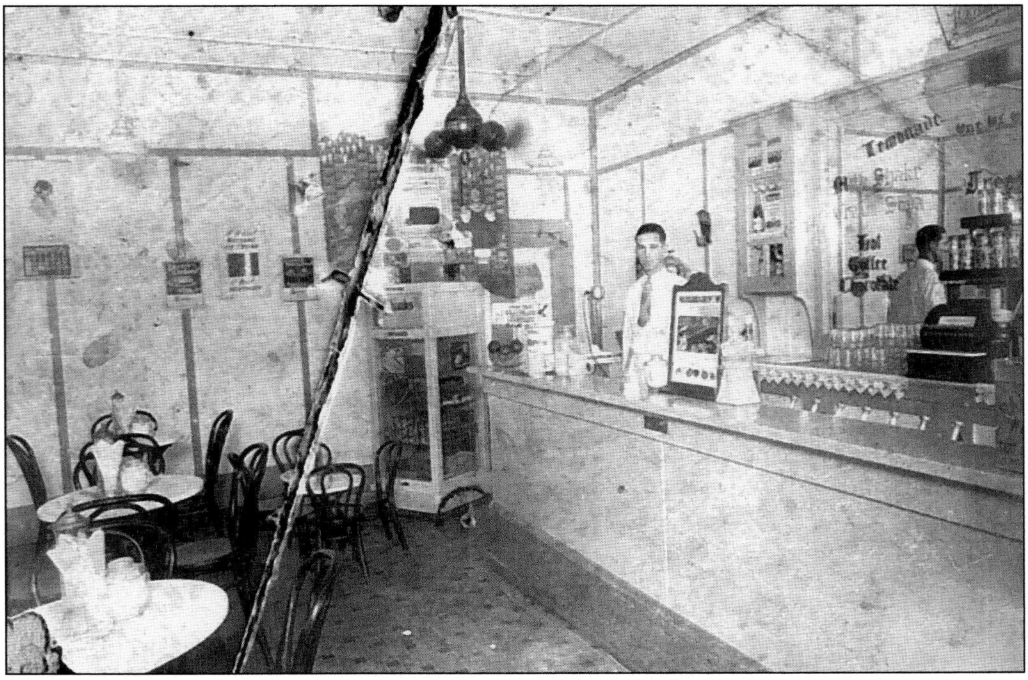

This is a rare inside view of People's Drug Store showing the first soda fountain in Rayne. The popular drinks advertised on the mirror include lemonade, hot coffee, and chocolate. Shown behind the counter is Alphonse Duclos. In 1904, he sold the store to Dr. J.P. Mauboles and Dr. M.A. Young, who later sold to Arnold Kahn. (Courtesy Marguerite Kahn Hoskins.)

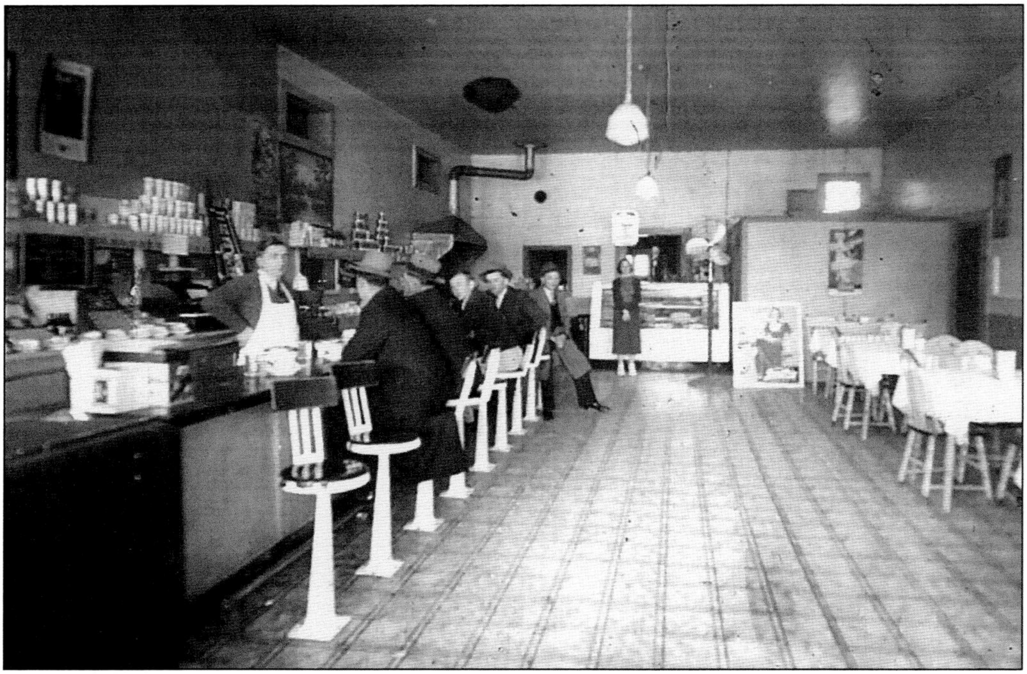

This early 1930s view of People's Café shows a very young Paco Borne behind the counter. Had he conjured up his famous recipe for biscuits yet? The cafe stayed relatively unchanged except for the addition of more tables and chairs for increased business. (Courtesy Rayne State Bank.)

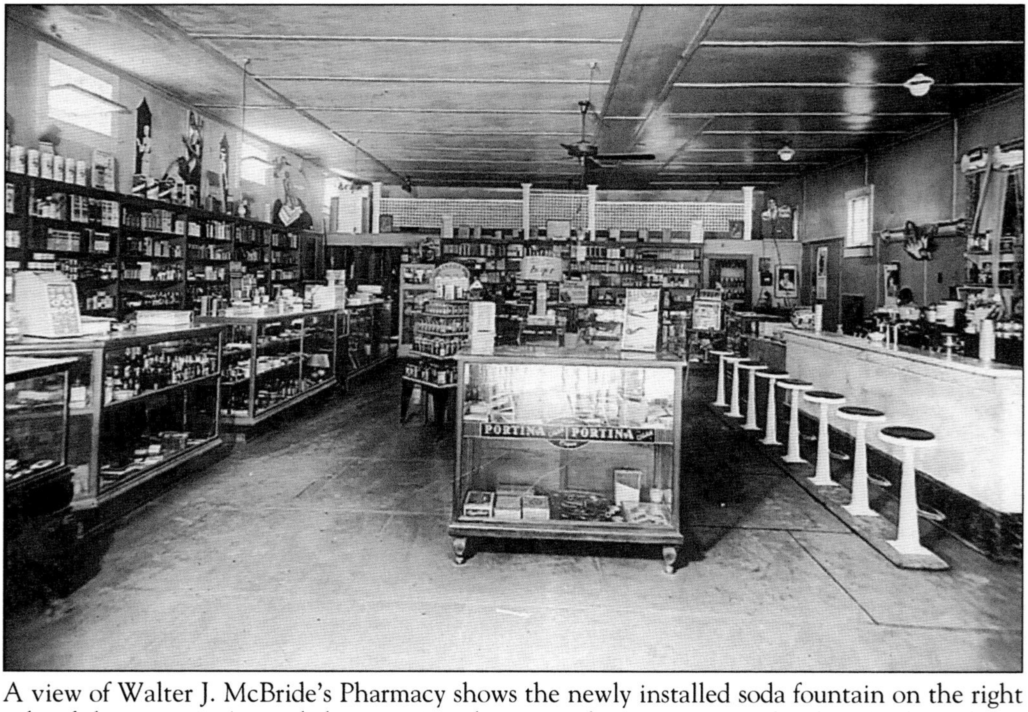

A view of Walter J. McBride's Pharmacy shows the newly installed soda fountain on the right side of the picture. Around the partition there was the waiting area for the Greyhound Bus Line, which picked up passengers at the back door leading to Devil's Alley. (Courtesy Jim & Mary Ann Bush.)

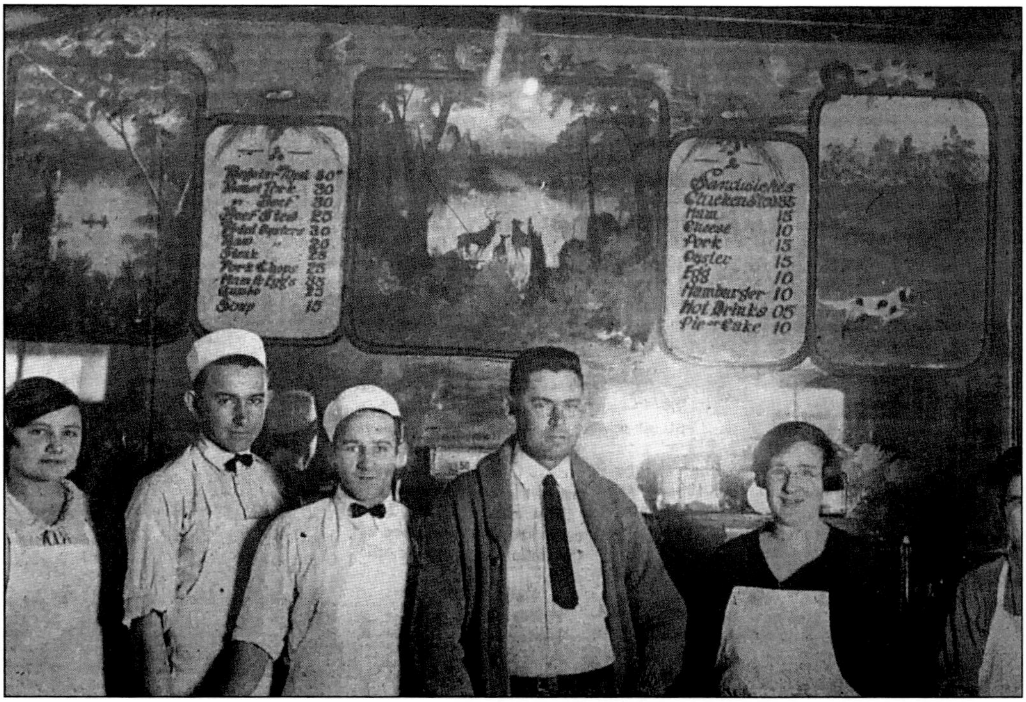

The old Farmer's Café was located next to where Russell's Furniture Mart is now located. In the picture above, third from left is Leo "Crip" Clement and fifth is Olezida Clement, his wife. (Courtesy Charles S. Stutes.)

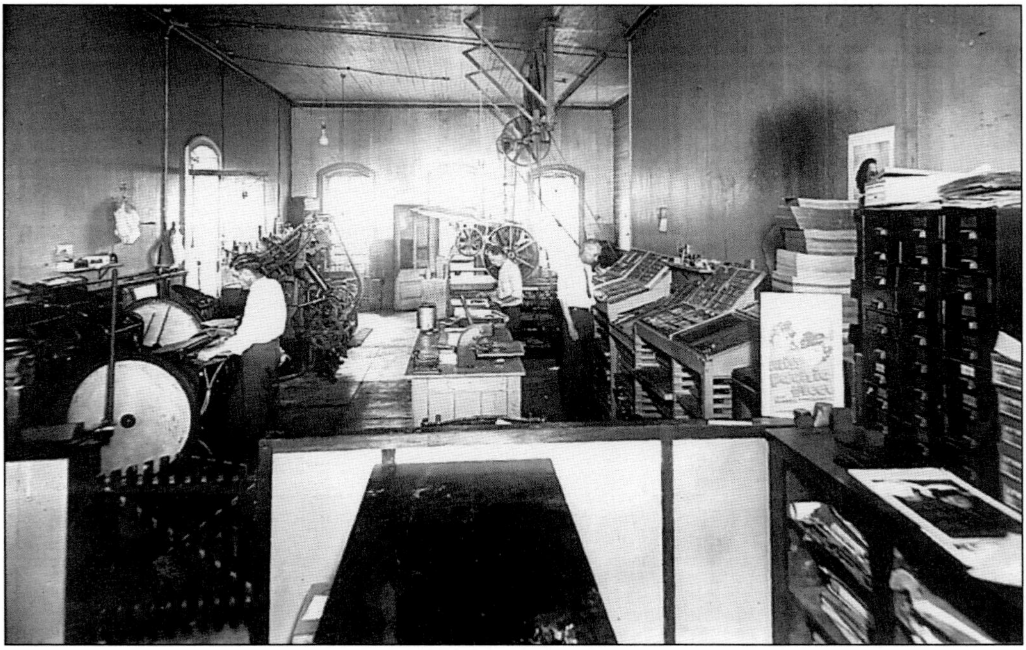

During the 1940s, *The Rayne Tribune* office was located between Broussard's Drug Store and Bank of Commerce. Shown operating the machines are Clinton Petitjean, Billy Wright, and Hugh Craig. Notice the poster for the war movie *Miss Pacific Fleet* on the counter. (Courtesy Donald Petitjean.)

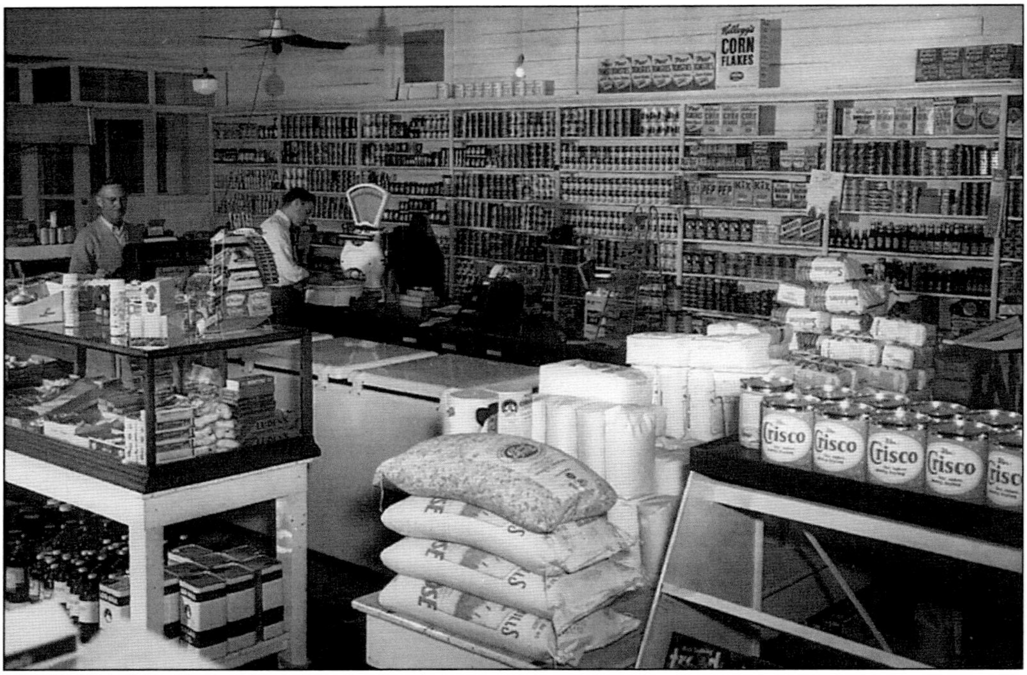

This is an inside view of Plattsmier's Grocery Store located on the corner of South Adams and West South First Street across from the Farmers True Value Hardware store. The building was originally built in 1901 by Anthony Plattsmier. Shown are George L. Plattsmier and Daniel Plattsmier at the scale. (Courtesy Louis Plattsmier.)

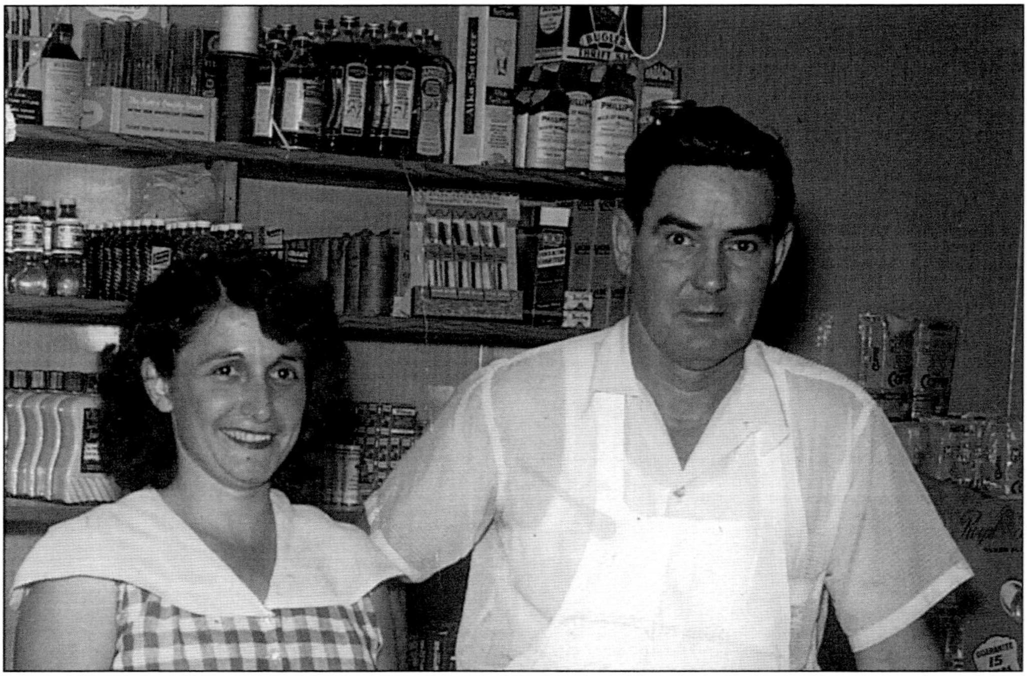

Shown behind the counter at the 1953 grand opening of T-Daigle Grocery and Market are Lucille and Theobert Daigle. The store was located at 302 Fourth Street and was in operation until 1983. (Courtesy Lucille Daigle.)

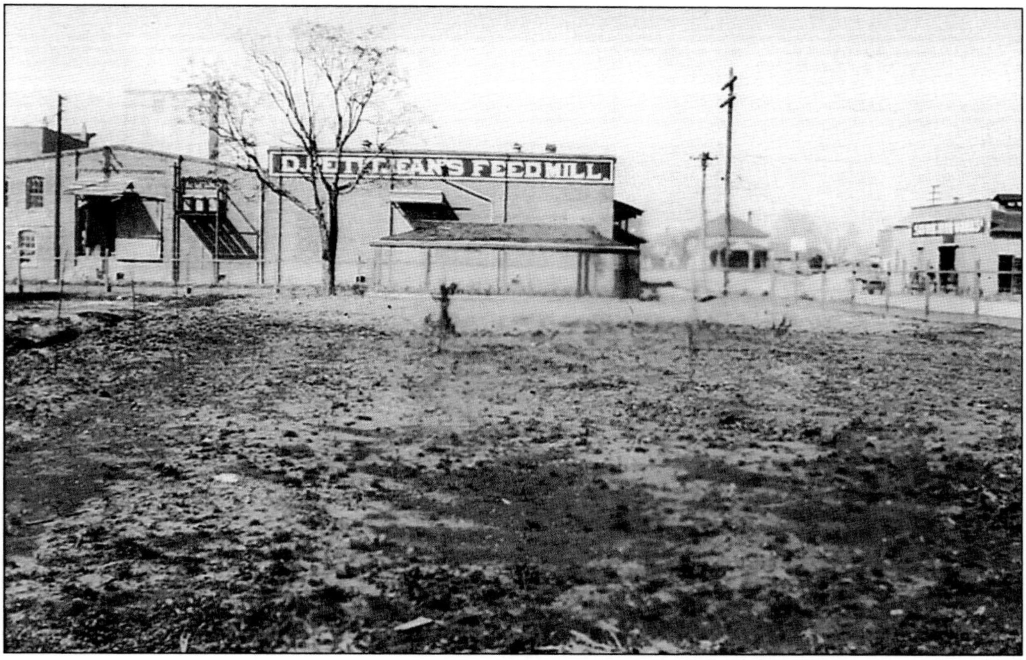

A picture looking north at Dave Petitjean Feed and Seed Warehouse is shown here. To the right you can see Savoie Iron Works and across the tracks, the old city hall. The business was later sold and renamed Hanks Warehouse. The walls of this warehouse are four bricks wide, which is probably the reason it still stands today. (Courtesy Margo Goertz.)

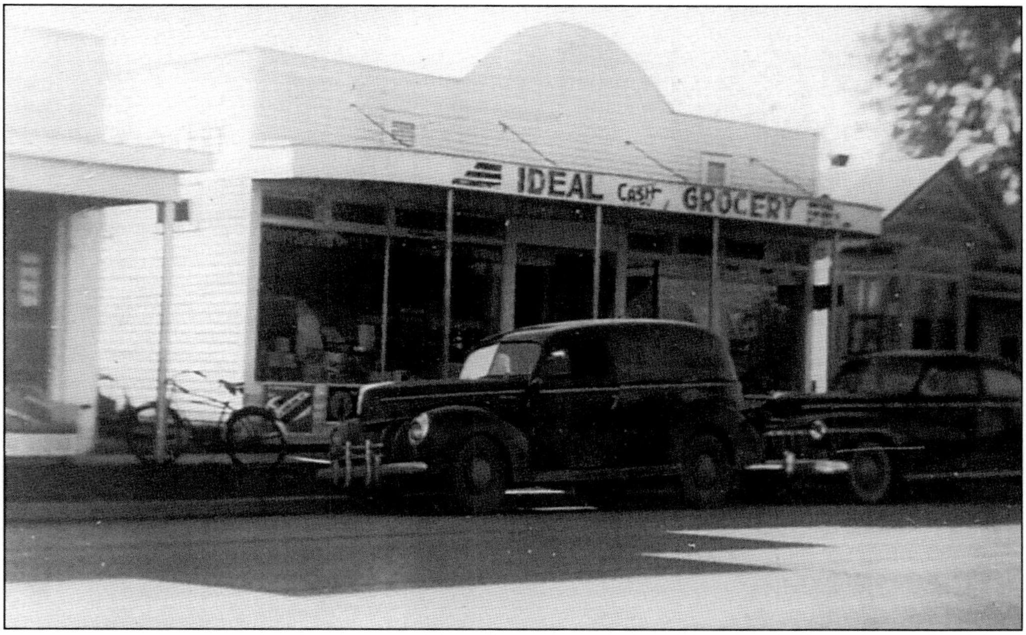

Ideal Cash Grocery was located across the street from St. Joseph's Catholic Church. It was owned by Rodney Baronet. On the right is the home of Dr. E.L. Bercier, and next door was his dentist office where he pulled teeth for 50¢. To the left of the grocery store was the Photo Shop operated by Leonard Laperouse, the best known photographer in the state during his time. (Courtesy Joyce Faulk.)

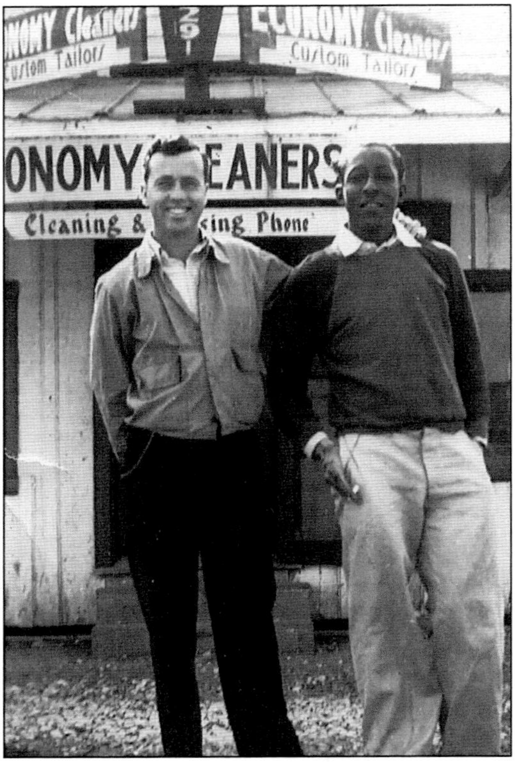

Herbert Thibodeaux, owner of Economy Cleaners, is shown with his only employee, Dallas Guidry. The business first opened on West Jeff Davis in 1938 and later moved to 102 West Louisiana Avenue in 1966. The business was later Sunshine Cleaners and is now J&J Cleaners. (Courtesy Hazel Prevost.)

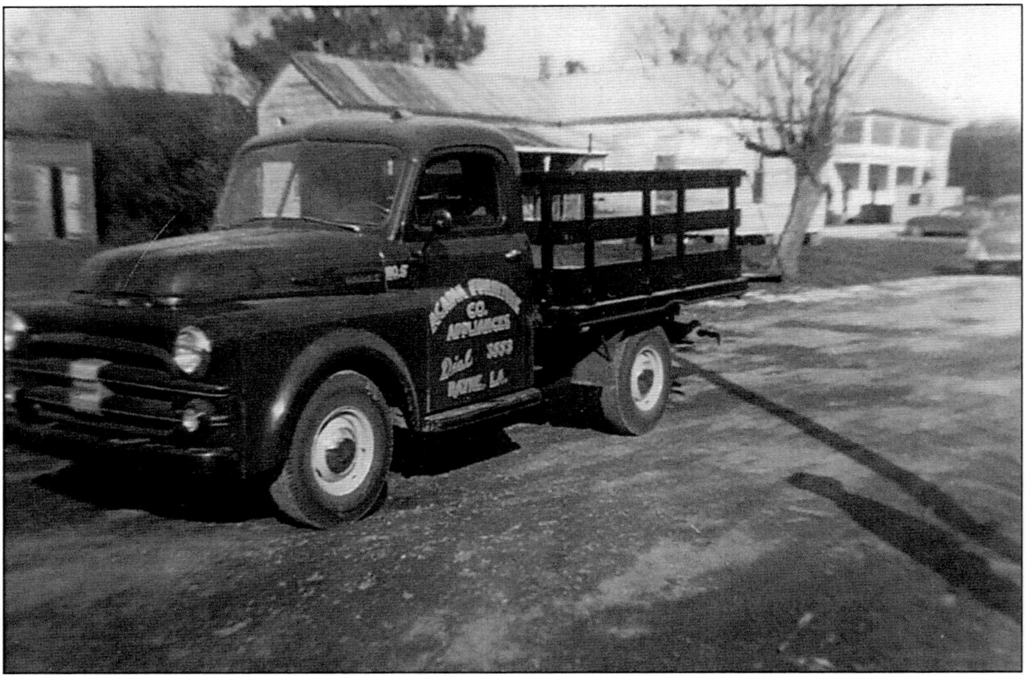

The Acadia Furniture Store truck is shown in this picture taken behind the store. The store was located across from St. Joseph's Catholic Church and you can see the old rectory in the background. After the store was closed it was purchased by the church and converted into a parish hall. (Courtesy Margie Breaux.)

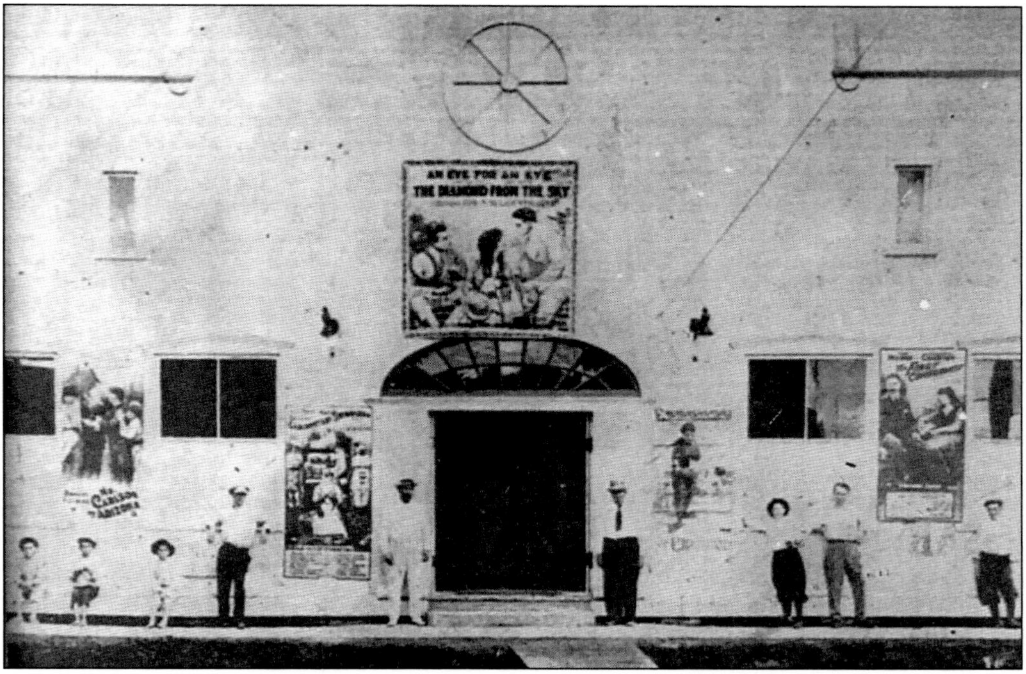

Rayne citizens were proud of their new Rayne Opera House, photographed after completion in 1915. From left to right are Frank DeLaune, Rene Besse, Ferdinand DeLaune, Hugh Craig, James L. Craig, A.P. McNeil (carpenter), Wheeler Bull, Earl Craig, Eugene Butaud, and Edmund Melancon. (Courtesy Fair Craig Hash.)

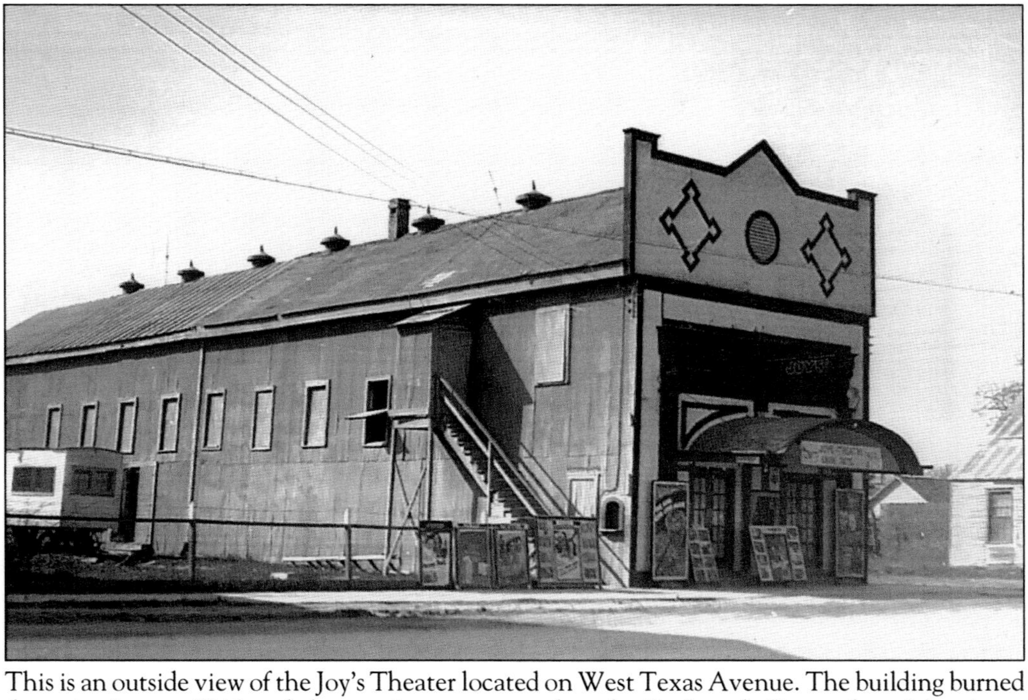

This is an outside view of the Joy's Theater located on West Texas Avenue. The building burned down in August 1946 and the movies were moved to the St. Joseph Gym, where Monsignor Lerschen allowed them to be shown. (Courtesy Andrus Fontenot.)

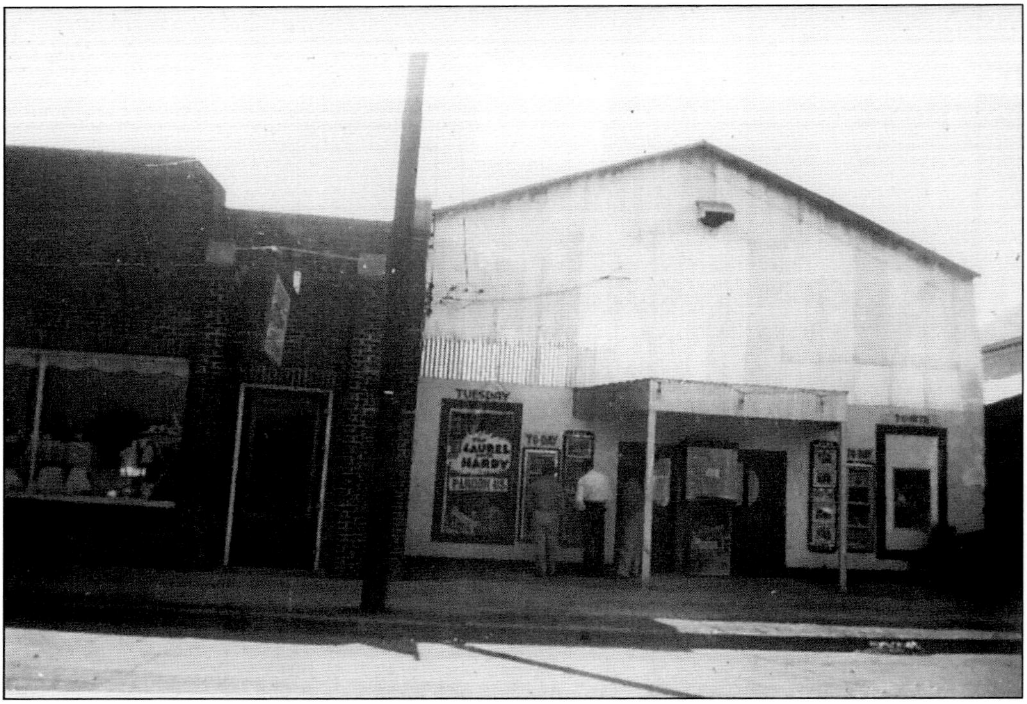

The Buck Theater opened and was operated by Buck Hardy upon his departure from the Joy Theater after a disagreement. It was open from 1946 to 1947 when he closed to run the Bruce Theater in the old Valverde Hotel Building, which closed down in 1948. (Courtesy Charles S. Stutes.)

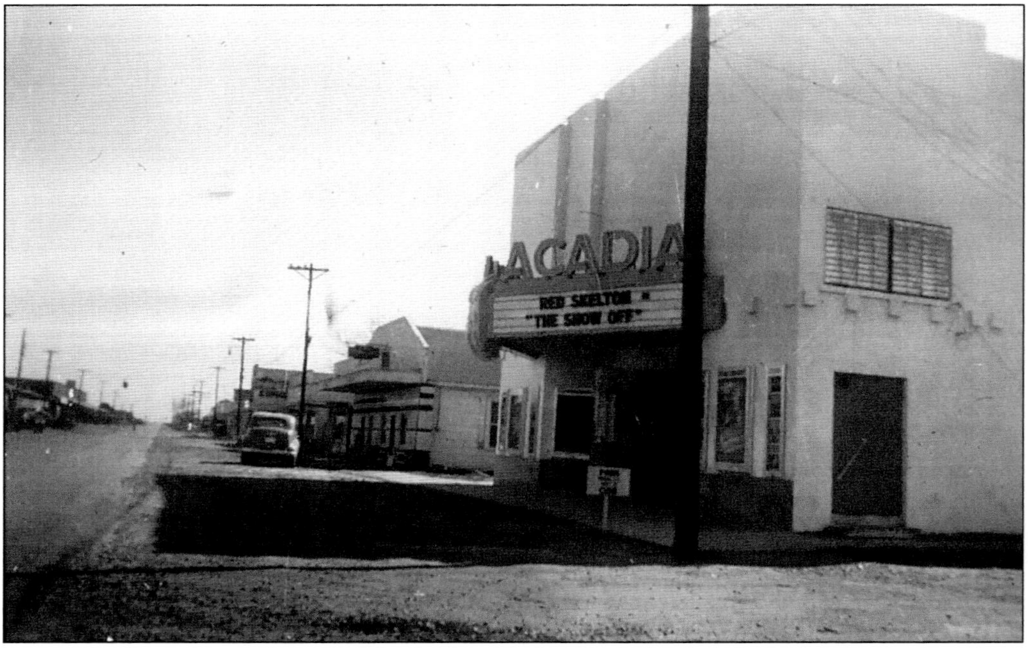

The Joy-Acadia Theater was built after the original Joy Theater burned down in 1946. It was operated by several people until the multi-theaters opened in Crowley and Lafayette and the theater could not survive. (Courtesy Charles S. Stutes.)

When Raynites felt the need for a home-cooked meal without the usual work, they could stop in at the Farmer's Café. Shown here is one of the cars from Comeaux's Taxi Cab Co., which was located next to the café. (Courtesy Charles S. Stutes.)

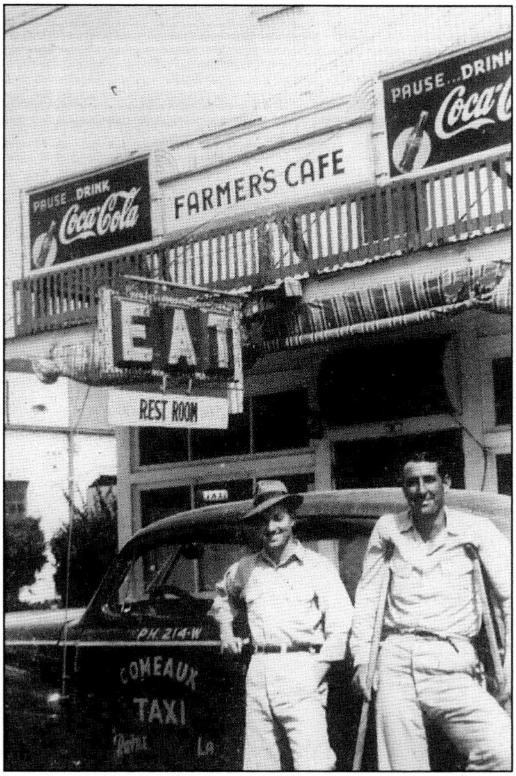

Around 1890, a French immigrant named Louis Privat opened a bakery in Rayne. Ownership of the bakery soon passed to his half-brother, Joseph Privat, shown here displaying a wedding cake for his daughter's wedding in 1949. (Courtesy Julie Ousse.)

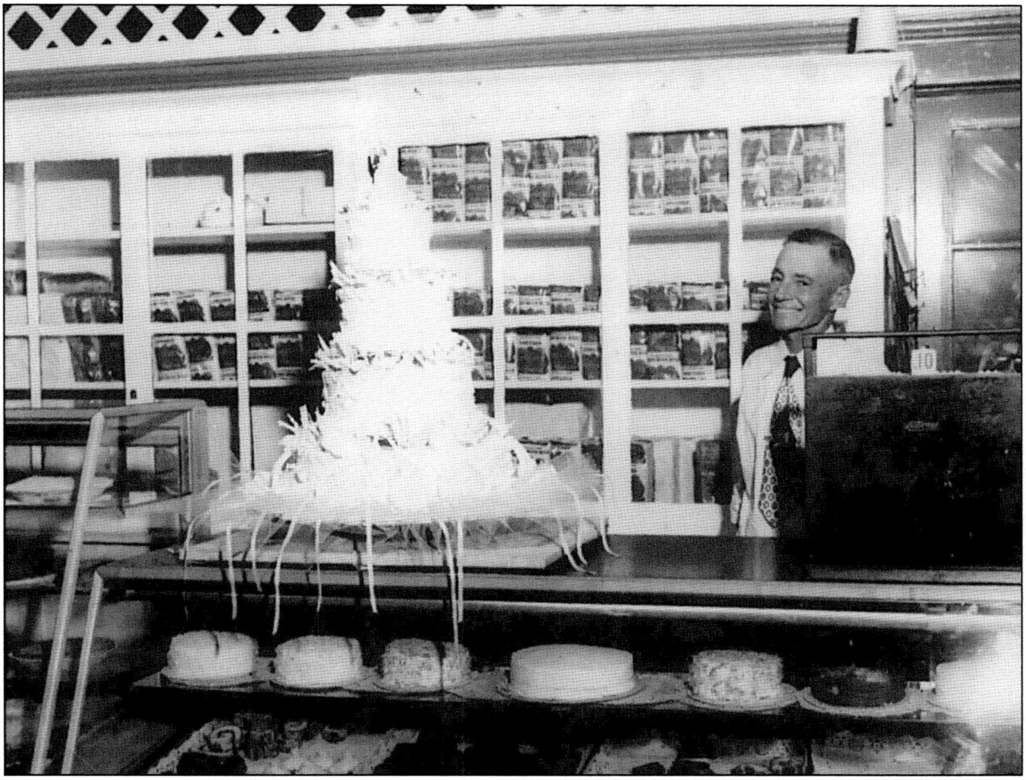

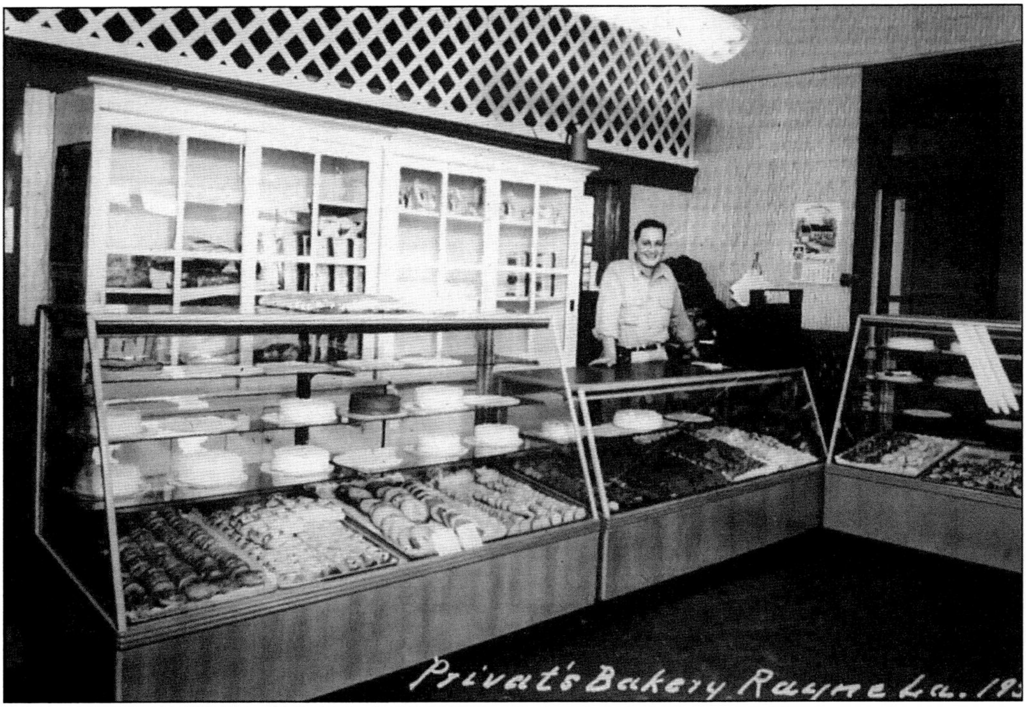

Anthony Privat, shown here in 1950, took over the bakery from his father. The Privat family serviced the community of Rayne for 78 years. Jo Cart tells the story of receiving the last loaf of French bread before they closed. (Courtesy Charles S. Stutes.)

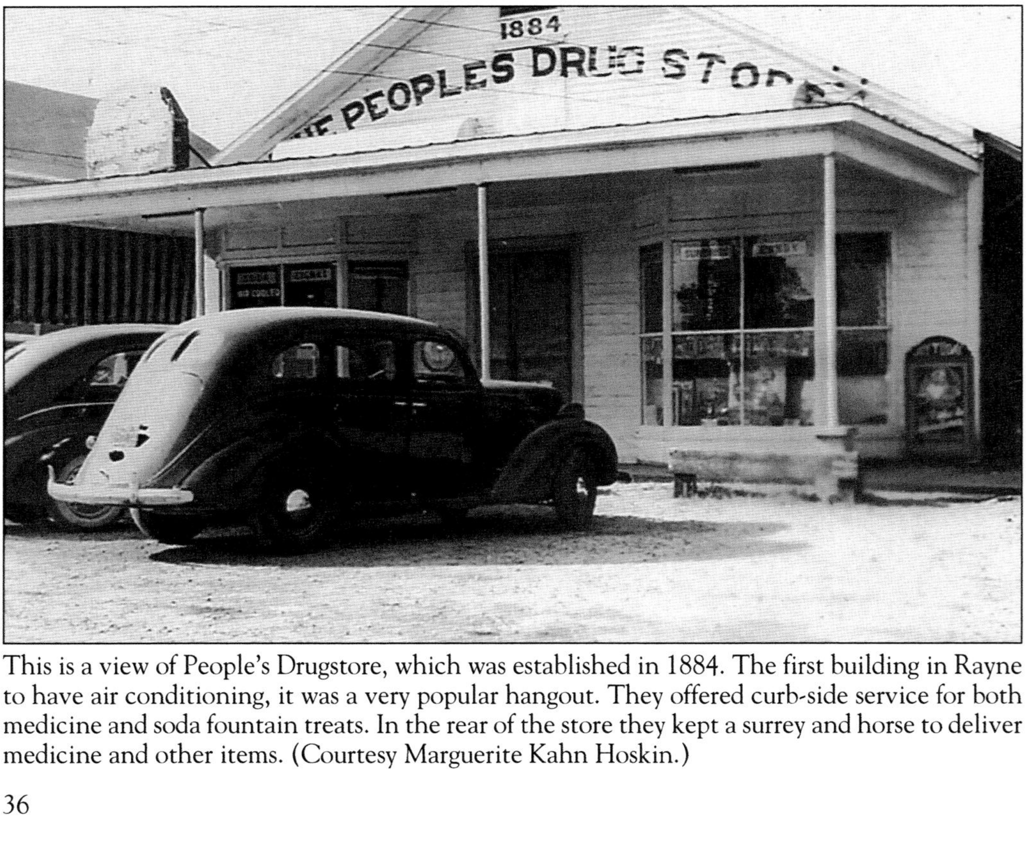

This is a view of People's Drugstore, which was established in 1884. The first building in Rayne to have air conditioning, it was a very popular hangout. They offered curb-side service for both medicine and soda fountain treats. In the rear of the store they kept a surrey and horse to deliver medicine and other items. (Courtesy Marguerite Kahn Hoskin.)

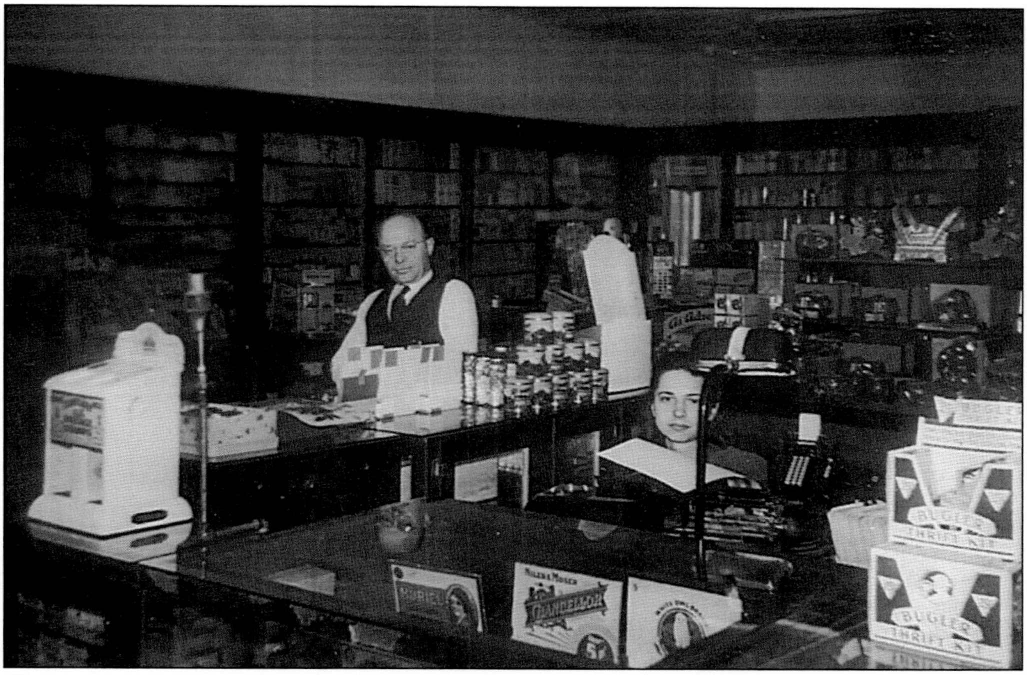

This is an inside view of People's Drug Store showing Arnold Kahn at the counter with Marcella Stagg, who was the bookkeeper. The drug stores of the day had every conceivable potion and elixir for every ailment. (Courtesy Marguerite Kahn Hoskin.)

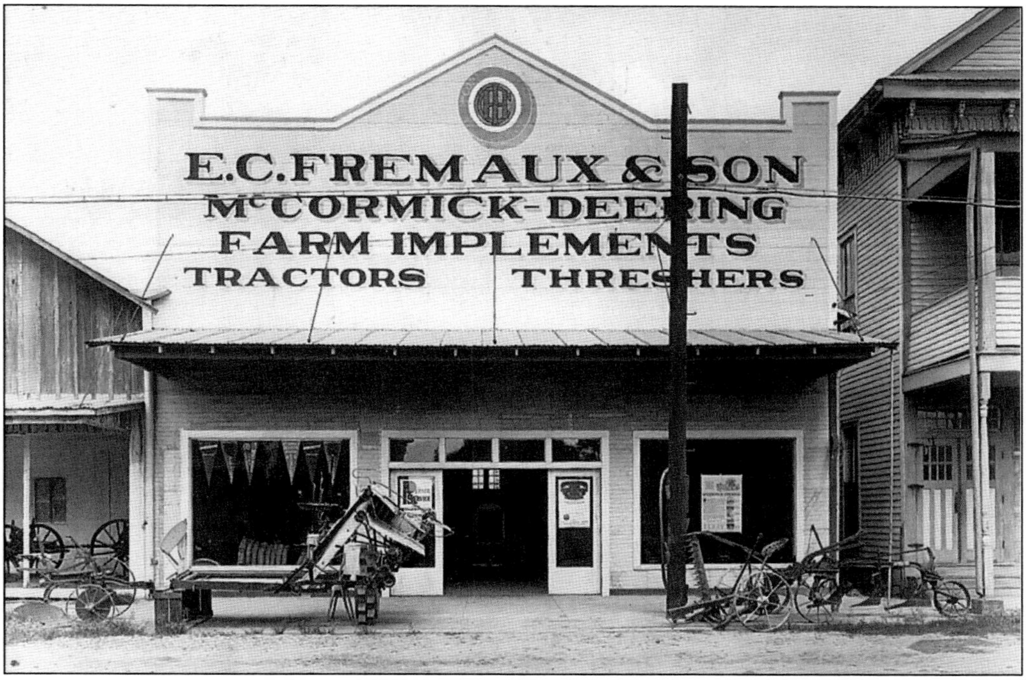

This is an outside view of E.C. Fremaux and Son Hardware and Implement Co., dealers in Mccormick-Deering implements. To the right you can see the Opera House and the Woodmen of the World Building. On the left is the Hebert Farm Implement Store, which was eventually bought by the Fremaux's. (Courtesy Fair Craig Hash.)

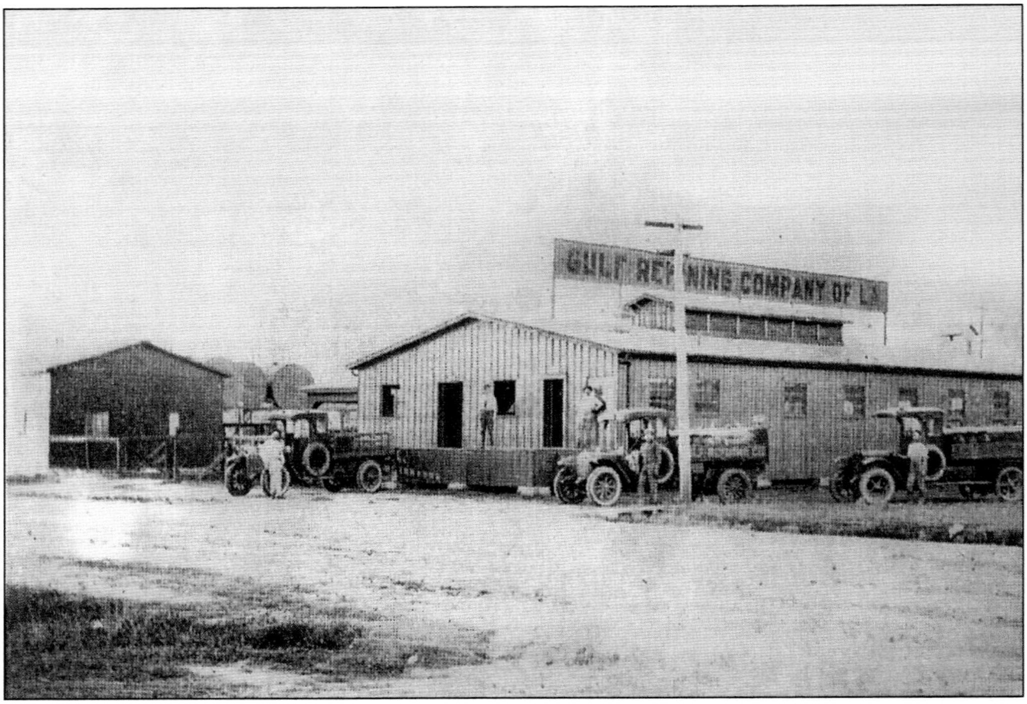

The Gulf Refining Co. of Louisiana located on Texas Avenue was owned by the Gaurdins and J.A. Pecot family. E.J. Gaurdin managed the plant, which later became the Rayne Oil Co. (Courtesy Fair Craig Hash.)

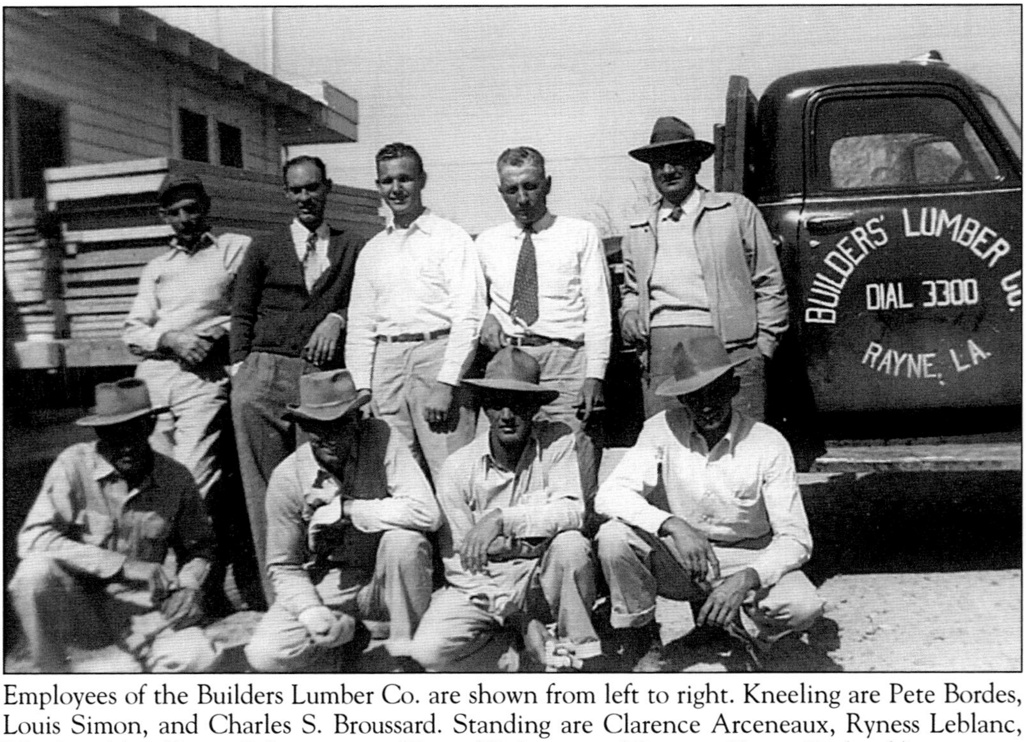

Employees of the Builders Lumber Co. are shown from left to right. Kneeling are Pete Bordes, Louis Simon, and Charles S. Broussard. Standing are Clarence Arceneaux, Ryness Leblanc, Jake Laughlin, Desire Babineaux, and Lionel Babineaux. (Courtesy Yvette Richard.)

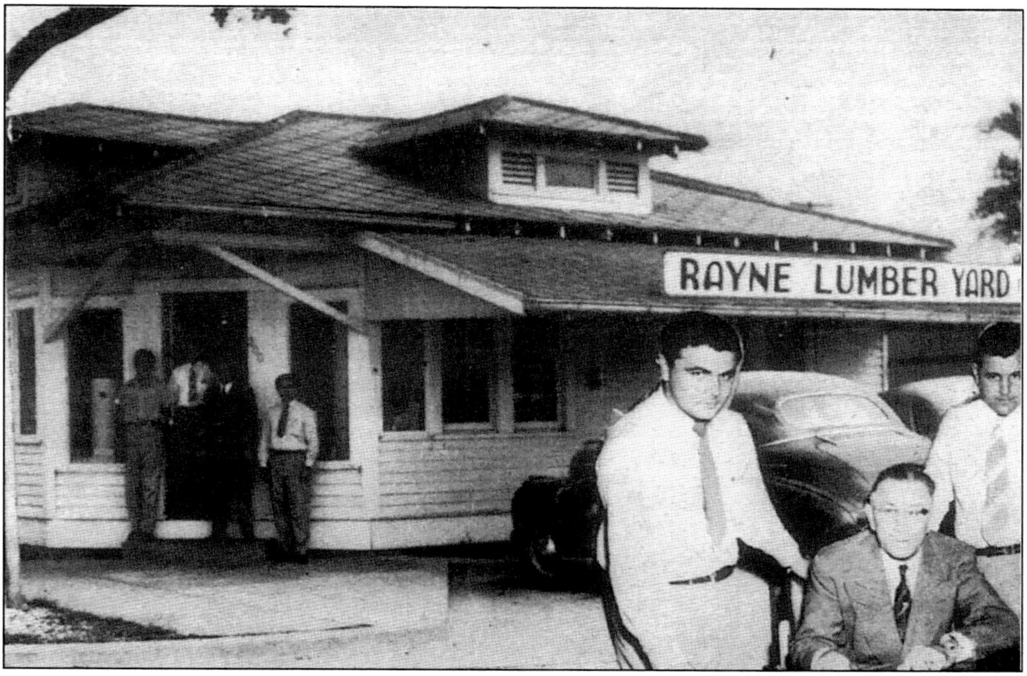

The Rayne Lumber Yard Inc. is shown with an inset view of Bill Gossen, Allen Gossen, and Richard Gossen. (Courtesy Charles S. Stutes.)

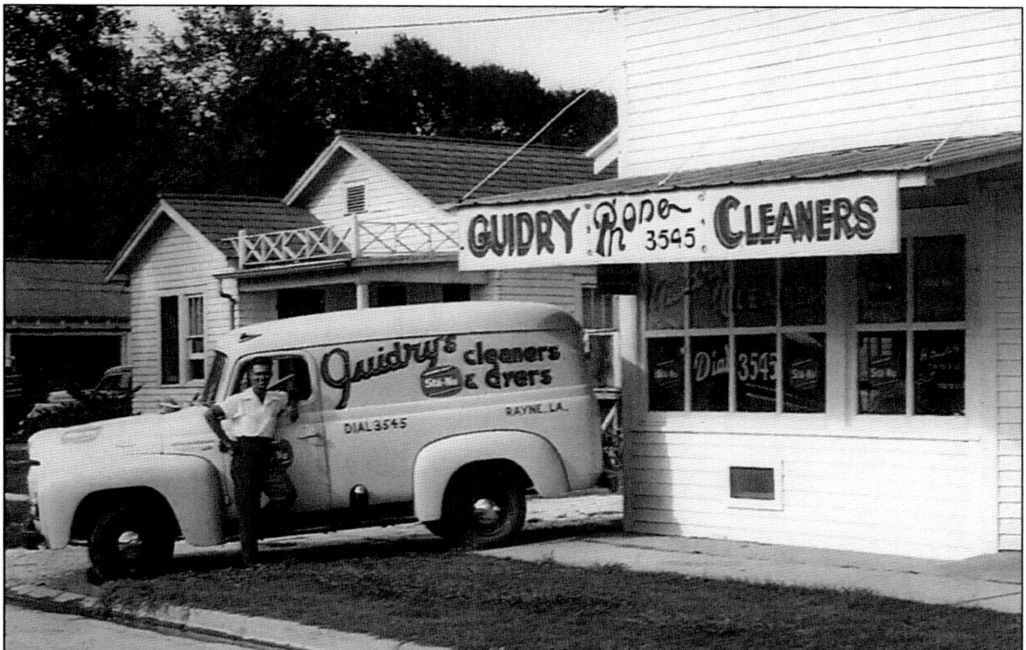

Owner Danny Domingue is shown outside of Guidry's Cleaners with his delivery truck. (Courtesy Lucille Barrows.)

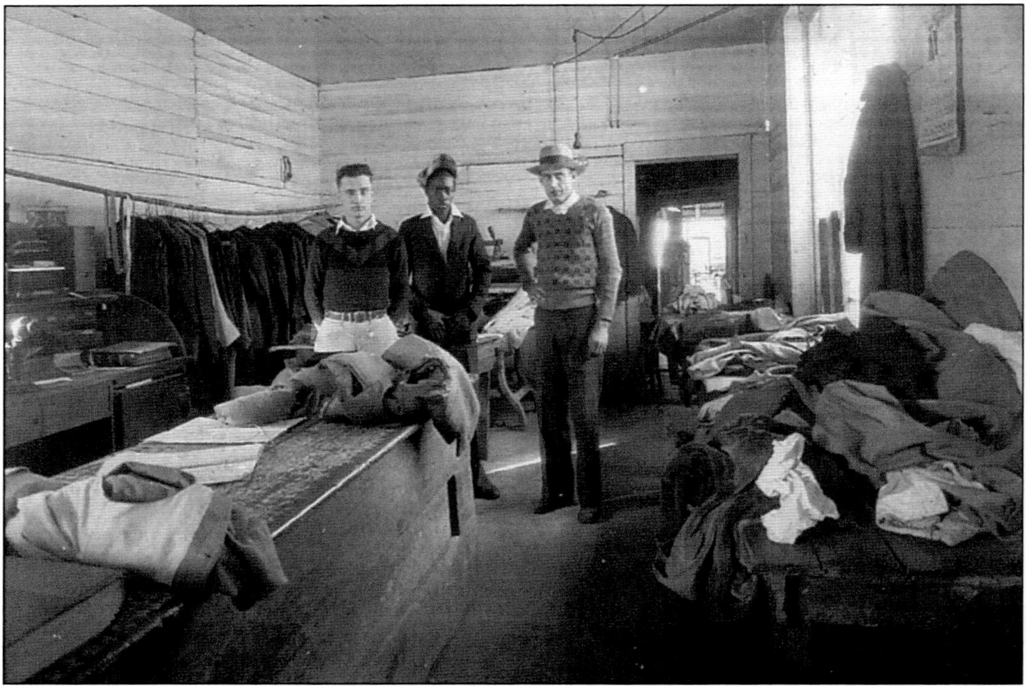

Clet Leblanc (manager), Charlie ?, and Eddie Floyd (who was notorious for his slot machines at local businesses) are shown inside Elite Tailors located at 208 South Adams Avenue in 1928. (Courtesy Steve Leblanc.)

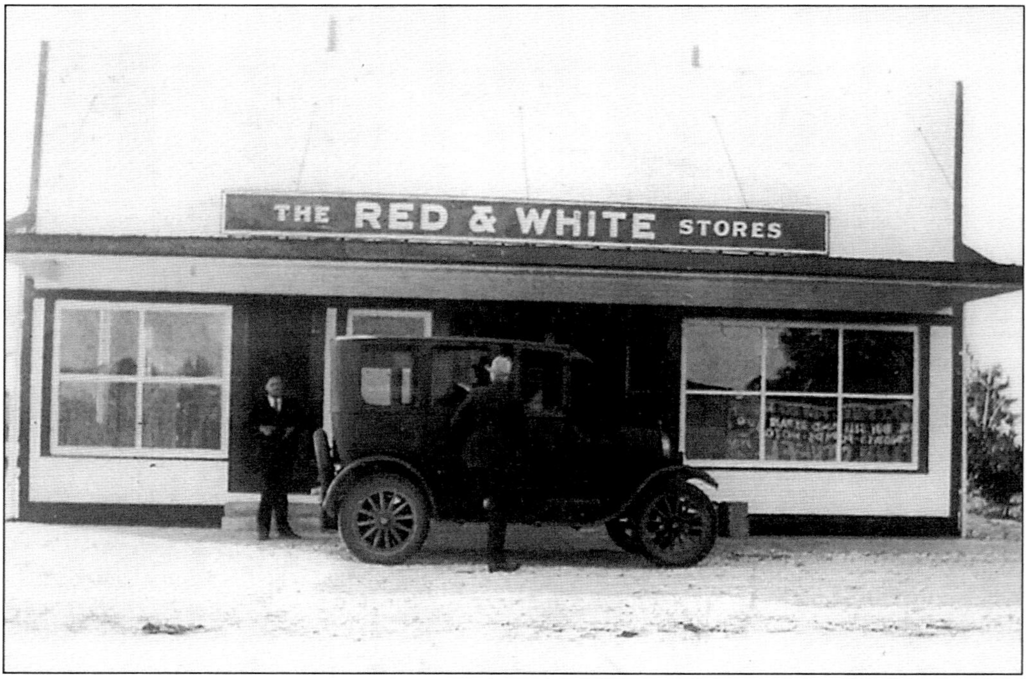

The Red and White store on the 600 block of South Adams Avenue later became Simoneaux's Bar. Then, it became popular as Mayance's (Leger's Bar). (Courtesy Nanette Leblanc.)

An unidentified youth with his bicycle is shown outside of Royal Cleaners picking up an order. (Courtesy Charles S. Stutes.)

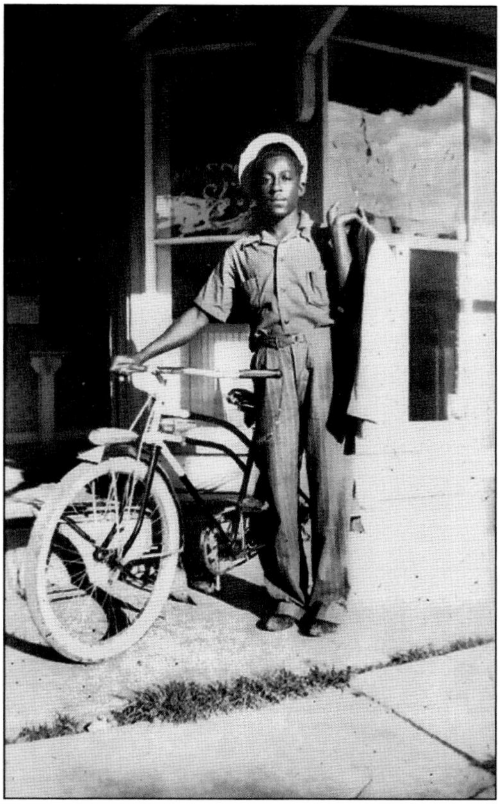

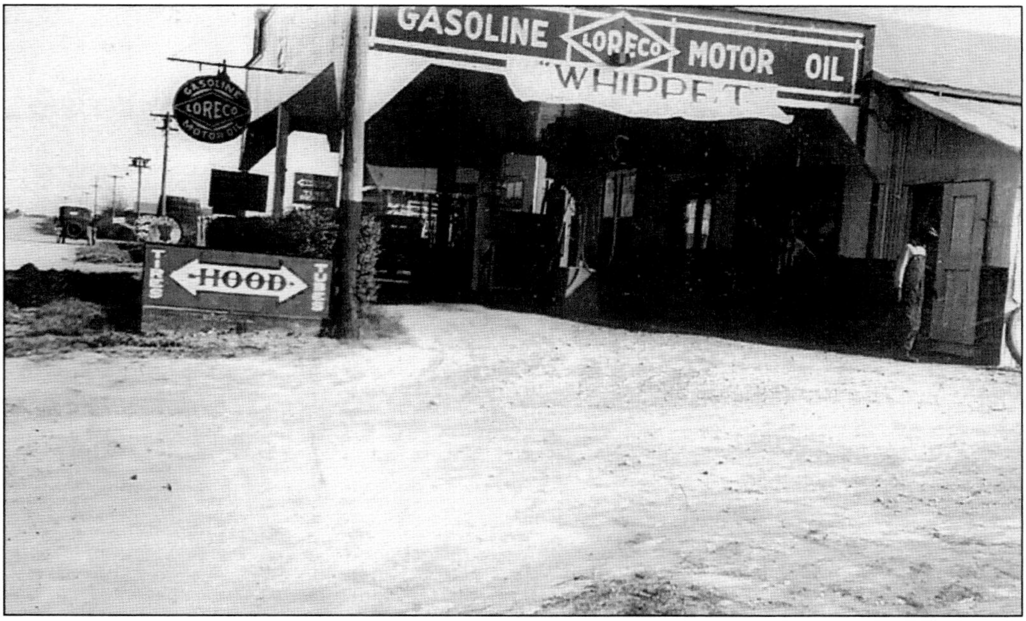

Dago Morgan's first gas station/garage was located on Jeff Davis Avenue between Arenas and Cunningham Streets and featured Loreco gasoline and motor oil. (Courtesy Freddie and Carolyn Morgan.)

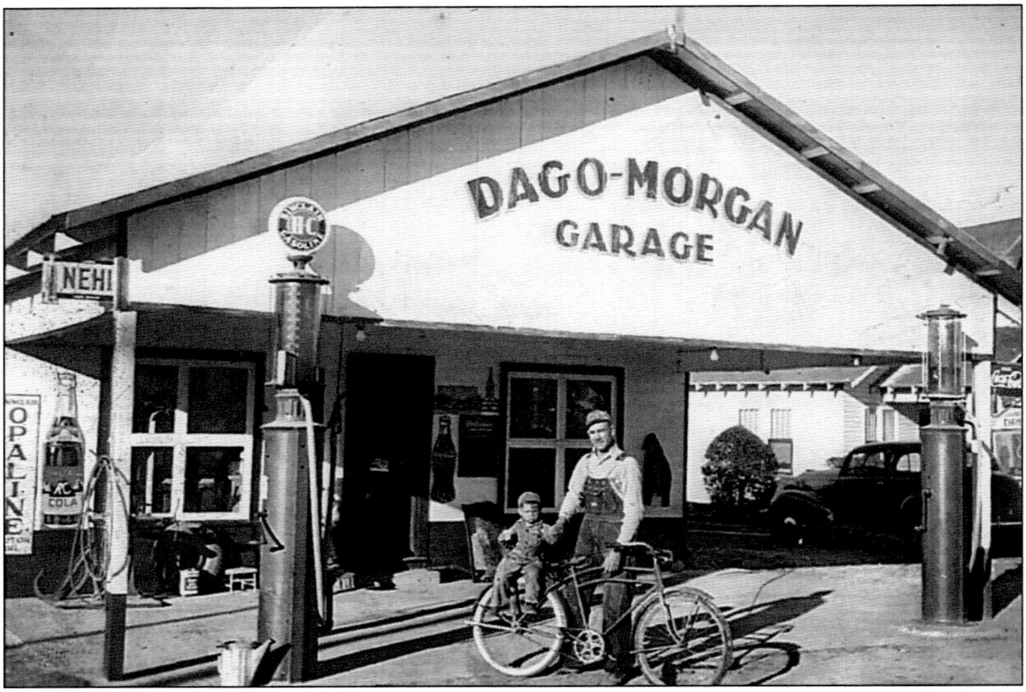

The more familiar Dago Morgan Garage on North Polk and Stadium Drive is shown here. In the picture is Dago Morgan and his son, Freddie "Bully" Morgan. At one time, sandwiches and snacks were sold from a drive-in window. (Courtesy Freddie and Carolyn Morgan.)

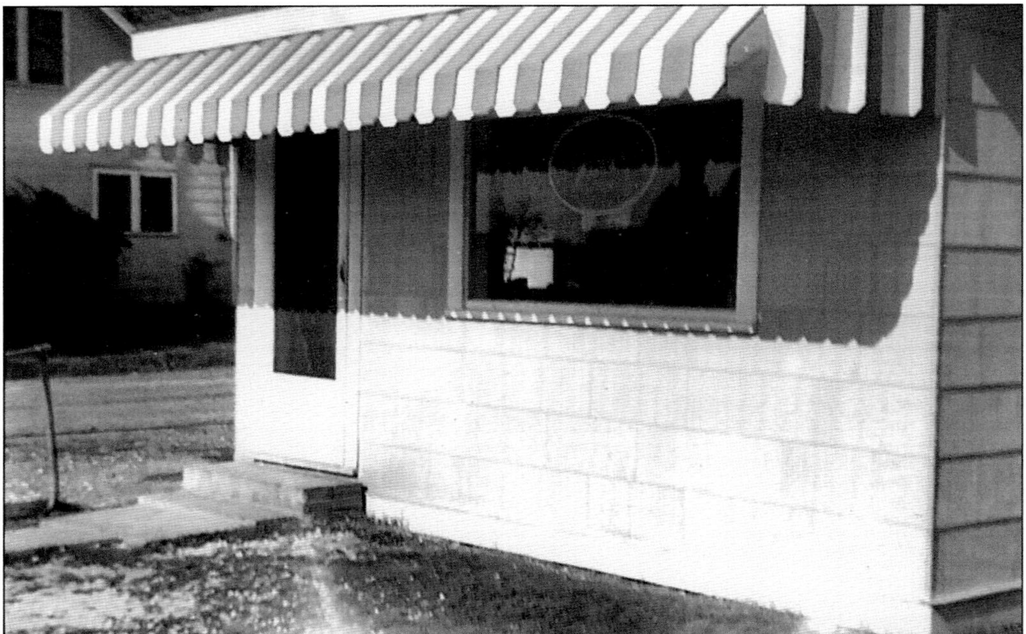

A familiar landmark and hangout for Rayne High students was the Domingue Hamburger Stand located across from the school on North Polk where jukebox music filled the air. (Courtesy Raymond Domingue.)

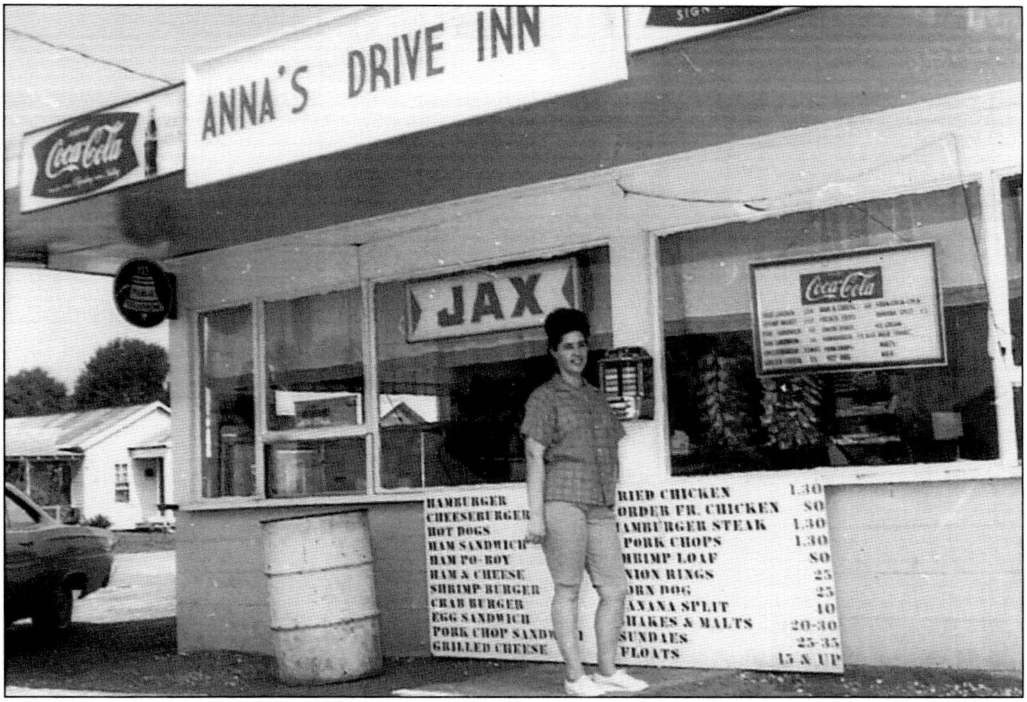

Anna's Drive-Inn, located on West Jeff Davis and Holt Street, was burned in the riots of the late 1960s. Pictured is Anna Louise Bourque Lavergne whose daughter, Glenda Faye, recounts stories of learning how to cook and make ice cream cones as a little girl. (Courtesy Fair Craig Hash.)

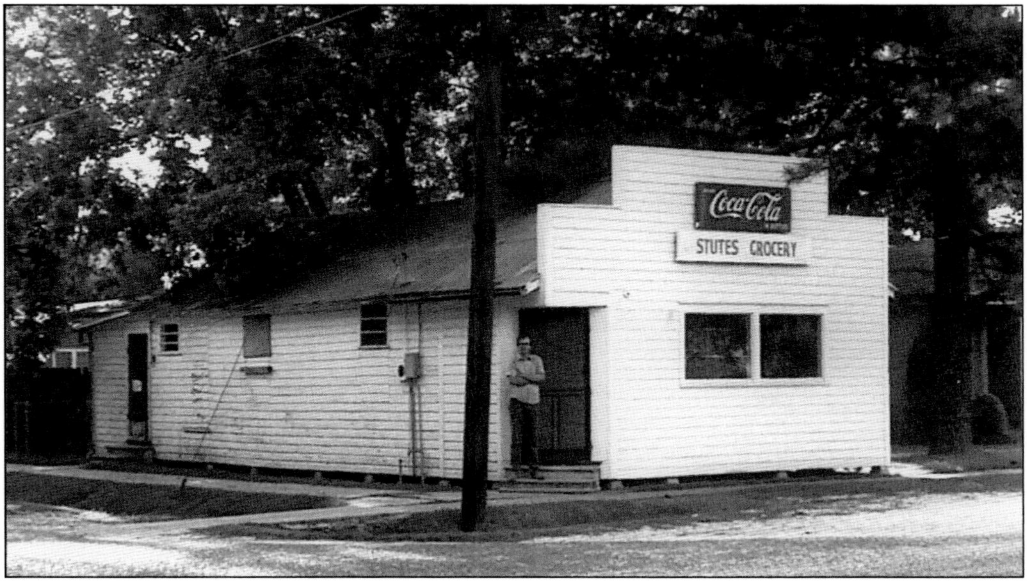

Ralph Stutes is pictured on the steps of Stutes Grocery, located on Lyman Avenue. The store was originally established in 1937 by Ralph's father, Ernest Stutes, who operated it from their home. In 1954 a rental house was purchased and converted into the second store. Ralph bought the business from his father and subsequently became the Mayor of Rayne. (Courtesy Charles S. Stutes.)

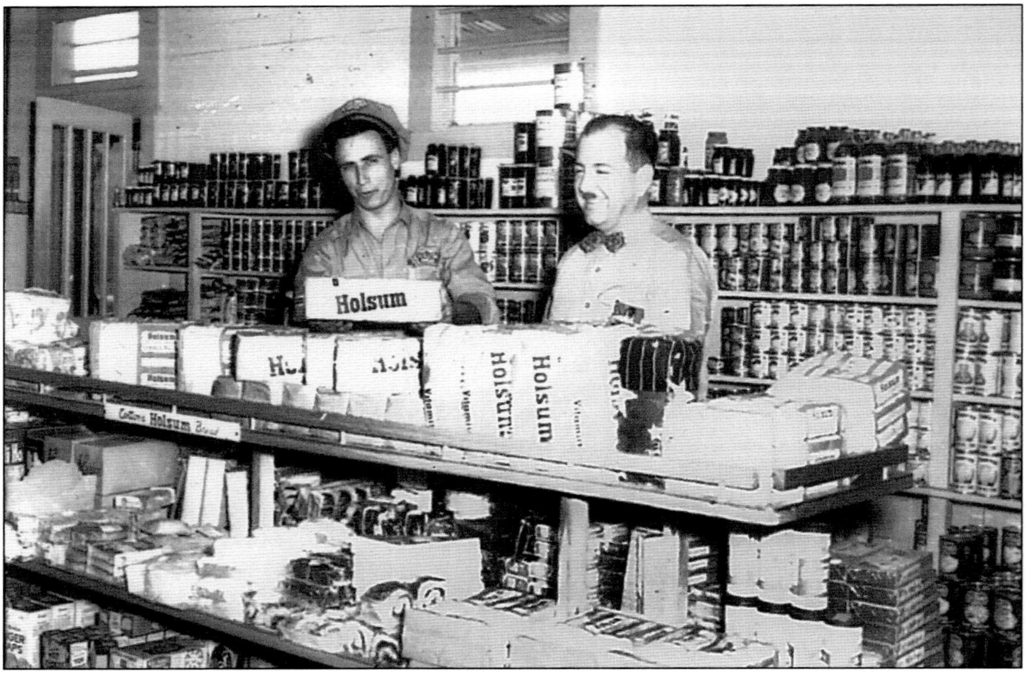

Batson Richard is shown with the Cotton Bread delivery man at one of the counters of his grocery store, which served the Rayne community for many years. Many remember that Batson would give a pack of gum to youngsters when their mother checked out. (Courtesy Jo Cart.)

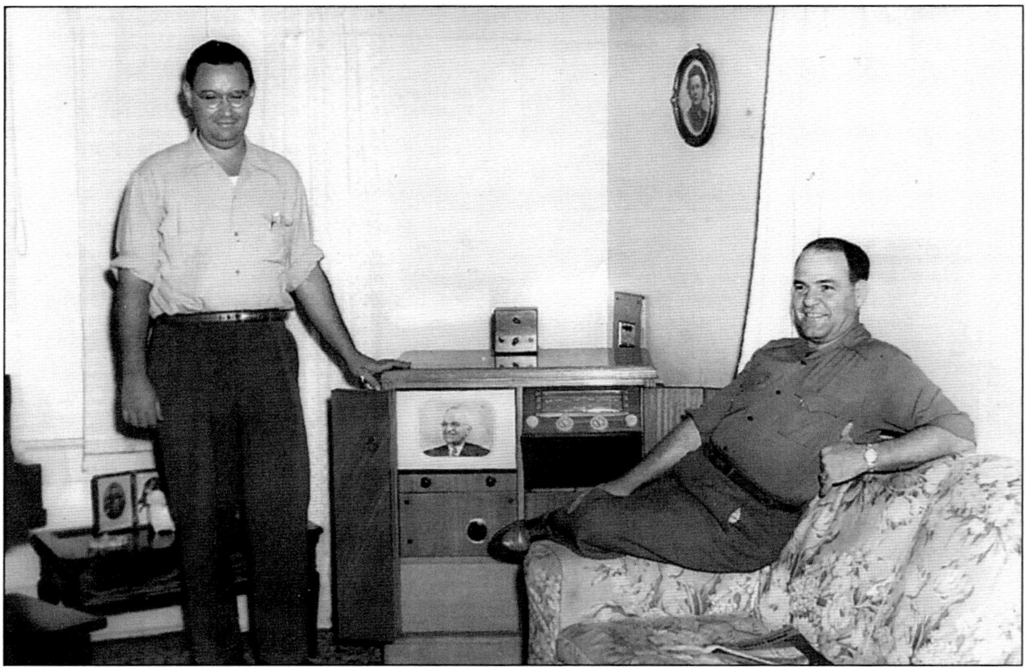

The latest in television was demonstrated by Leon T. Siadous (seated) and Robert Frank (standing) of the firm Siadous Radio Sales and Service located on South Adams Street. They are displaying the new Howard Console showing Harry Truman, then President of the United States. (Courtesy Donald Petitjean.)

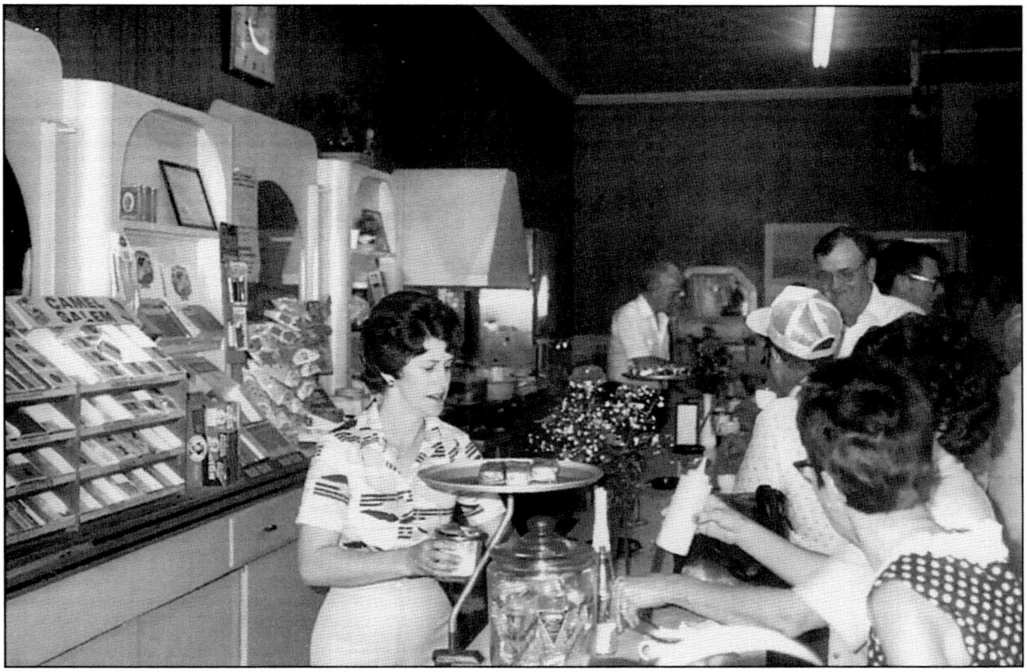

This was a common sight at Paco's Café lunch counter—Evelyn Leger and Jesse Breaux serving the lunch crowd. It was a popular gathering place for businessmen, politicians, and anyone who wanted to know the latest news on the street. (Courtesy Rayne State Bank.)

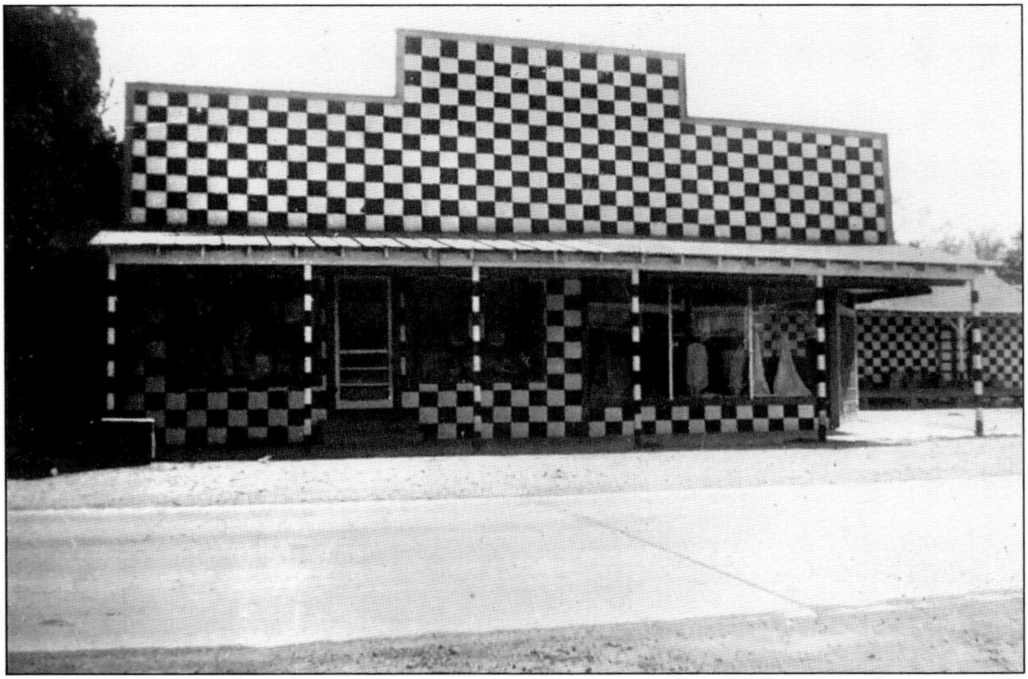

Lee Mayeaux's many businesses included this Red and White Purina Checkerboard Store, which was later Petitjean Radio and TV Repair. It was then torn down and was located where Galaxy Chinese Restaurant now stands. (Courtesy Charles S. Stutes.)

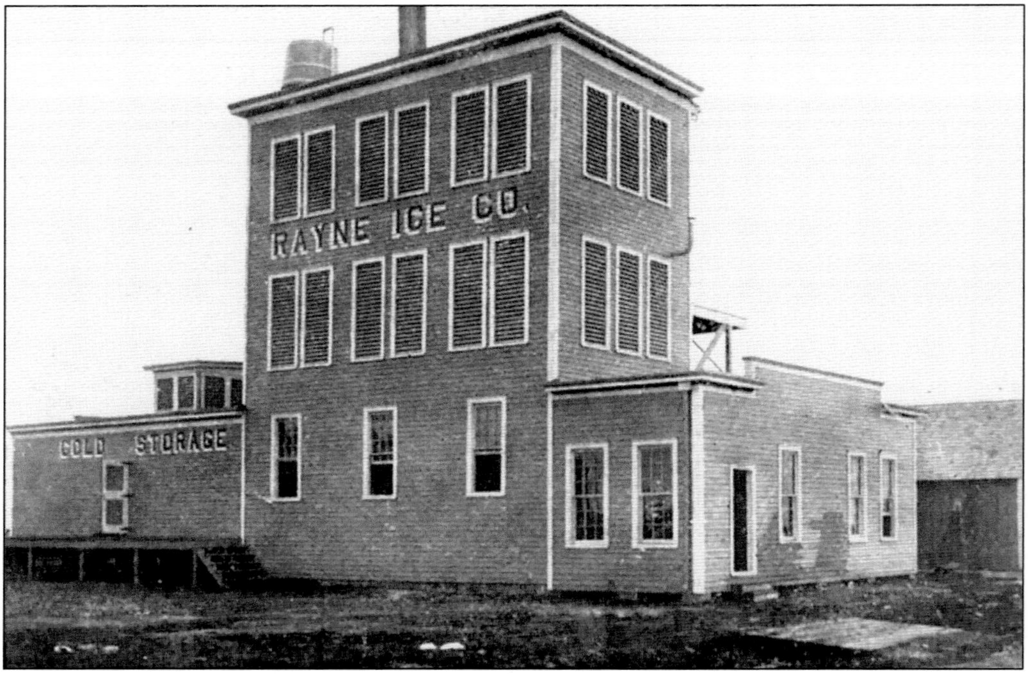

The old steam ice plant, Rayne Ice Co. was originally operated as Gossen and Leonards and was classed among the best in this part of the state. It had a daily capacity of 20,000 pounds and a large cold storage room for the preservation of meats, fruits, butter, and eggs. (Courtesy Charles S. Stutes.)

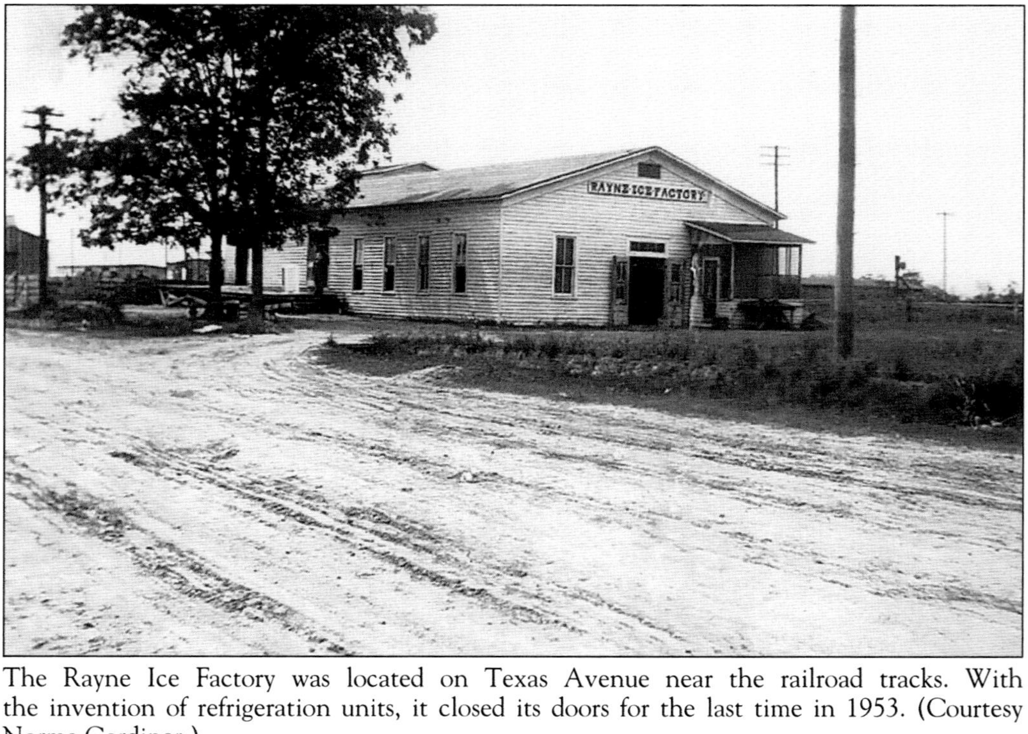

The Rayne Ice Factory was located on Texas Avenue near the railroad tracks. With the invention of refrigeration units, it closed its doors for the last time in 1953. (Courtesy Norma Gardiner.)

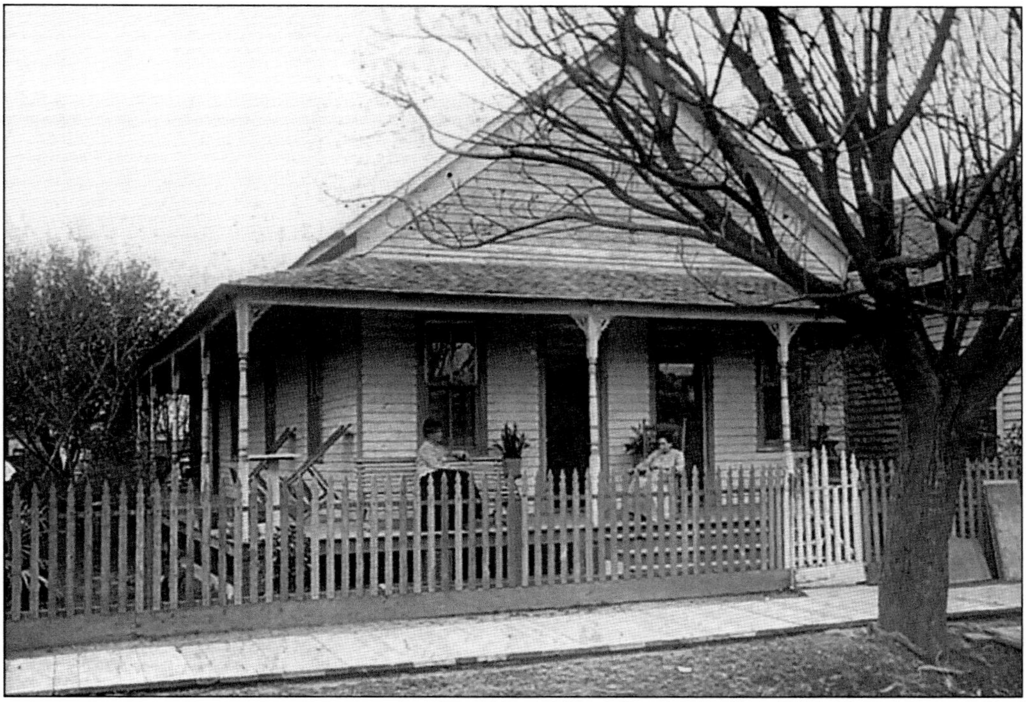

Shown above is the home of P.F. Besse on Adams Avenue, approximately where Mr. Gatti's now stands. Shown in the bottom photo is Besse Furniture Store, which was directly next door to the Besse Home. Shown sitting on the front porch is Louise Burns Besse (Mrs. P.F. Besse) and "Tante Zine," who lived and worked at the Commercial Hotel. Notice the boardwalks along the front of the house that were the early walkways lining the main street. (Courtesy Margaret Zaunbrecher.)

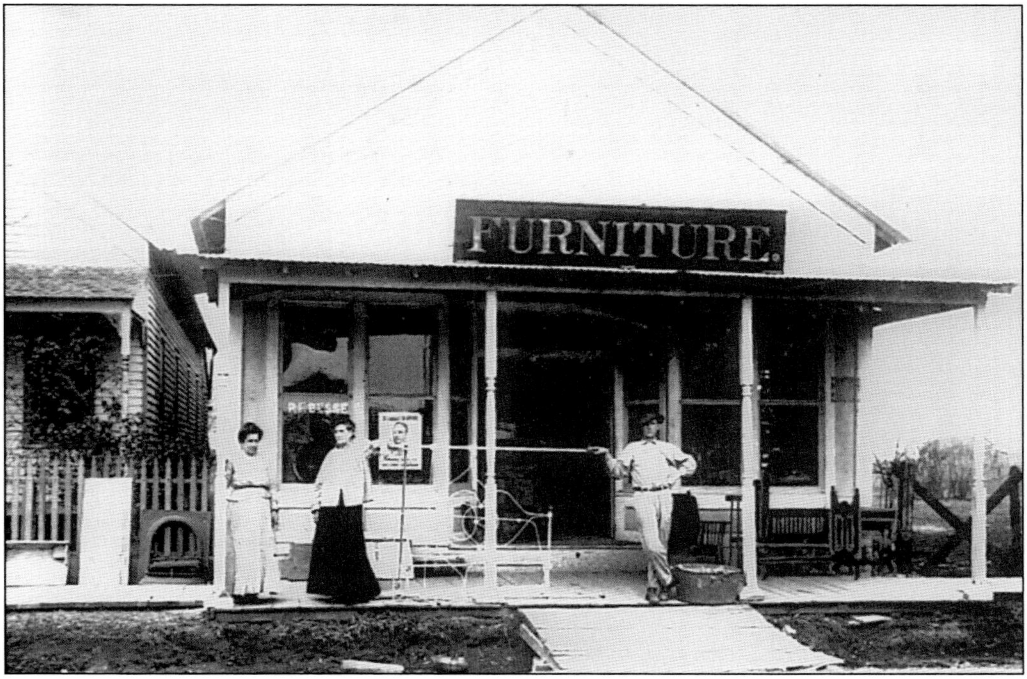

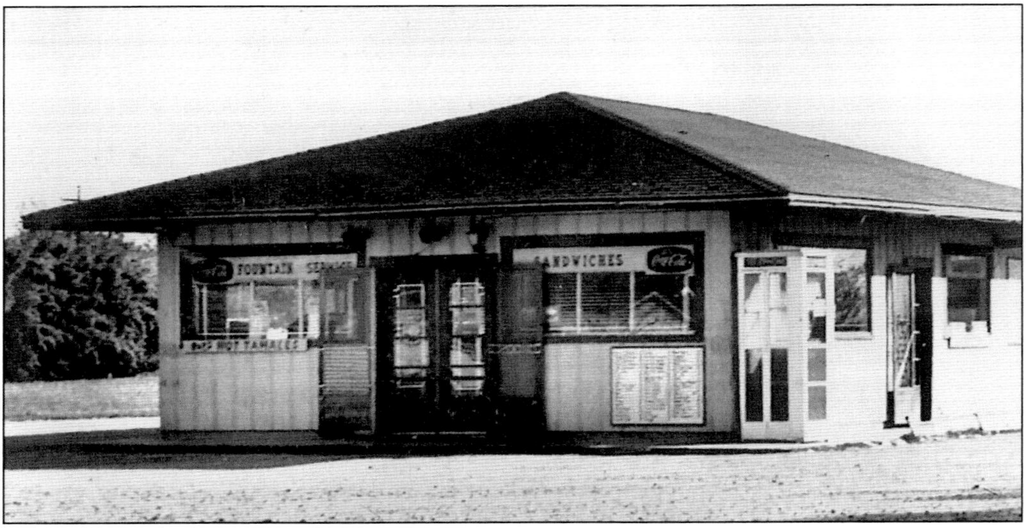

Johnson's Drive-In, a "mecca" for teenagers in the 1950s, was owned and operated by Glady and Flemon Johnson. It was located on South Adams and Branche Street. (Courtesy Tom Johnson.)

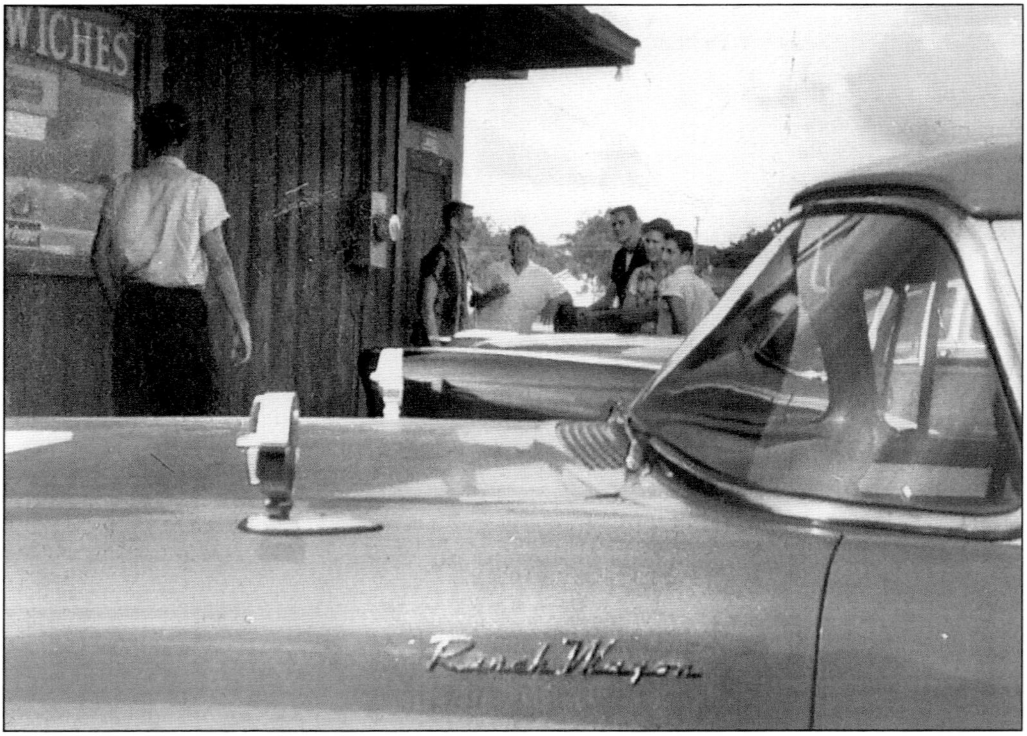

Several local youths are enjoying the day outside at Johnson's Drive-In. Pictured from left to right are Winston Petitjean (walking), Gus Leblanc, Myron Chaisson, Carroll Mouton, Frank Privat, and Alex Joe Lacroix. (Courtesy Tom Johnson.)

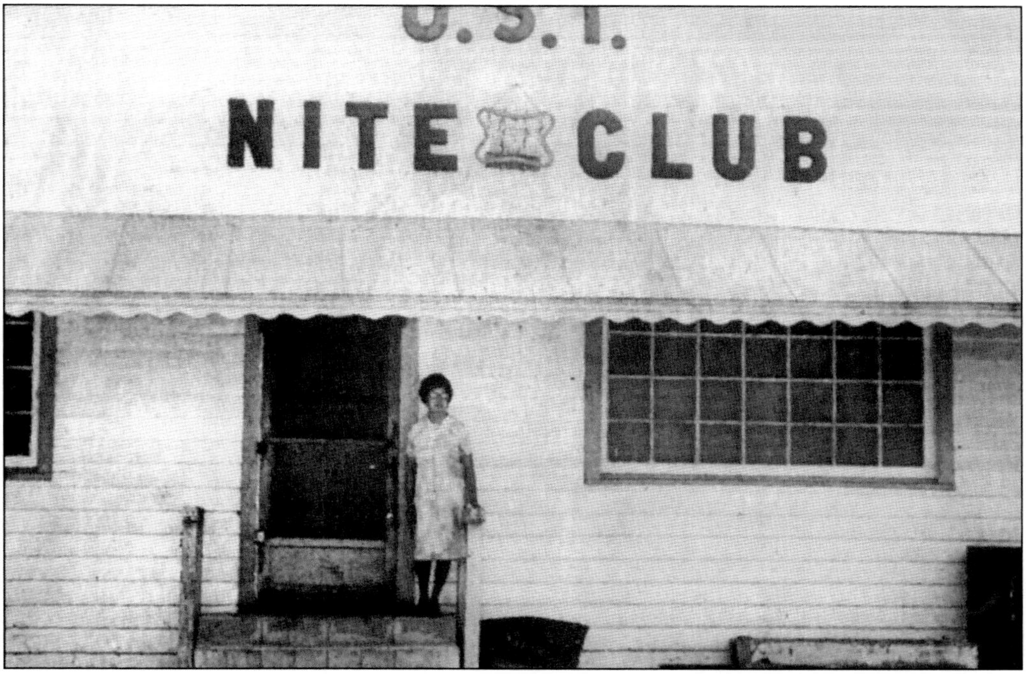

Mrs. Joe Latour is pictured on the steps of the famous O.S.T. Dance Hall located on South Arenas Street, so named for the original site located at the Old Spanish Trail, the road coming through Rayne as a principal "highway" in those years. It was moved to its location on South Arenas Street when increased traffic along the trail, which was absorbed by Highway 90, made necessary parking no longer available. (Courtesy Charles S. Stutes.)

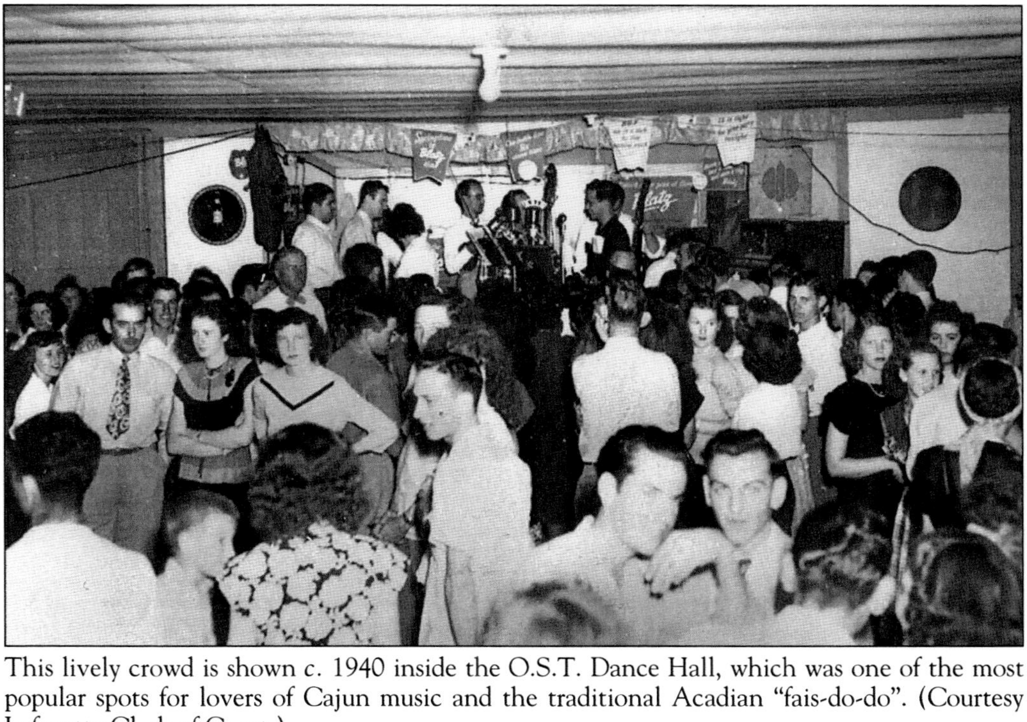

This lively crowd is shown c. 1940 inside the O.S.T. Dance Hall, which was one of the most popular spots for lovers of Cajun music and the traditional Acadian "fais-do-do". (Courtesy Lafayette Clerk of Court.)

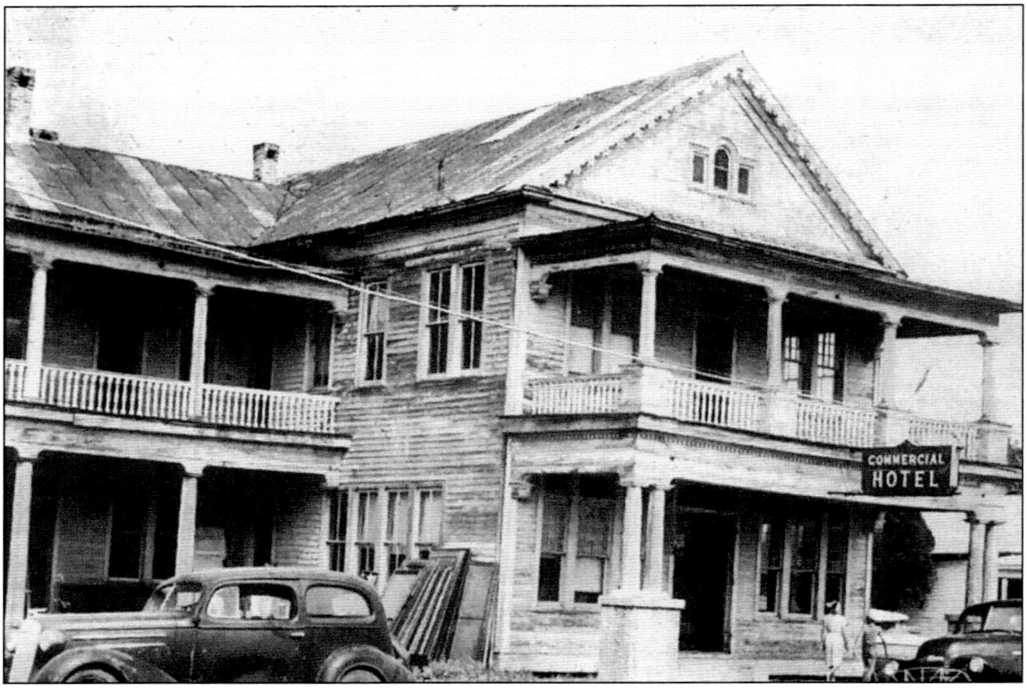

The Commercial Hotel, Rayne's most famous establishment for overnight lodging, is pictured above. It catered to traveling salesmen, and across the street was a livery stable. The salesmen could rent a horse and buggy there to travel around the area to make their sales calls. Celebrities such as Tex Ritter, Lash LaRue, and Sunset Carson stayed there during their promotional tours. Local youth would wait in the lobby for their favorite stars in hopes of getting an autograph. The building was later purchased and torn down in 1952 by Jack Koury to build his jewelry store. (Courtesy Charles S. Stutes.)

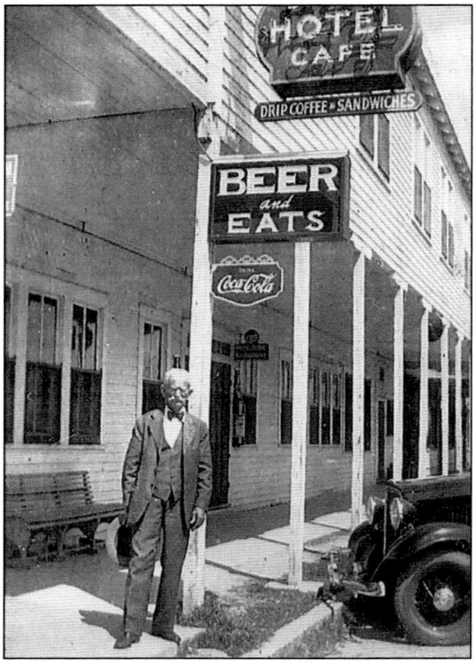

The Besse Hotel, owned by Camile Besse, was the precursor to the Town House. The restaurant was on the ground floor. The second floor space on the front side housed the old telephone company where the switchboard operators facilitated phone calls before being moved to the second floor of Broussard's Drug Store. The back part of the second floor served as the hotel. Shown standing in front is P.F. Besse. (Courtesy Margaret Zaunbrecher.)

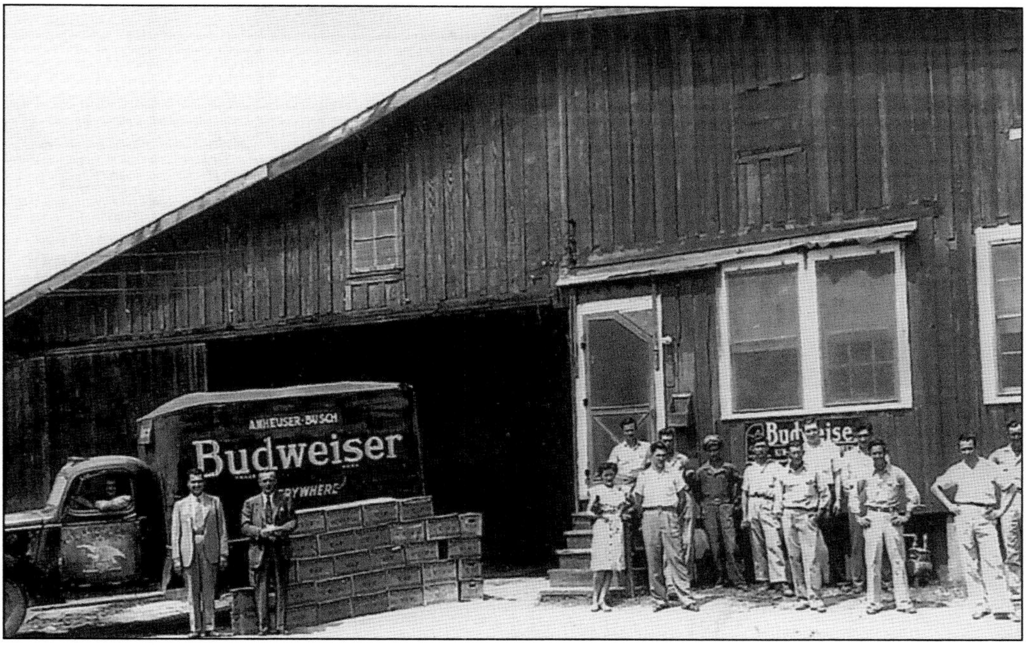

Rayne Wholesale Distributing had the local Budweiser distributorship and is shown here with the Budweiser delivery truck and many of their employees. The business was started in 1928 at the intersection of West Texas and Second Street. Pictured, from left to right, are Bill Comeaux in truck, Fred Darby (manager), an unidentified person, Irene Darby, Woody Gaspard, Francis Mier, an unidentified person, Edias Royer, Lloyd Guidry, Adam Hargrove, Edwin Spell, Lawrence Guidry, and Wilson Broussard. (Courtesy Lawrence Guidry.)

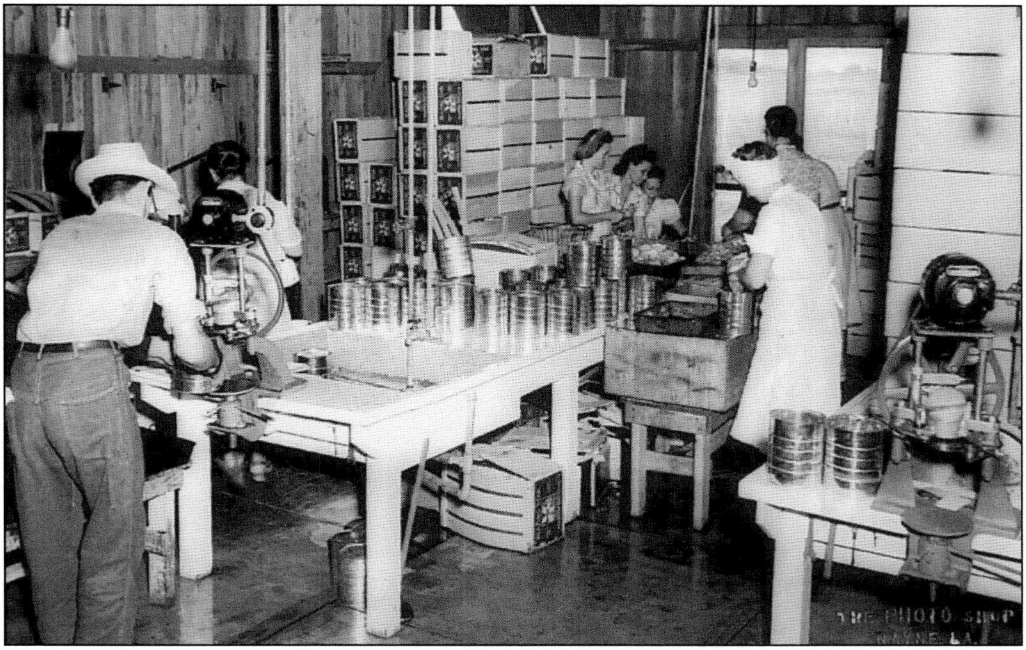

Associated Distributing Co. packers are shown stacking Blazing Star Bartlett pears, one of the many products packaged. The packing business was started in 1950 and was a subsidiary of Rayne Wholesale Grocery. (Courtesy Donald Petitjean.)

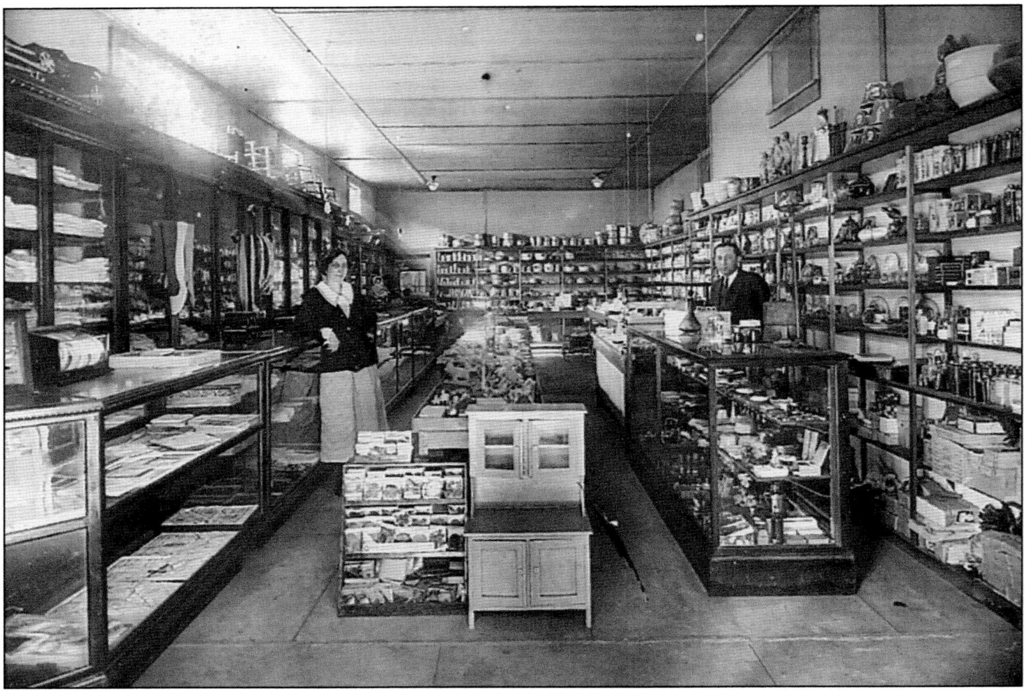

Walter McBride at the right is shown with his sister, Ella, inside McBrides's Pharmacy on South Adams next to Robichaux's Meat Market. (Courtesy Jim and Mary Ann Bush.)

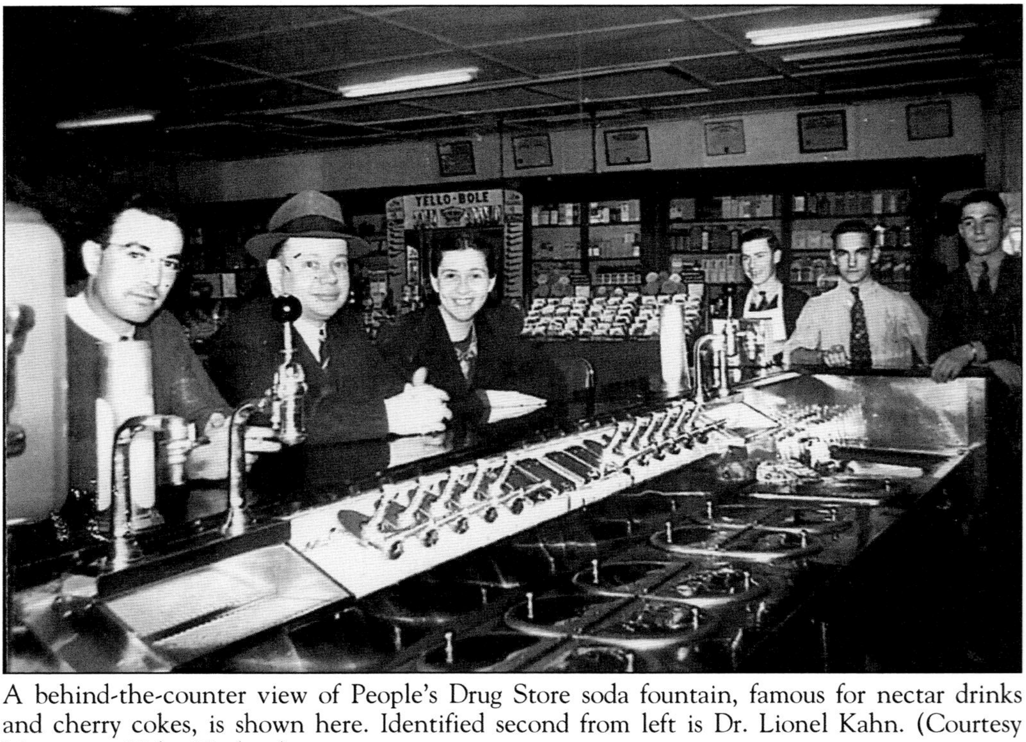

A behind-the-counter view of People's Drug Store soda fountain, famous for nectar drinks and cherry cokes, is shown here. Identified second from left is Dr. Lionel Kahn. (Courtesy Marguerite Kahn Hoskin.)

Lynn LeBlanc Horse and Mule Dealers opened in 1919 near the railroad tracks and later moved to its current location on Highway 90 when the city started to grow toward the south. The name was changed to LeBlanc Saddlery and Western Wear in the early 1970s when they stopped selling horses and mules. Pictured is Lynn LeBlanc. (Courtesy Jeremy Granger.)

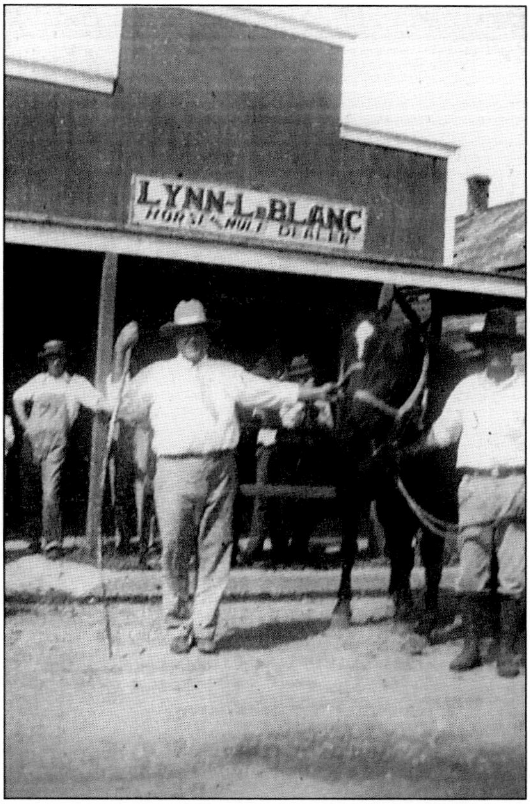

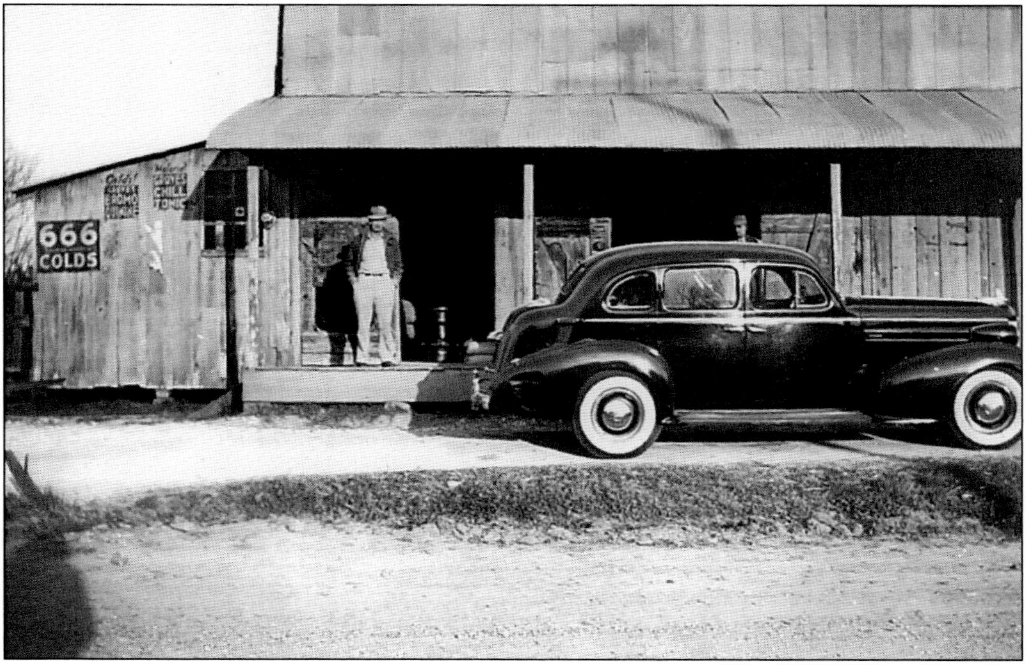

Pictured is L.C. Soileau in front of the Soileau Feed Warehouse located on the corner of North Polk and East F Street. The warehouse was located at the front of the property and the mill was directly behind. (Courtesy Virginia Soileau.)

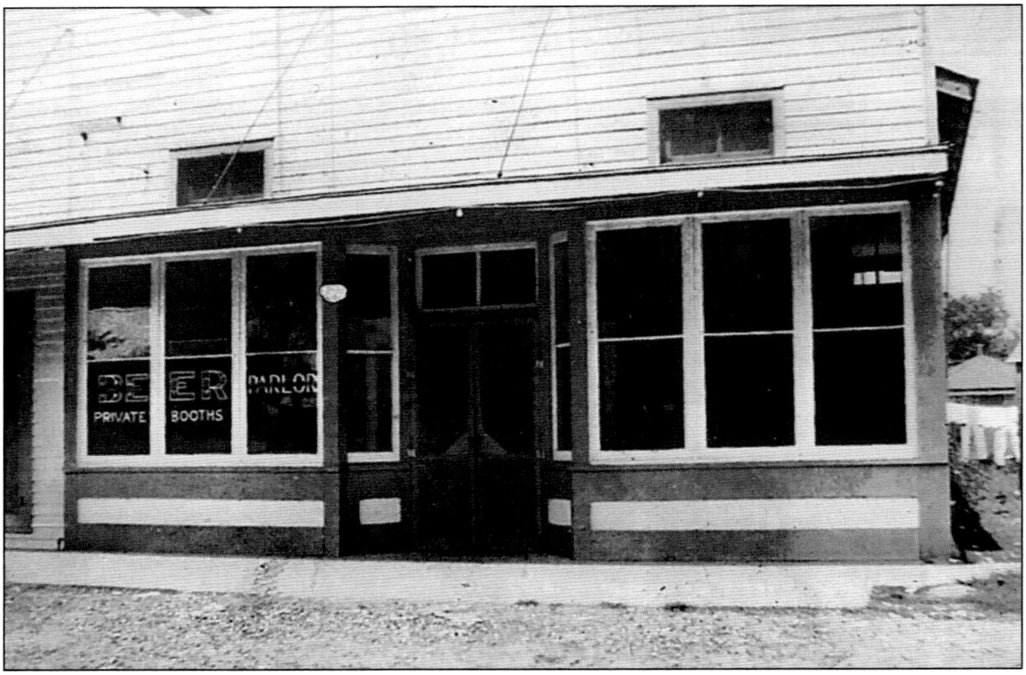

Pop and Herb's Place is shown in 1938. The business was located on West Texas Avenue behind the old Bank of Commerce building. The building later became City Bar. (Courtesy Fair Craig Hash.)

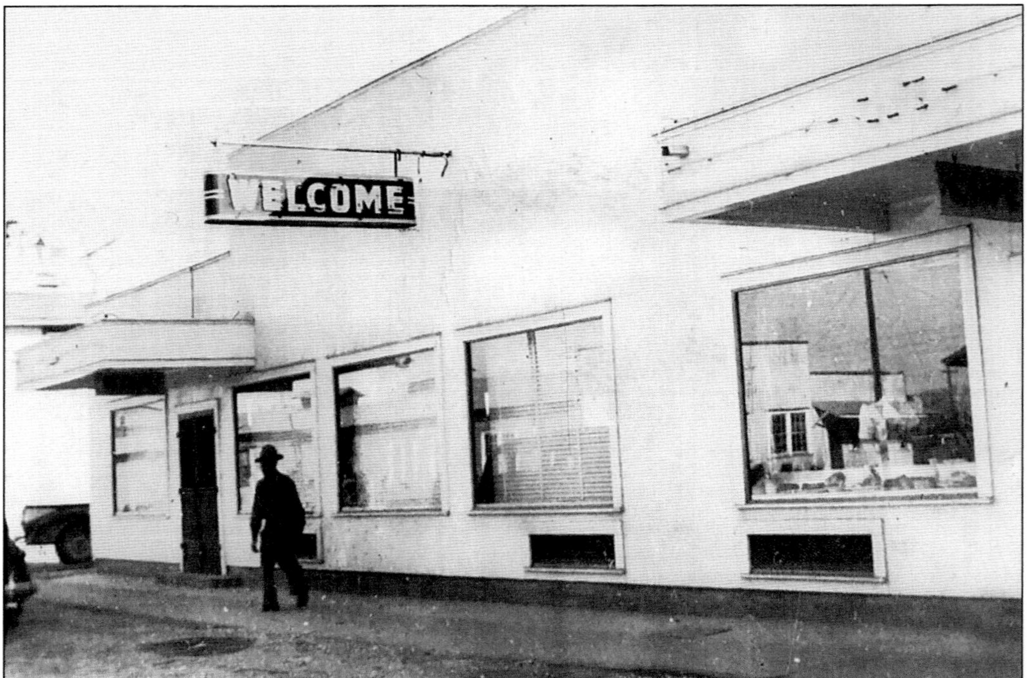

This is an exterior view of Gladys Robichaux's Welcome Bar and Café. Gladys would later turn the building into Robichaux's Five and Dime and would go on to build Robichaux Furniture. She is considered to be one of Rayne's greatest businesswomen. (Courtesy Fair Craig Hash.)

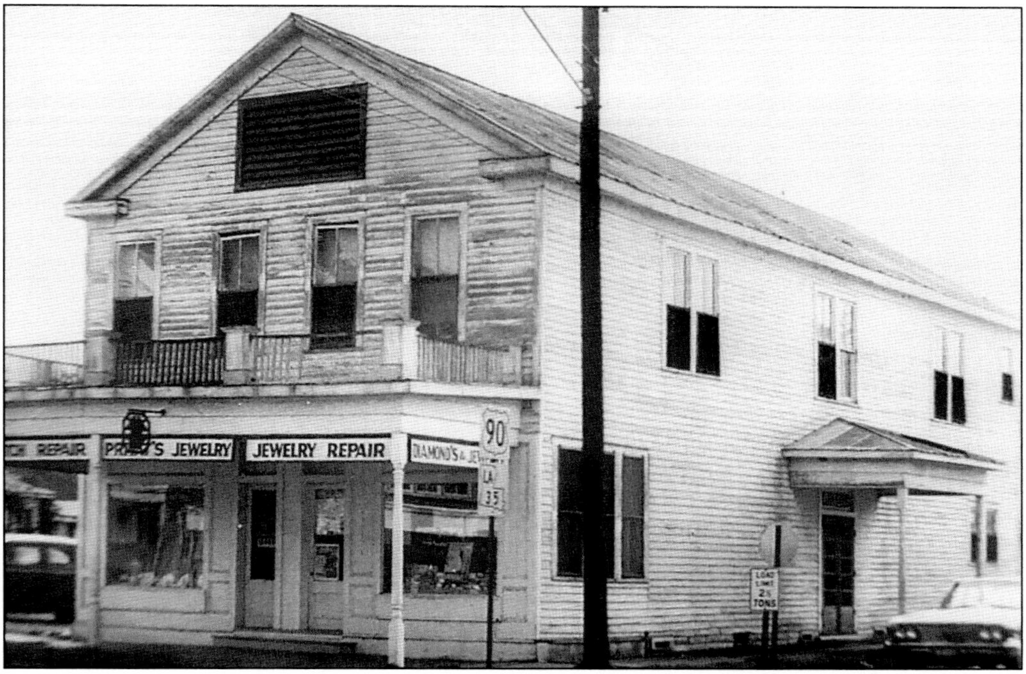

This building housed Privat's Jewelry Repair on the bottom floor and to the right is the stairwell that led upstairs to the Knights of Columbus Council's 1897 meeting space. The Boy Scout troop held their meetings at one time on the second floor. This building was later torn down and is now the site of the new Knights of Columbus home. (Courtesy Charles S. Stutes.)

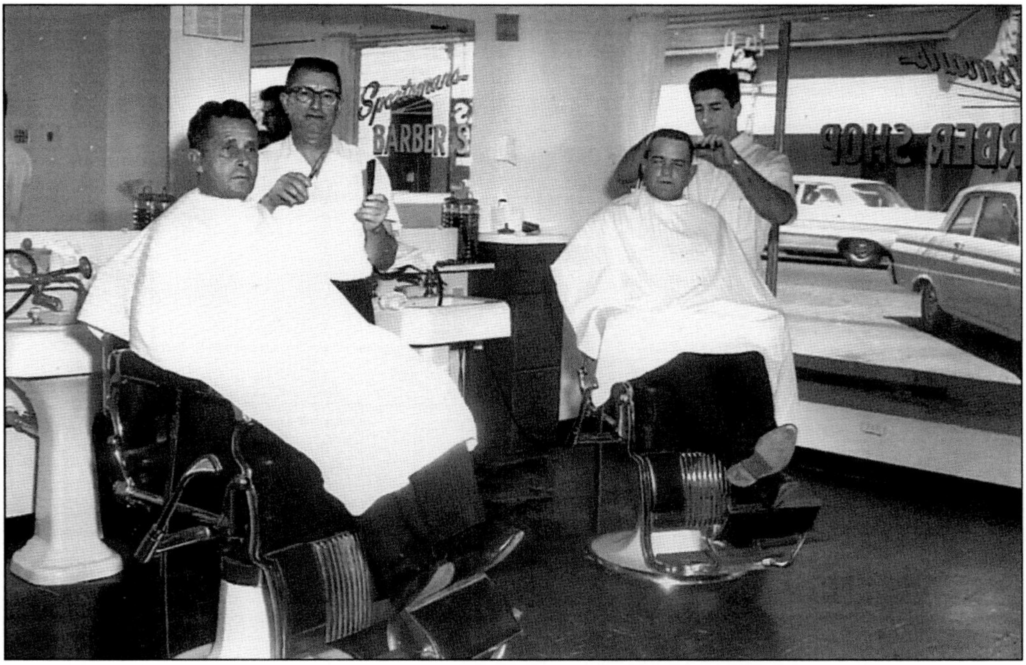

On September 4, 1964, the Sportsman's Barber Shop opened on East Texas Avenue. On the left is Lawrence "Pee Wee" Romero Jr. cutting the hair of Wedes Bourque. Alex Joe Lacroix is cutting the hair of George Monceaux. (Courtesy Fair Craig Hash.)

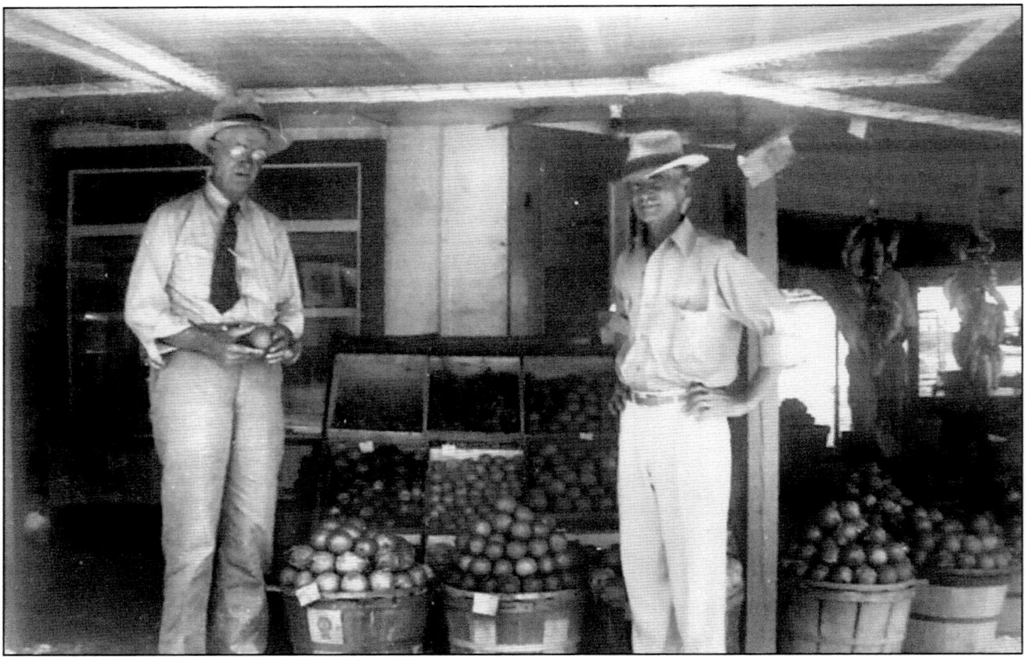

Privat's Fruit Stand, located on the 700 block of South Adams, was owned by Joe Privat (right) and managed by Ed Lancaster (left). His farm was located off Edwin Drive. He also had fruit stands in Lafayette and Crowley and would sell to local grocery stores from his truck. (Courtesy Julie Ousse.)

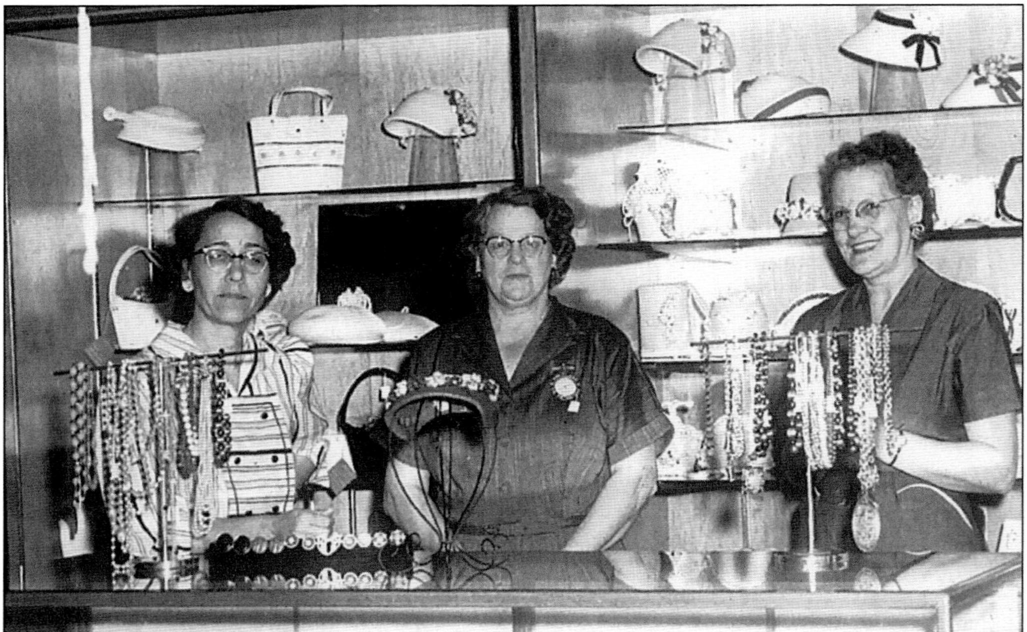

Catherine's ABC shop was owned and operated by Catherine Kahn and was on East Texas Avenue across from the depot square. Shown in this 1956 picture are, from left to right, Goldie Hebert, Catherine Kahn, and Ethel Winters. The shop was known for their handmade items. (Courtesy Albert Owers.)

"Newt" Hebert, wearing overalls, is shown walking in front of Sol Kahn Co., Inc., which was later Weill's Department Store and is now occupied by Dollar General Store. In late 1925, Sol Kahn leased the old "T" Miers Billiard Room from H.E. Bruner to expand his business to a ladies ready-to-wear. (Courtesy Ray Hebert.)

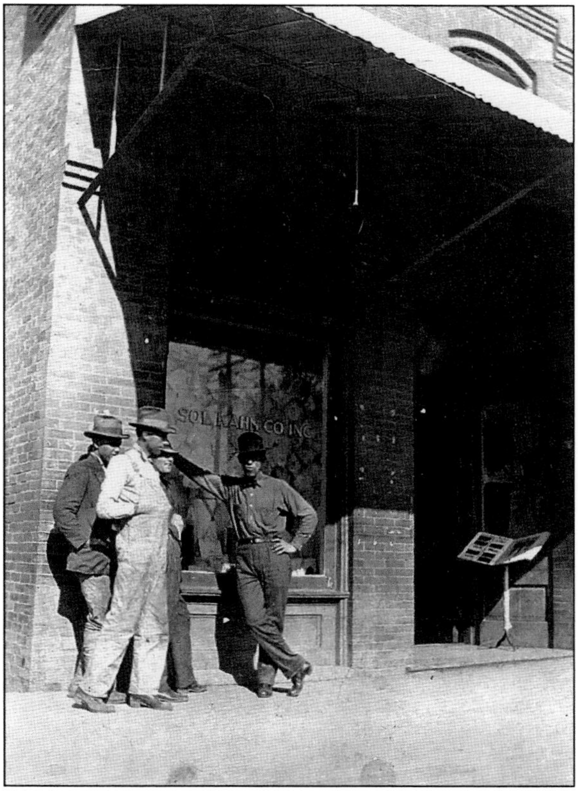

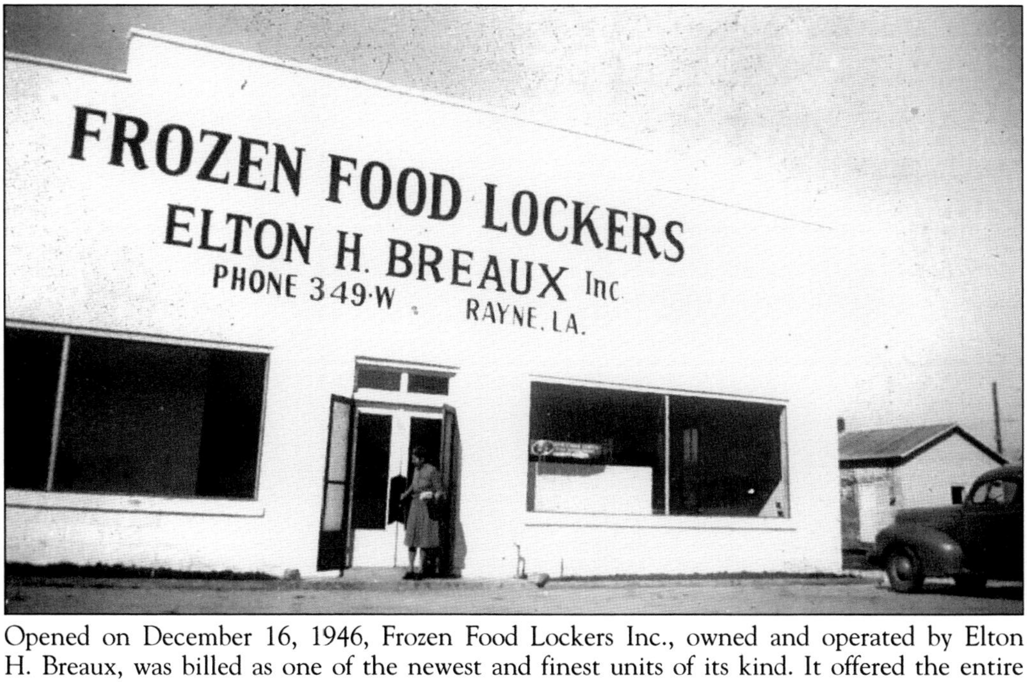

Opened on December 16, 1946, Frozen Food Lockers Inc., owned and operated by Elton H. Breaux, was billed as one of the newest and finest units of its kind. It offered the entire community the very latest in locker and frozen foods service, one of the most successful of all recent innovations in the food industry. The establishment was located on South Adams Street, which now houses the Slush Puppie offices. (Courtesy Charles S. Stutes.)

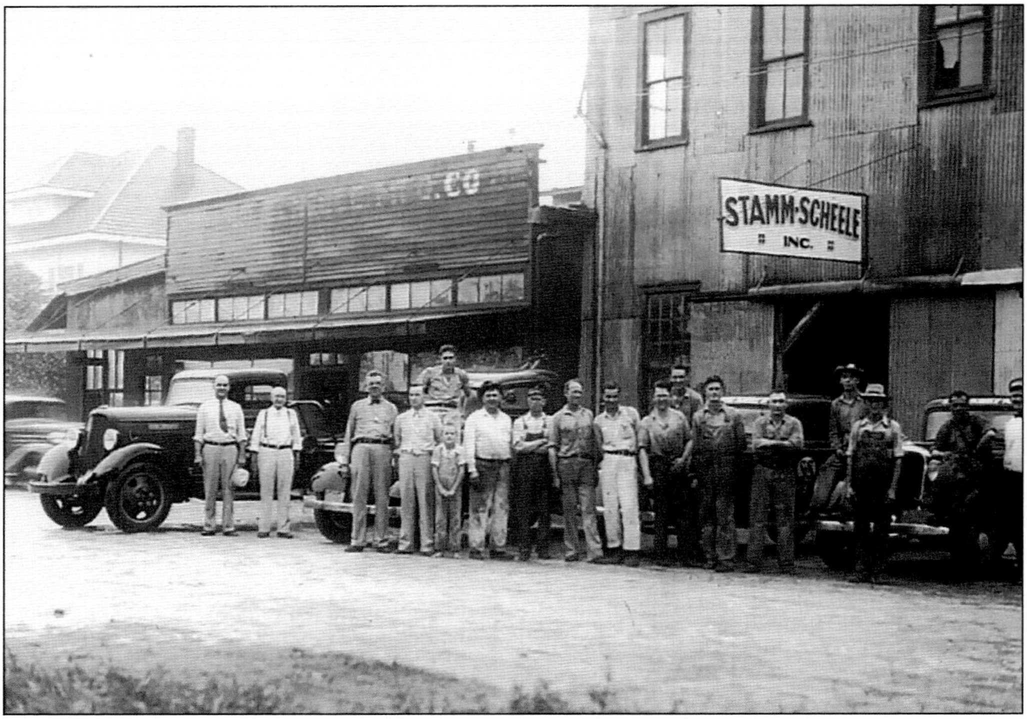

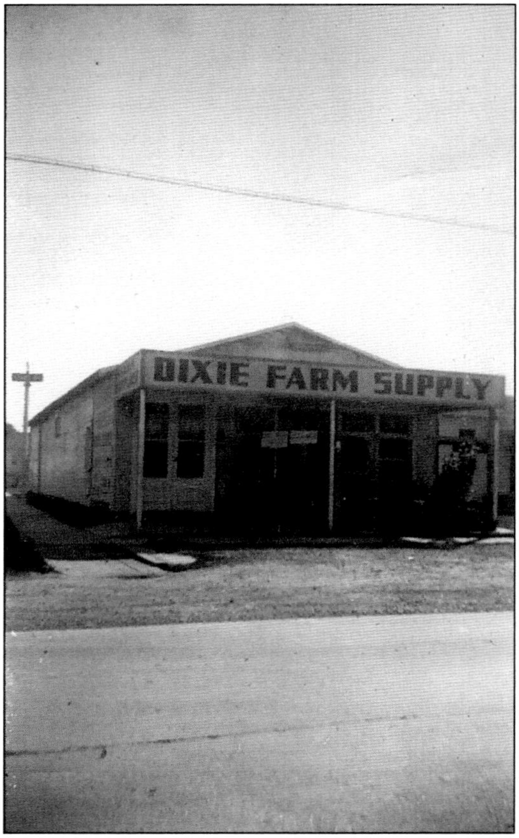

Employees of Stamm Scheele are shown standing in front of the old shop on Edwards Street. The house in the background belonged to Dr. Bruner. (Courtesy Tucker Johnston.)

This 1946 picture of Dixie Farm Supply, owned and operated by Leroy Bihm, was located on South Adams and Bull Street. They sold seed, feed, and farm supplies. (Courtesy Charles S. Stutes.)

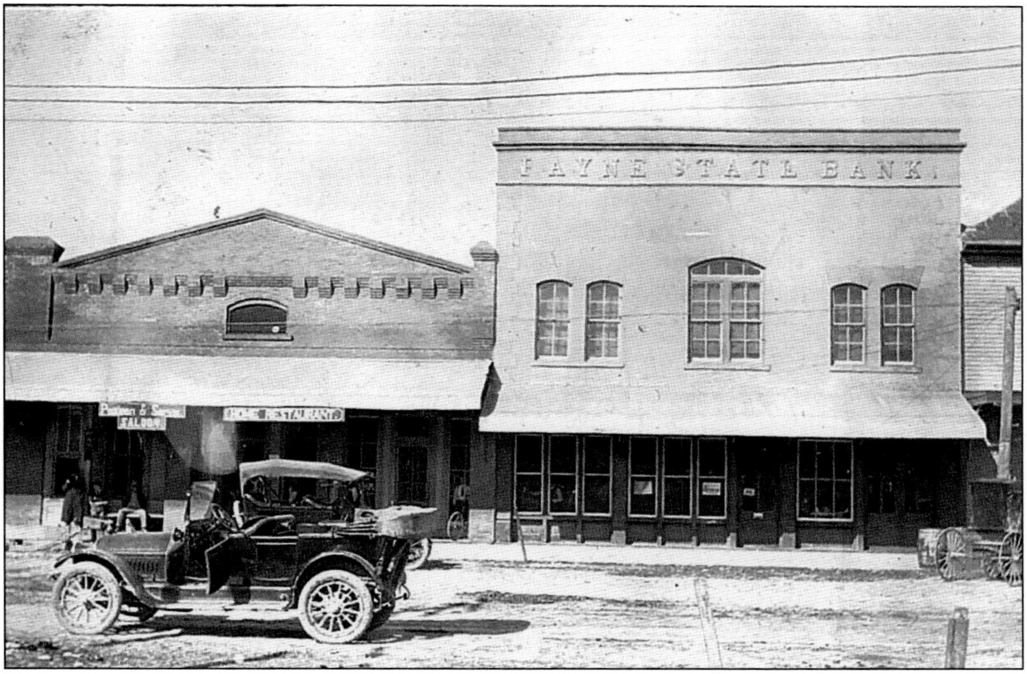

This Louisiana Avenue scene shows, from left to right, the Petitjean and Servat Saloon, the Home Restaurant, and the Rayne State Bank. (Courtesy Albert Owers.)

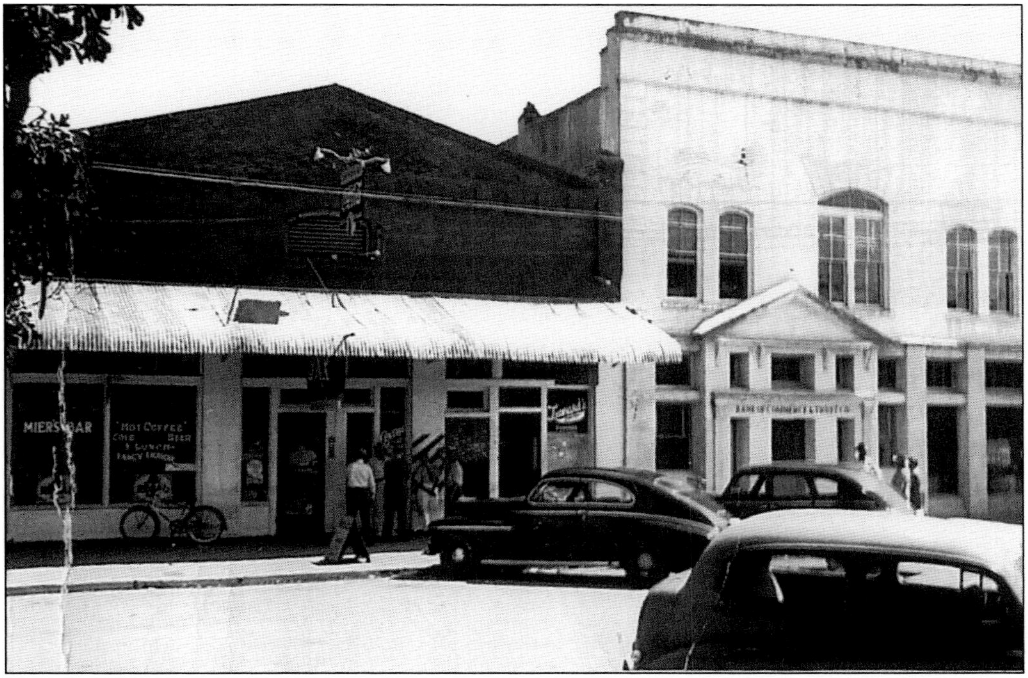

From left to right are T-Miers's Pool Hall and Billiard Parlor, Central Barber Shop, and Leonards Jewelry, which was owned by Leonard Hebert, in one building. To the right is the Bank of Commerce and Trust Co., which bought out the former Rayne State Bank. (Courtesy Fair Craig Hash.)

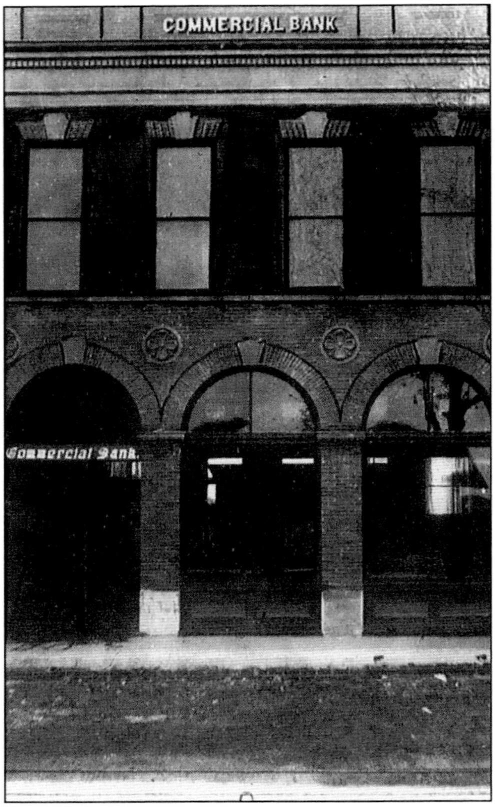

The Commercial Bank is shown here before it was shut down during the Depression. This brick building was located on the 100 block of East Texas Avenue where Fontenot Insurance now stands. In 1907, the bank advertised a capital stock of $25,000 and a $5,000 surplus. Olivier Broussard Sr. was president, David Levy was vice president, and R.C. Holt Jr., cashier. (Courtesy Charles S. Stutes.)

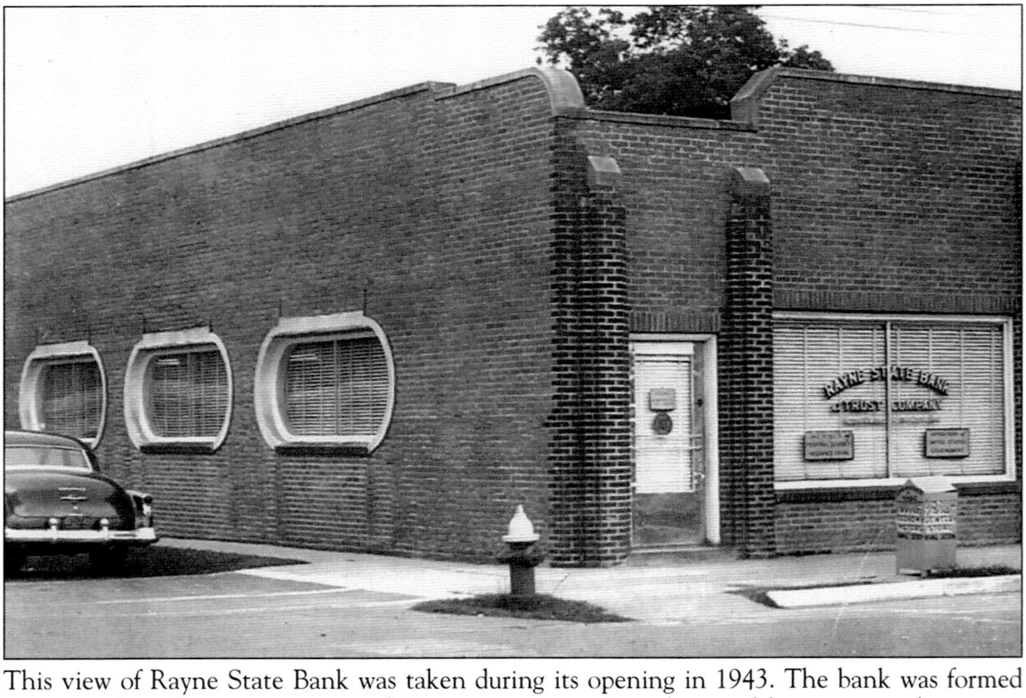

This view of Rayne State Bank was taken during its opening in 1943. The bank was formed by Betrand Nash Sweeney Sr. Paul Fremaux was vice president and became president upon Sweeney's death. (Courtesy Rayne State Bank.)

Three

EDUCATIONAL FOUNDATION

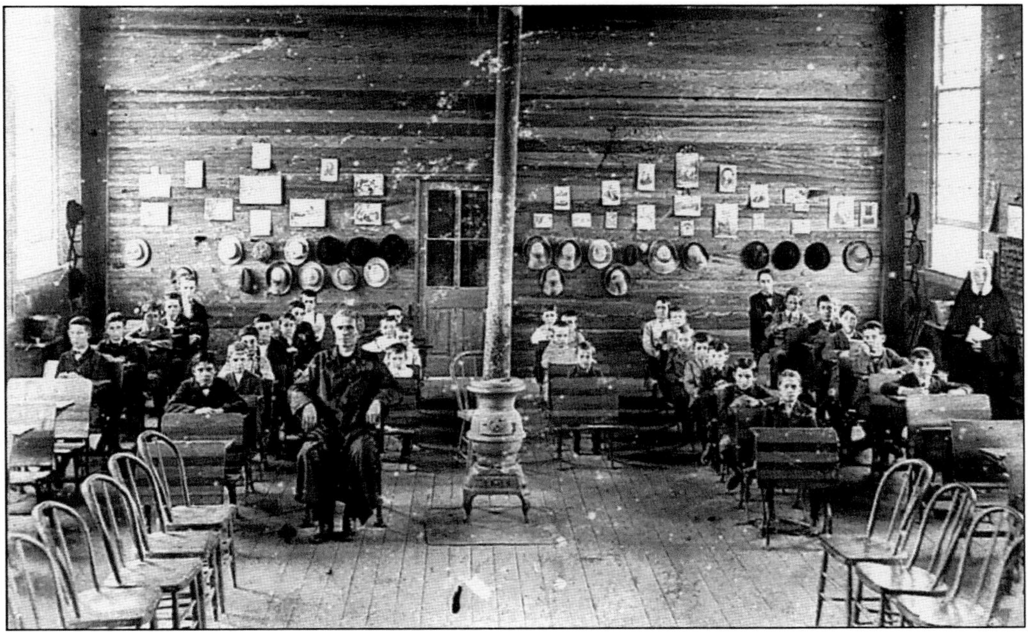

One of the first classes of St. Joseph School proves the important role of the school in the community by this impressive list of "early students" names, all of whom have played a wonderful part in the growth and progress of Rayne through the years. Included are Rev. A.S. Doutre, pastor of St. Joseph Church and Sister M. Angelica with Louis Toups, Blaise Boudreaux, Leo Kahn, Isaac Broussard, Joe Knipping, Laurent J. Guidry, Joe Hebert, Eucled Claude Barrilleaux, Arnold Kahn, Julian Kahn, Rodney Toups, John Taylor, Raoul Besse, Oday Couvillion, Blaise Chappuis, Henry Bull, George Dunion, Ulysses Landry, Arnold Stamm, Lionel Barrilleaux, Milo Daboval, George Mouton, Winfred Plattsmier, Albert Love, Ovide Bernard, Toncrelle Junot, Philip Caillouet, and Luke Caillouet. (Courtesy Charles S. Stutes.)

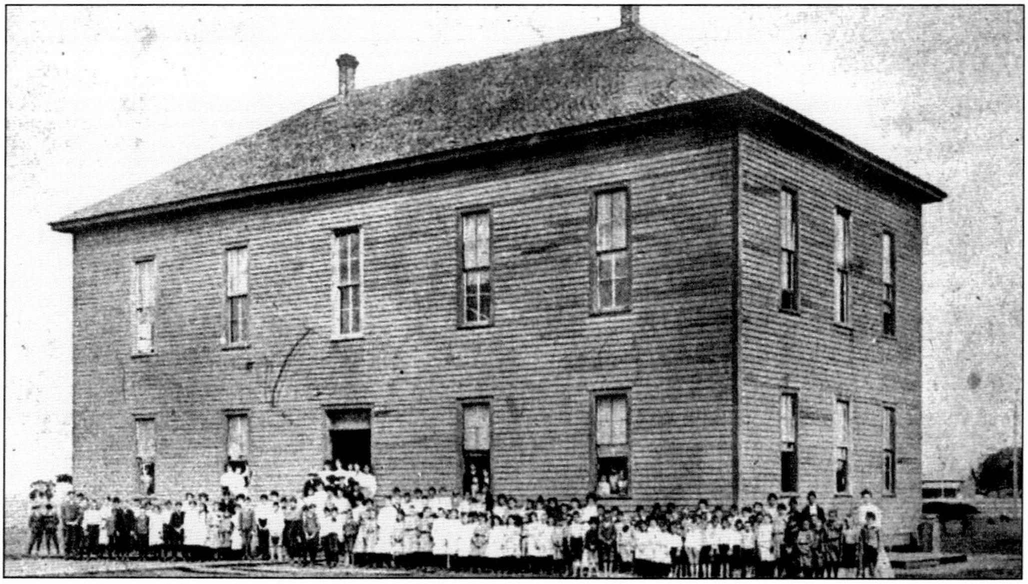

Rayne's first public school, Rayne Grade School, shown here in 1902, was located where Rayne Central Kindergarten now stands, faced south, and had eight rooms. The School Improvement Board paid $4 for 10 oaks to be planted. The school was moved and housed the Acadia Parish Training School for black children in 1888. (Courtesy Charles S. Stutes.)

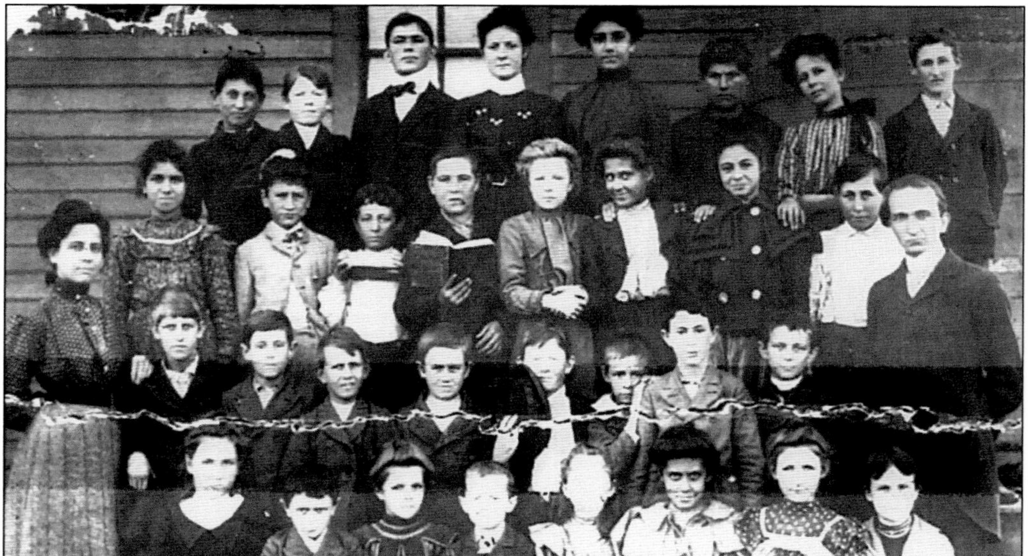

Pictured above are students of Rayne Grade School in 1902. From left to right, they are (first row) Nettie St. John, Julien Kahn, Florence Pierce, Arnold Kahn, Julia Bull, Dora Morales, Dora Dickinson, and Kathleen Johnson; (second row) Conrad Hoffpauir, Bowden Manouvrier, Eugene Hawkins, Henry Addison, Henry Bull, Clyde Bruner (Dr.), Tresmond Soileau, and Leo Kahn; (third row) Miss Nellie Cunningham, Eugenia Marlowe, Winfred Carver, Walter McBride, Alfred Locock, Dalton Fauste, Mercides Morales, Flossie Kahn, unidentified, and Prof. Thomas McGregor (principal); (fourth row) Jules Julin, Reeves Bull, Rev. Brown's nephew, Agnes Richard, Inez Morales, E.J. Peitijean (Dr.), Louella Hawkins, and Leon Hoffman. (Courtesy Jo Cart.)

Sadie Kahn played basketball and shows her spirit with a basketball and pennant from Rayne High School. (Courtesy Charles S. Stutes.)

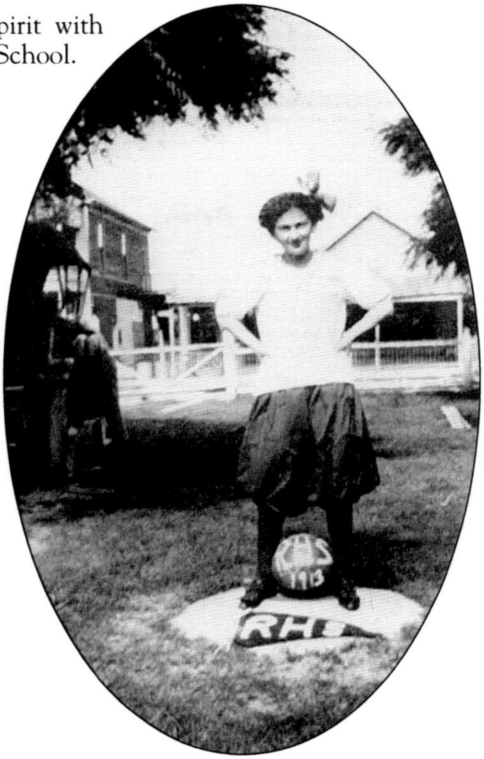

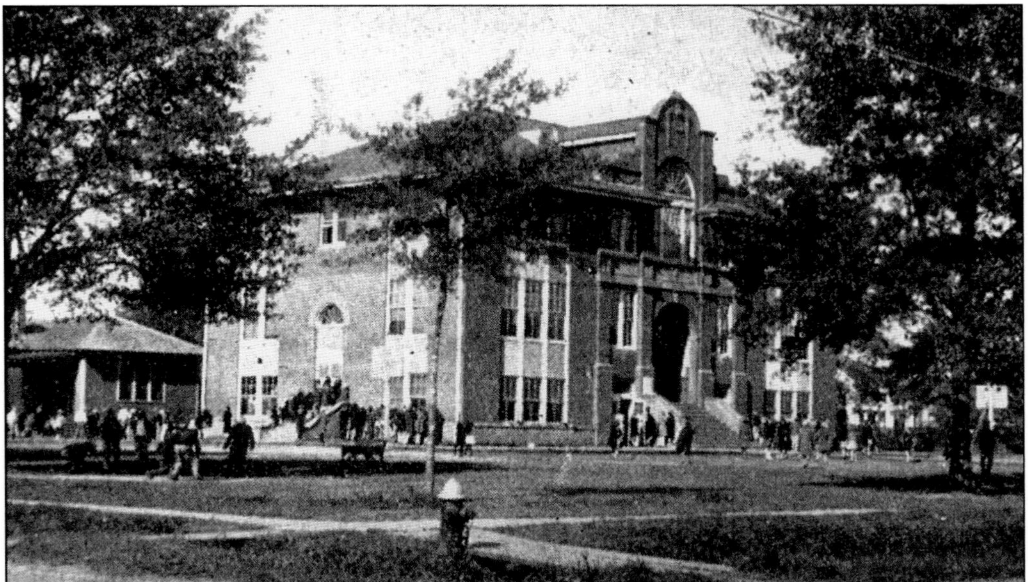

The old three-story Rayne High School building was red brick and faced east. The 10 oaks that were planted can still be seen. The Home Economics building, on the left rear, was torn down in the early 1960s. Movies were shown in the third floor auditorium. (Courtesy Charles S. Stutes.)

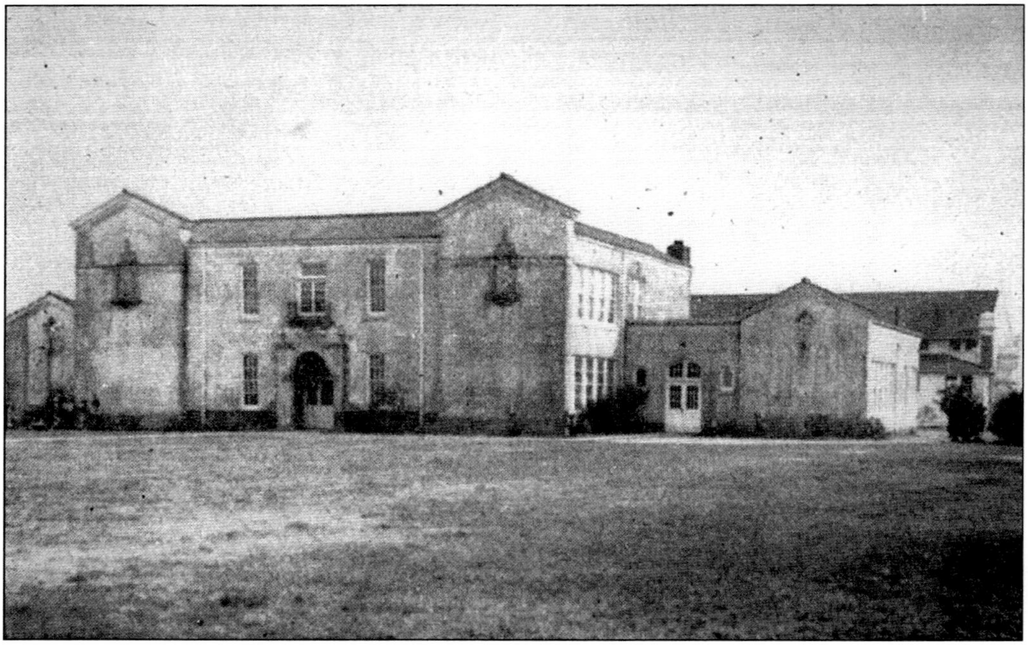

This beautiful building was South Rayne Elementary school on Branche Street. It is unknown why the building was torn down. It can be surmised that it was condemned for health reasons. The present school was built on the same location in 1963. (Courtesy Charles S. Stutes.)

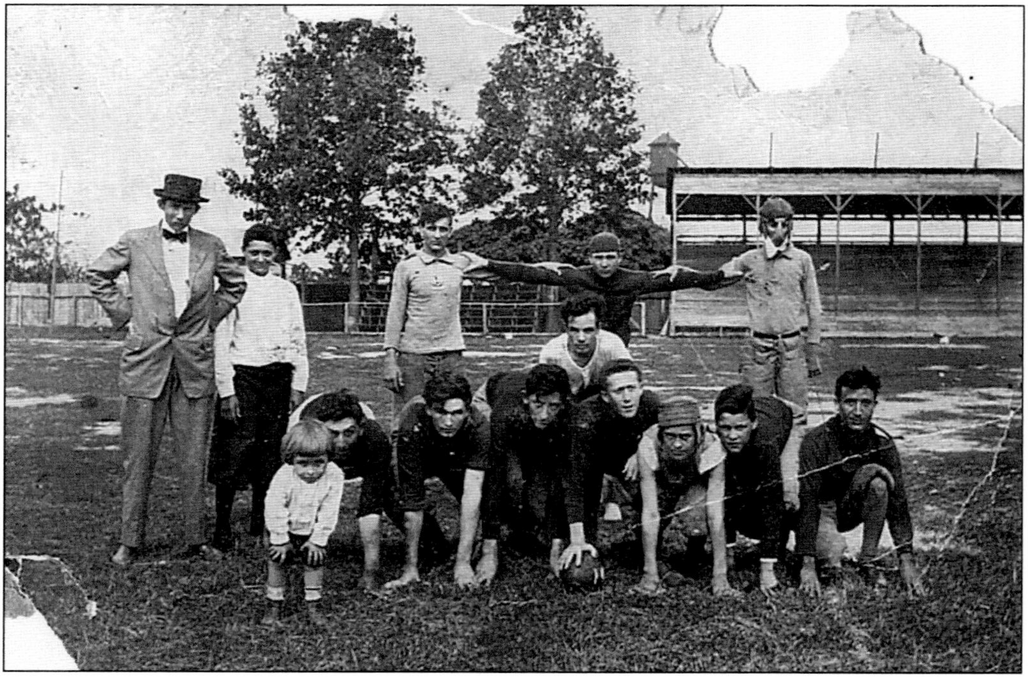

This 1913 photo of a pick-up football team is shown on the field at the baseball park on Fourth Street where the Rayne baseball teams would play. You can see the grandstands in the background. Some of the identified people are Gabe Servat, Lester Jenkins, Lenis Hollier, George Mouton, Clovis Bailey, Winnie Plattsmier, and Hugh Craig (with helmet.) (Courtesy Donald Petitjean.)

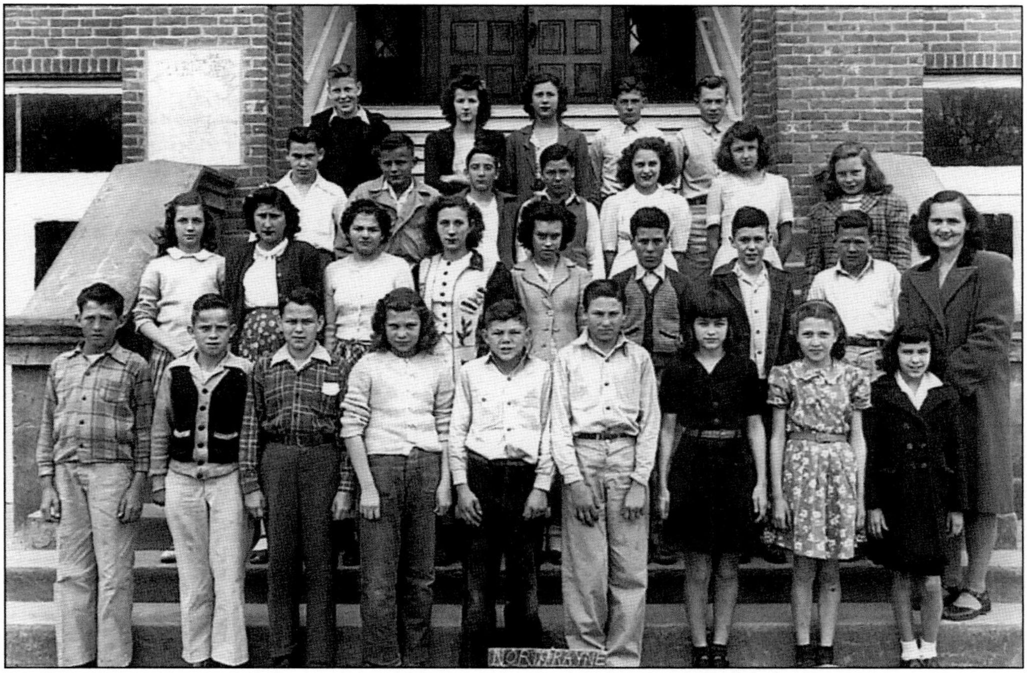

Willie Etta Servat is shown on the right of this photo of the 1946–1947 class of North Rayne Elementary. (Courtesy Doug Vincent.)

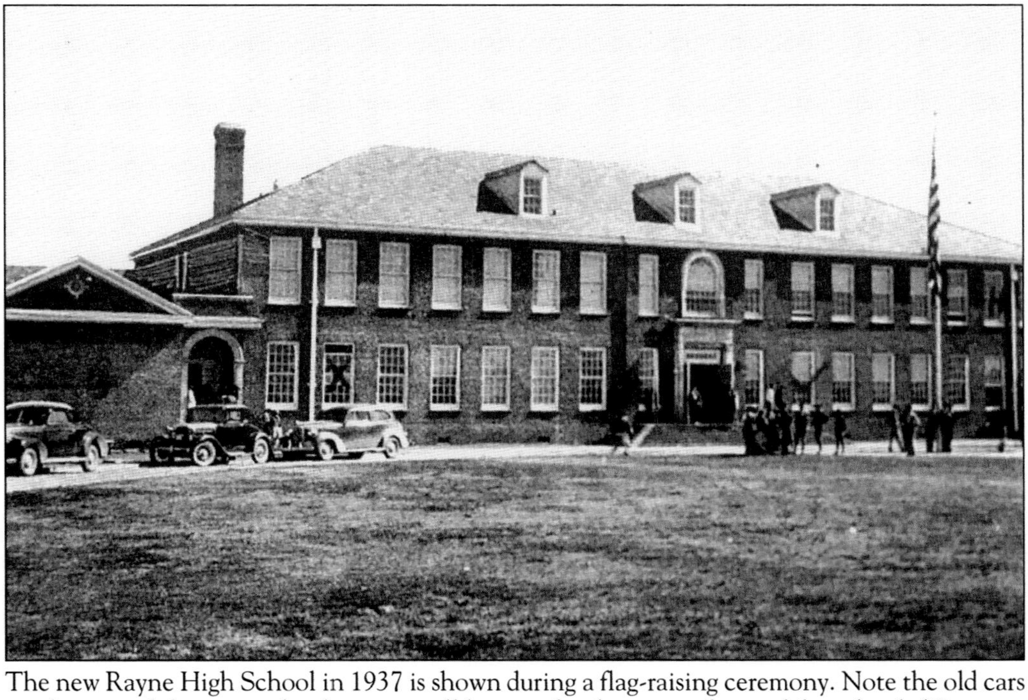

The new Rayne High School in 1937 is shown during a flag-raising ceremony. Note the old cars on the curved driveway, the driveway still being a focal point in front of the school. (Courtesy Charles S. Stutes.)

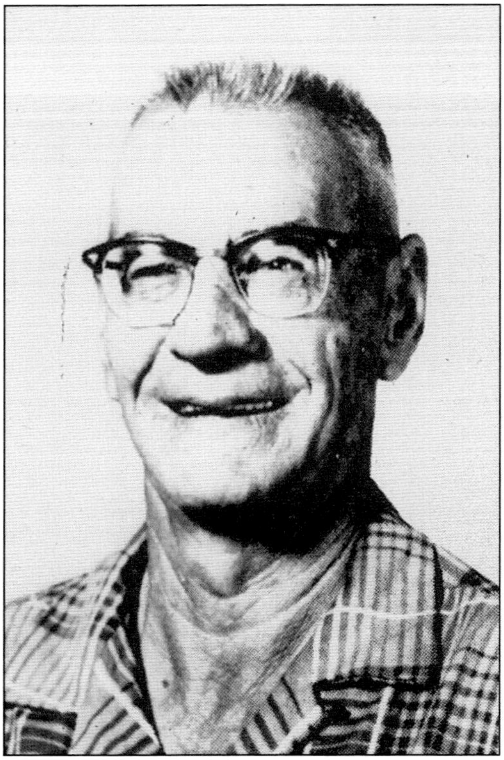

Raoul Sonnier, a.k.a. "Chief," was the janitor at Rayne High School for 40 years and lived on the school property. Thousands of Rayne High students will always remember this man for his friendly demeanor.

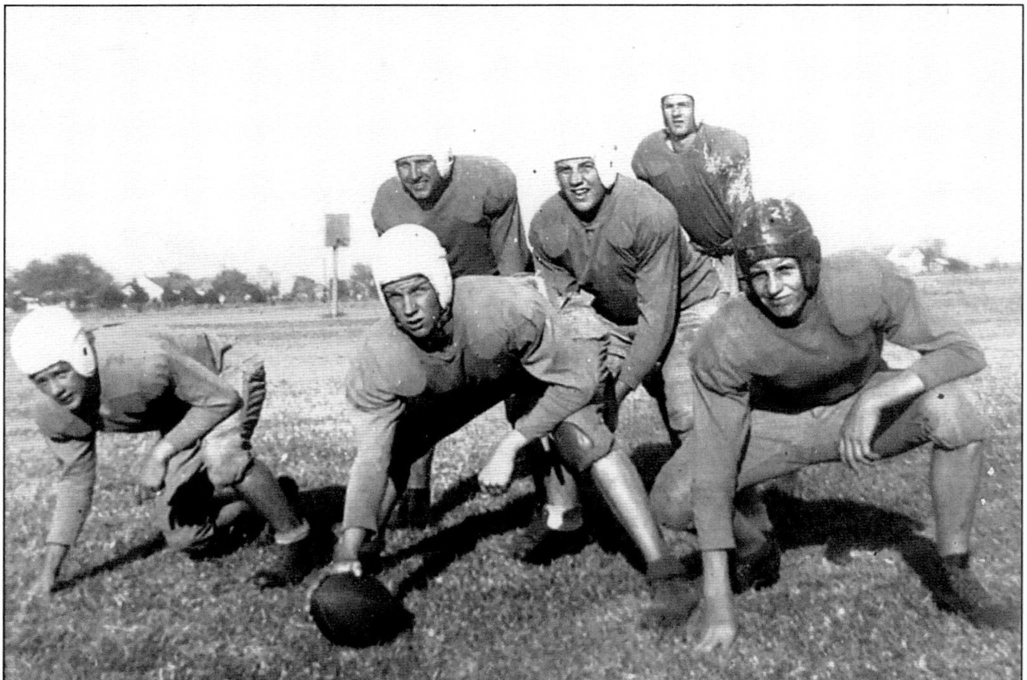

The 1944 Rayne High School championship team members are, from left to right, (front) Maxie Navarre, Bob Craig, and Buddy Moody; (back) Rodney Hoffpauir, Tommy Petitjean (quarterback), and Buddy Gilbert. (Courtesy Fair Craig Hash.)

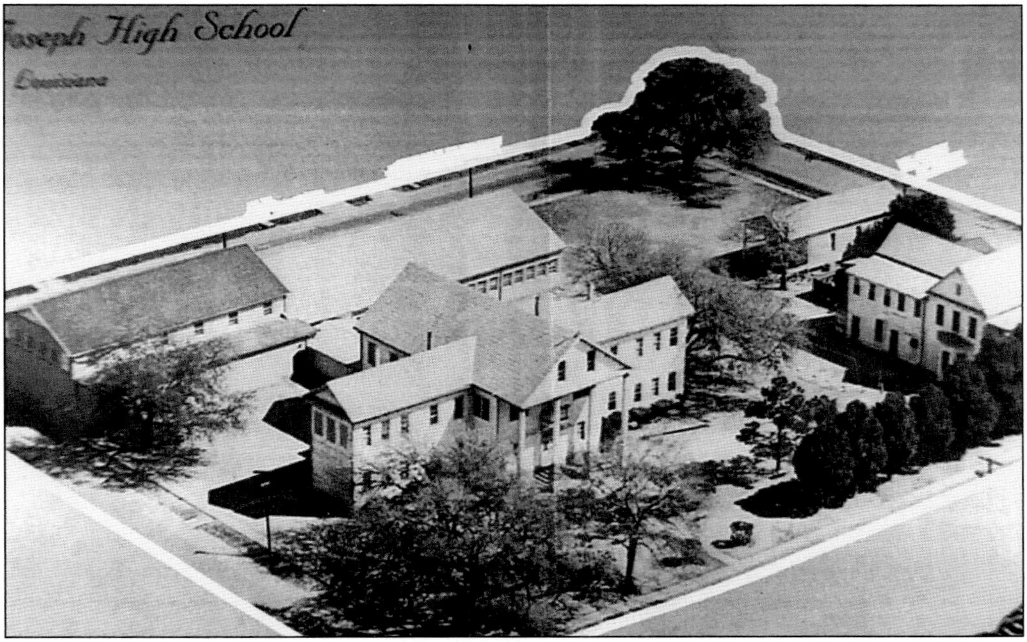

This is an aerial view of the St. Joseph High School campus in the early 1950s. To the right you can see the band room/snack shop, which was a favorite spot for the students. (Courtesy Charles S. Stutes.)

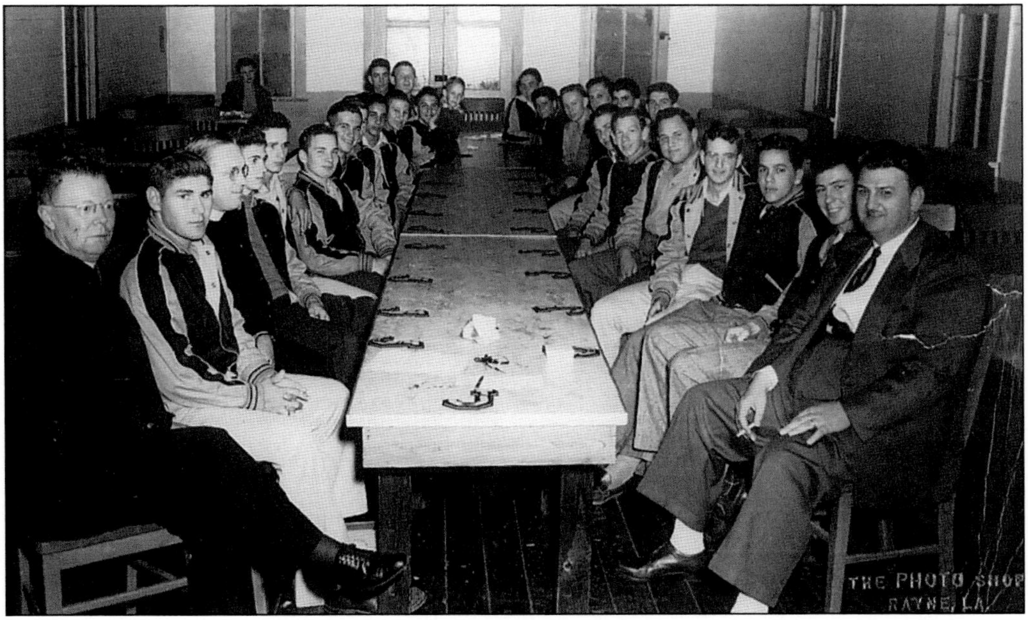

The 1949 St. Joseph Tiger football team attends a banquet in their honor. From left to right are Rev. Msgr. Hubert Lerschen, Dudley Leblanc, Rev. Fr. Daniel Habetz, Patrick Hoffpauir, Gus Richard, Jimmie Barousse, John Allen Petitjean, Glenn Zaunbrecher, Larry Babineaux, P.J. Gidry, Clarence Arsement, Norman Faulk, Richard Mier, Milton Pharr, Elton Arceneuax, Reginald Simoneaux, Leo Van Amerongen, Norman Hanks, Nookie Gilbert, John Charles Matthew, Richard Broussard, Jerome Simoneaux, Thomas Hebert, Harold Prevost, Edroy Broussard, Tanny Lacroix, and Lee Mayeaux. (Courtesy Fair Craig Hash.)

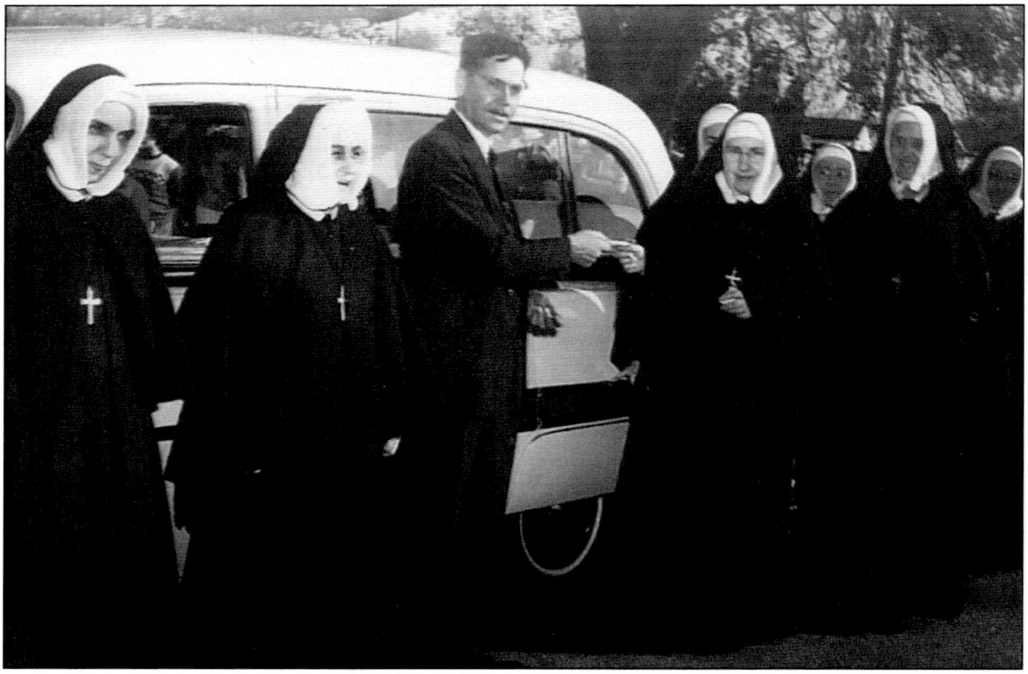

St. Joe Tiger Backer Howard Perrodin presents the keys of a 1954 station wagon to Mother Stanislaus of St. Joseph. Identified nuns are Sister Jeanne, Sister Edith, and Sister Claudia. (Courtesy Jim and Mary Ann Bush.)

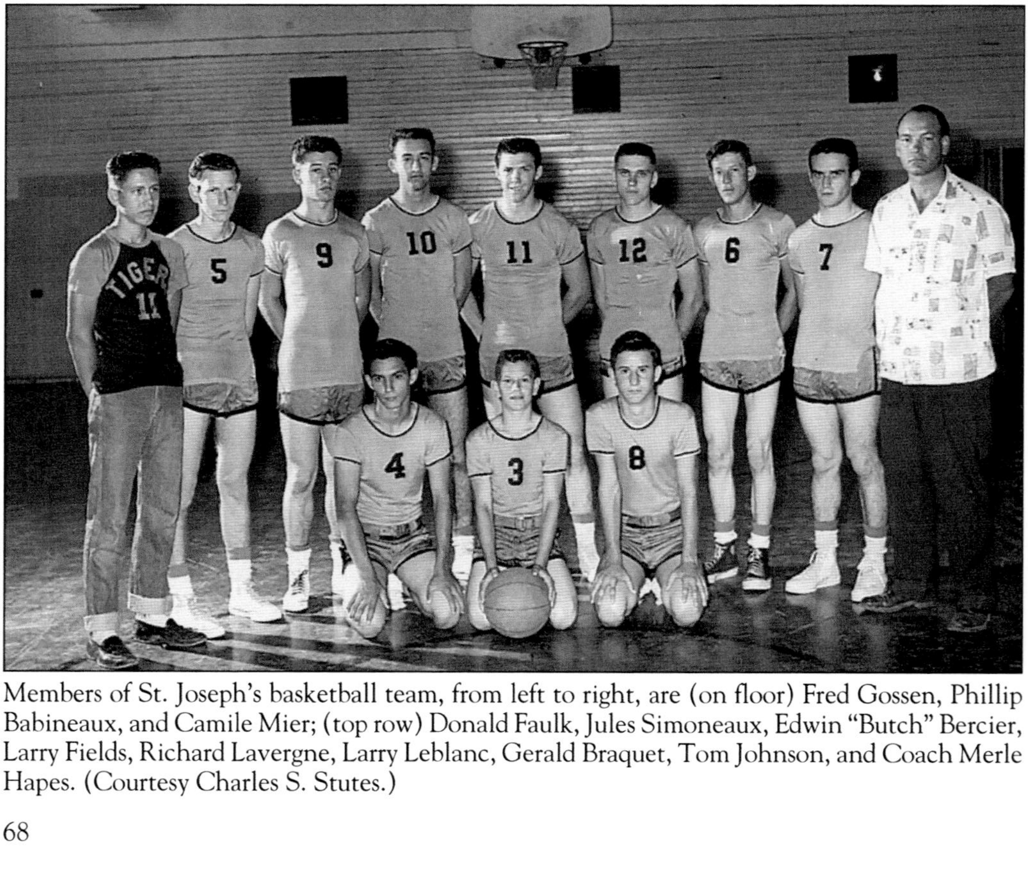

Members of St. Joseph's basketball team, from left to right, are (on floor) Fred Gossen, Phillip Babineaux, and Camile Mier; (top row) Donald Faulk, Jules Simoneaux, Edwin "Butch" Bercier, Larry Fields, Richard Lavergne, Larry Leblanc, Gerald Braquet, Tom Johnson, and Coach Merle Hapes. (Courtesy Charles S. Stutes.)

Four

Fabulous Frogs

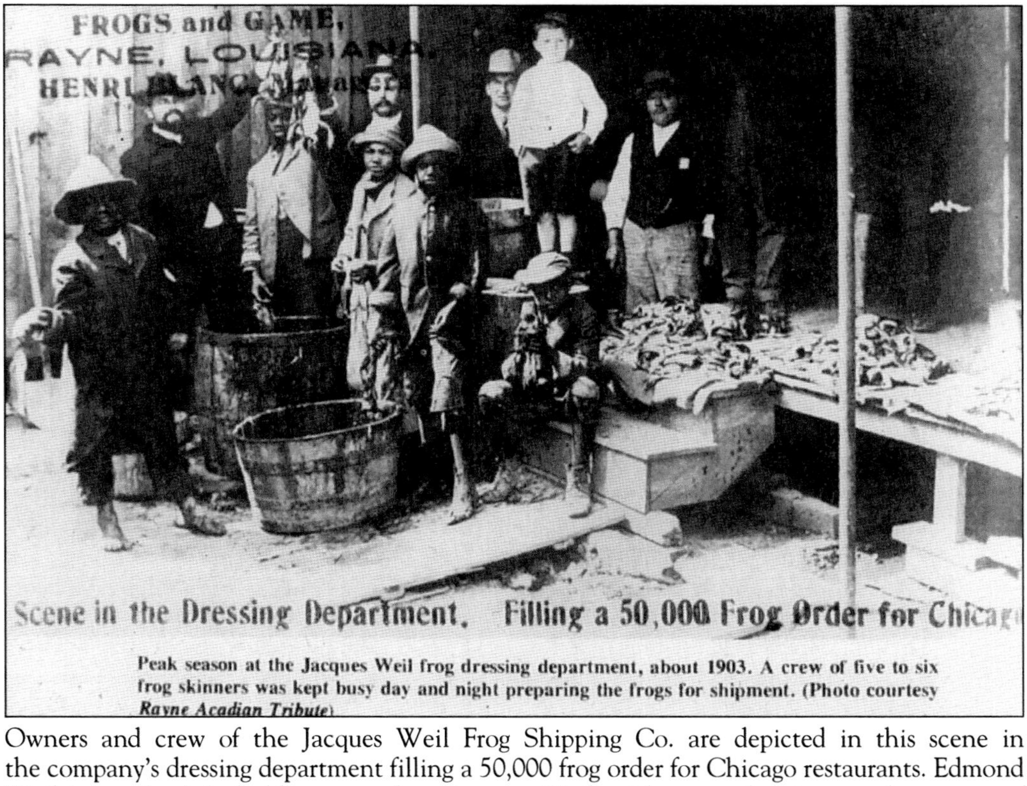

Owners and crew of the Jacques Weil Frog Shipping Co. are depicted in this scene in the company's dressing department filling a 50,000 frog order for Chicago restaurants. Edmond Weil is on the left, holding up a frog. Jacques Weil, with mustache, is near the center of the photograph. Manager Henri Blanc is kneeling on the porch. Young Jacques, Edmond's son, is standing on the porch, wearing a sweater and cap in this 1903 photo. (Courtesy Charles S. Stutes.)

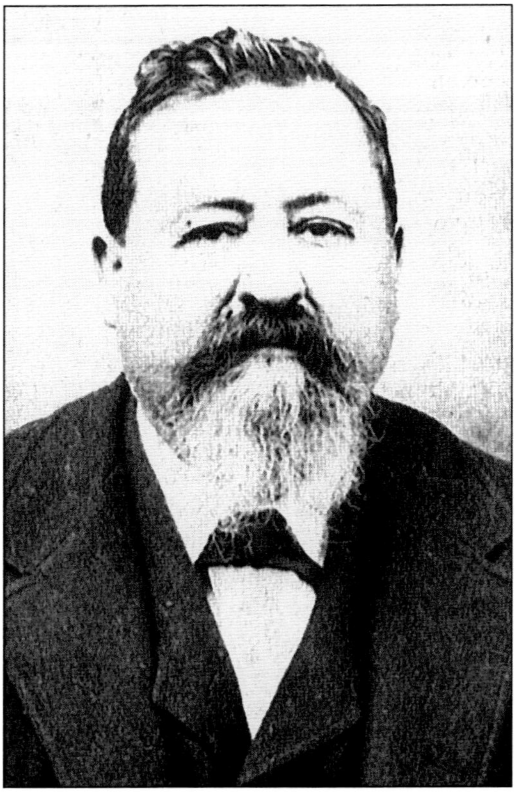

Shipments of frogs from Rayne to New Orleans were reported as early as 1887. Donat Pucheu was probably the first resident of Acadia Parish to engage in the business of shipping frogs. A native of France, Pucheu settled with his family in Rayne in 1887. (Courtesy Fair Craig Hash.)

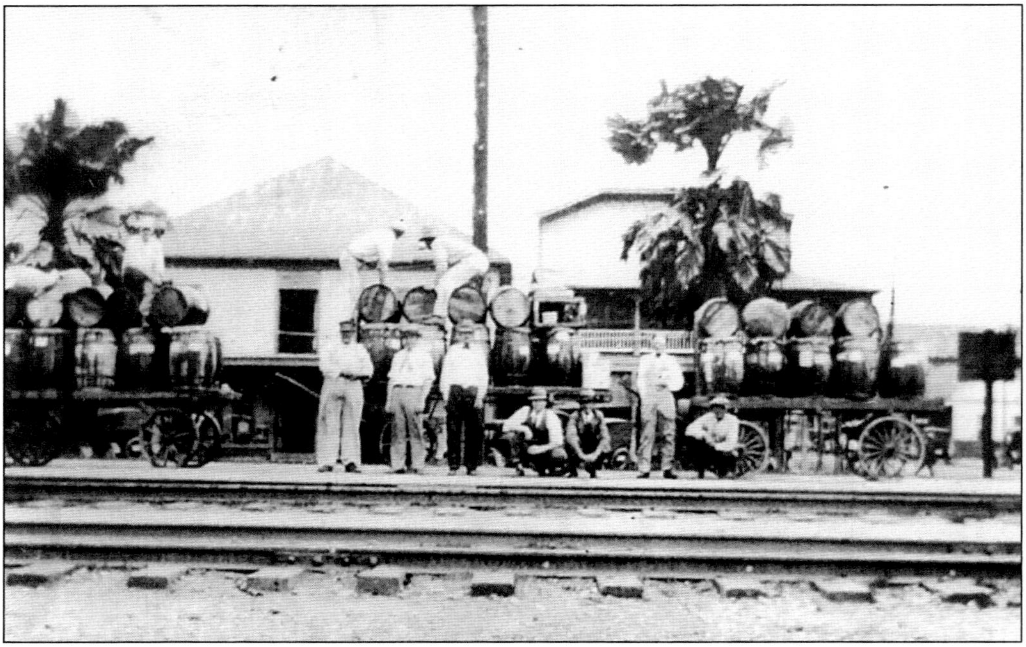

This photo depicts one of the scenes repeated many times over in the early days of Rayne as barrels of freshly cleaned frogs awaited shipment to markets across the country from the Rayne depot. This scene has been painted on the side of Koury's Jewelry Store as part of the city's mural program. (Courtesy Fair Craig Hash.)

Jacques Weil was the original owner and founder of Jacques Weil, Boudreaux, and Leger. Shown with Weil is his wife, Mathilde, in this photo taken at their home in Rayne. (Courtesy Charles S. Stutes.)

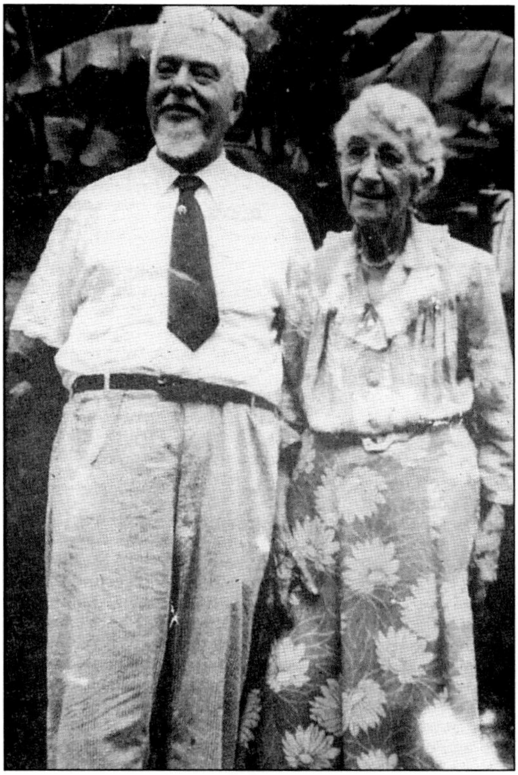

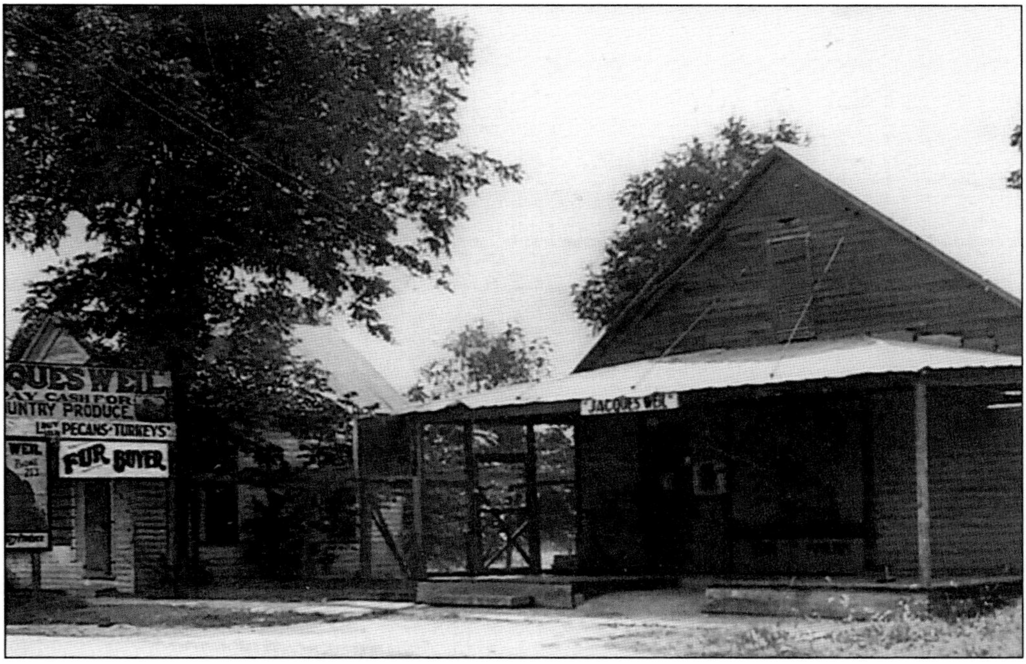

A native of France, Jacques Weil and his brothers, Edmond and Gontron, came to Rayne from Paris about 1901. Jacques became the senior partner in the firm Jacques Weil, Boudreaux, and Leger. The firm shipped frogs, poultry, eggs, and produce to New Orleans and other larger cities. The business firm became a landmark in the area. (Courtesy Donald Petitjean.)

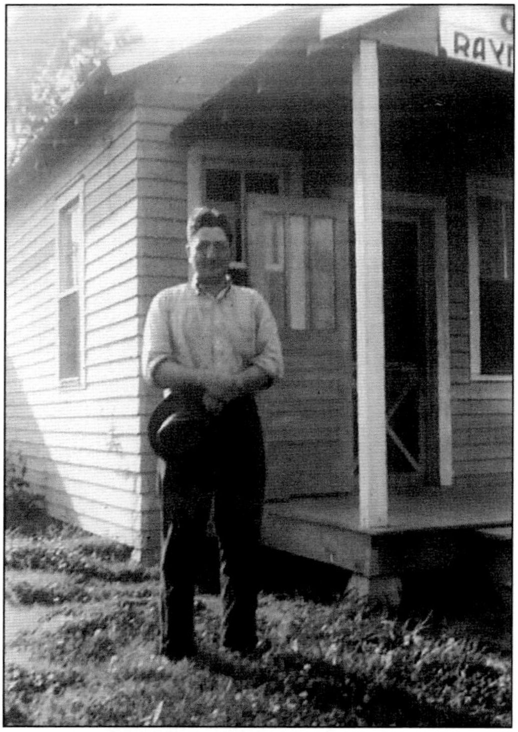

Lionel Babineaux is shown in front of the Rayne Frog Co., which was located on the 700 block of South Adams next to where Rayne Food Center now stands. He was later elected Mayor of the City of Rayne. (Courtesy Sue Stutes.)

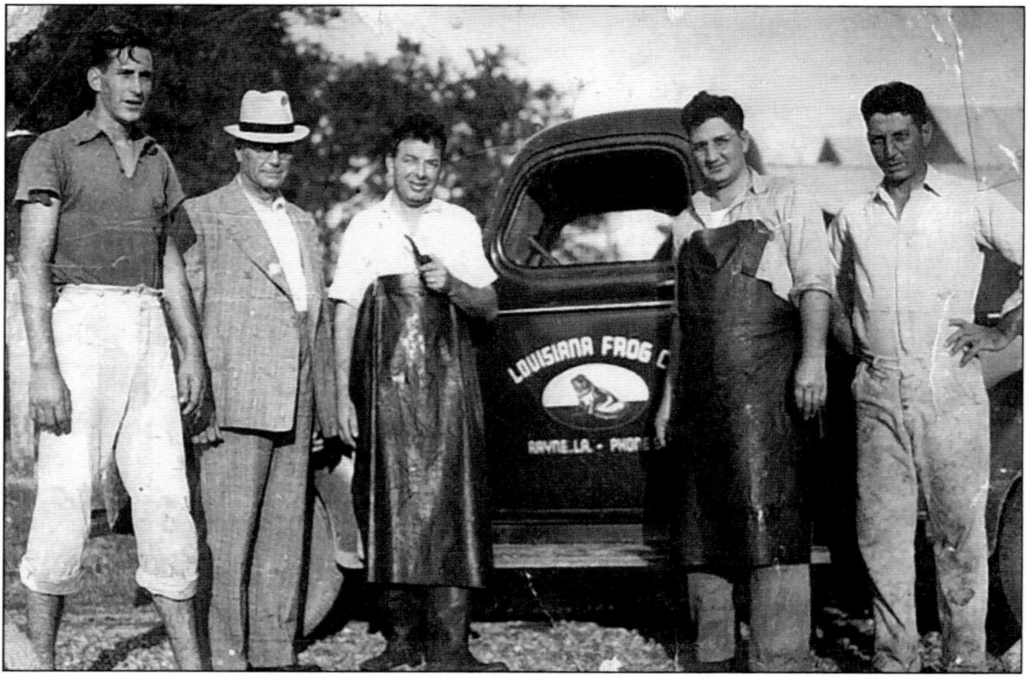

The Louisiana Frog Co. was established in 1928. Lionel Babineaux was the owner of this business, which was first located in Mermentau, along the river. The American Frog Industries, a subsidiary of Louisiana Frog Co., prepared a brochure on raising jumbo bullfrogs in 1933. Shown are Saul Touchet, an unidentified person, Louis Baer, Lionel Babineaux, and Pete Babineaux. (Courtesy Sue Stutes.)

This publicity photo for the Lions Club Frog Derby was taken in the late 1940s and shows one of the frog jockeys, Fair Craig Hash, in the Louisiana Frog Co. frog pit holding up two "oua-oua-rons." (Courtesy Pete Babineaux.)

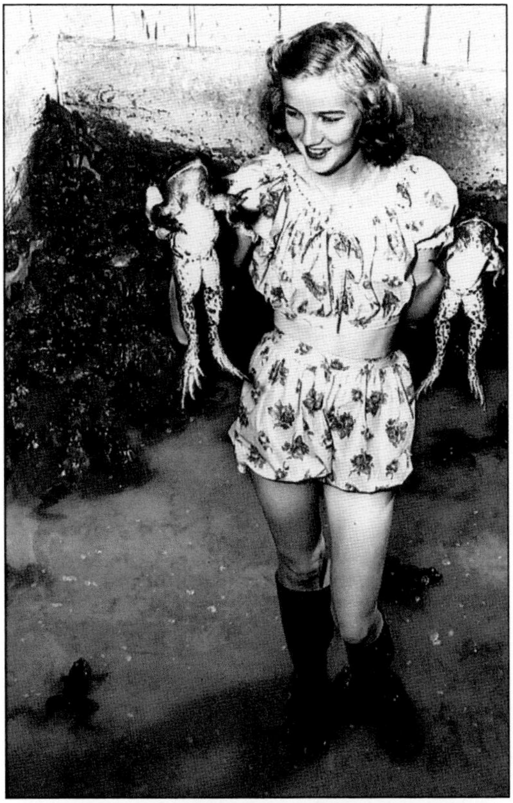

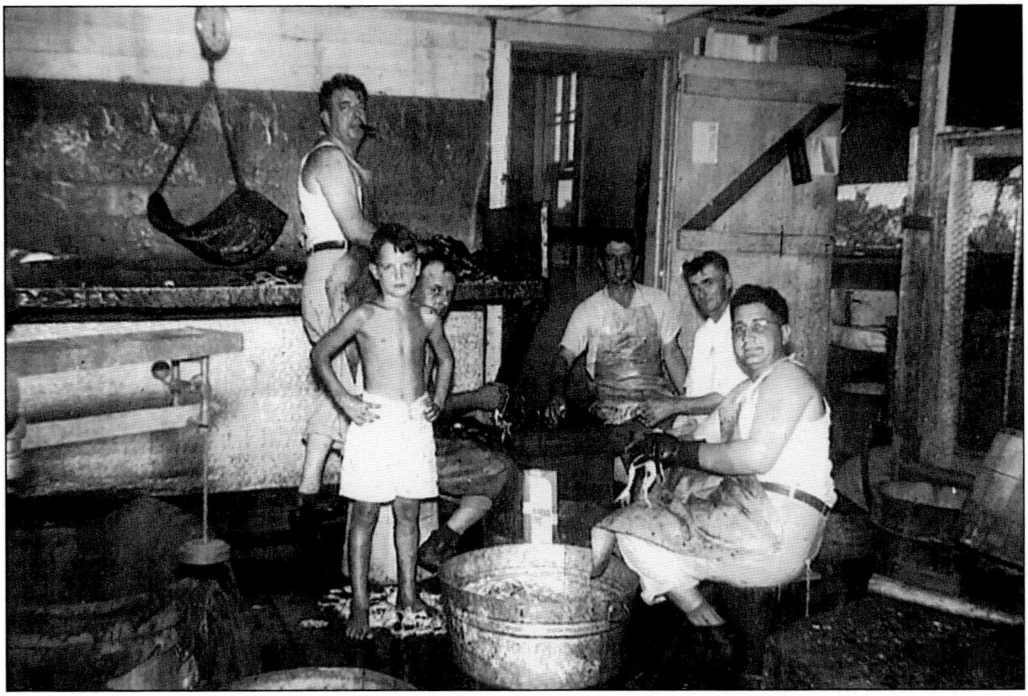

This 1939 picture from Louisiana Frog Co. shows Louis Baer, Max Baer, Murphy Molbert, Desire Babineaux, Saul Touchet, and Lionel Babineaux cleaning frogs. (Courtesy Jo Cart.)

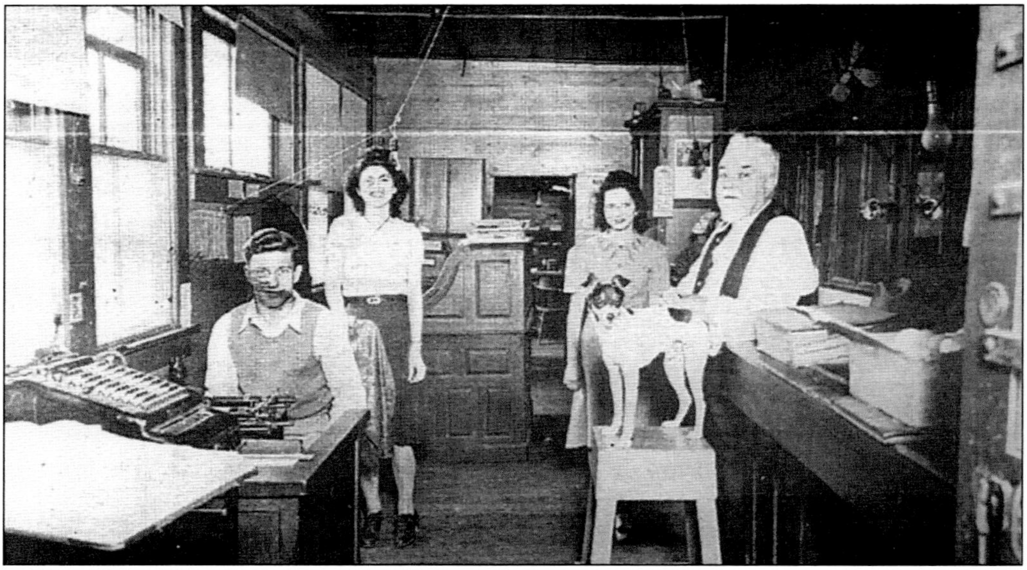

This picture, taken just before the start of World War II, showed the continued importance of Jacques Weil and the frog industry to Rayne. These were the original offices where the firm was started, then still in operation by Wiltz J. Chatelain. Seated to the left is Georges Weil, son of Mr. and Mrs. Edmond Weil. Jacques is standing to the right and the two young ladies who assisted in the office are, from left to right, Mrs. Irene Broussard Doty and Mrs. Percy Alleman, the former Mildred Perrodin. (Courtesy Fair Craig Hash.)

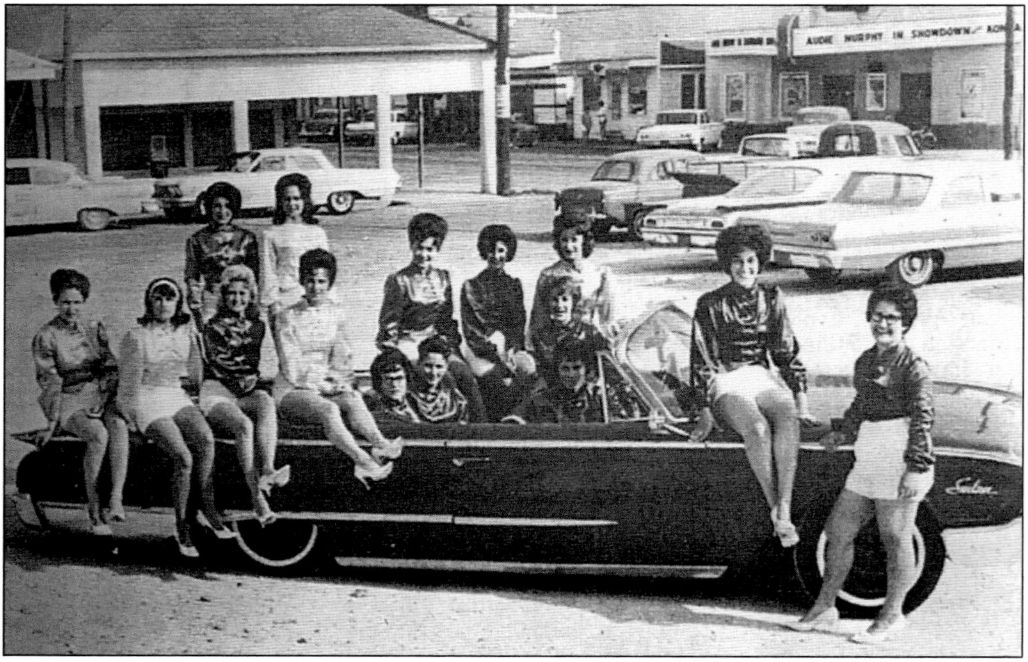

The red convertible belonging to Jack Koury was worth its weight in the lovely legs of the Frog Derby entries in 1963. Shown in the front are Judy Hoffpauir, Dianne McCarty, Shirley Jagneaux, Judy Bearb, Charlene Guidry, Jeannette Guidry, Mary Lou Moore, Betty Guidry, and Anna Marie Cormier. Shown in the back are Barbara Boudreaux, Jean Seaux, Mary Daigle, Cathy Laurent, and Diane Saltzman. (Courtesy Fair Craig Hash.)

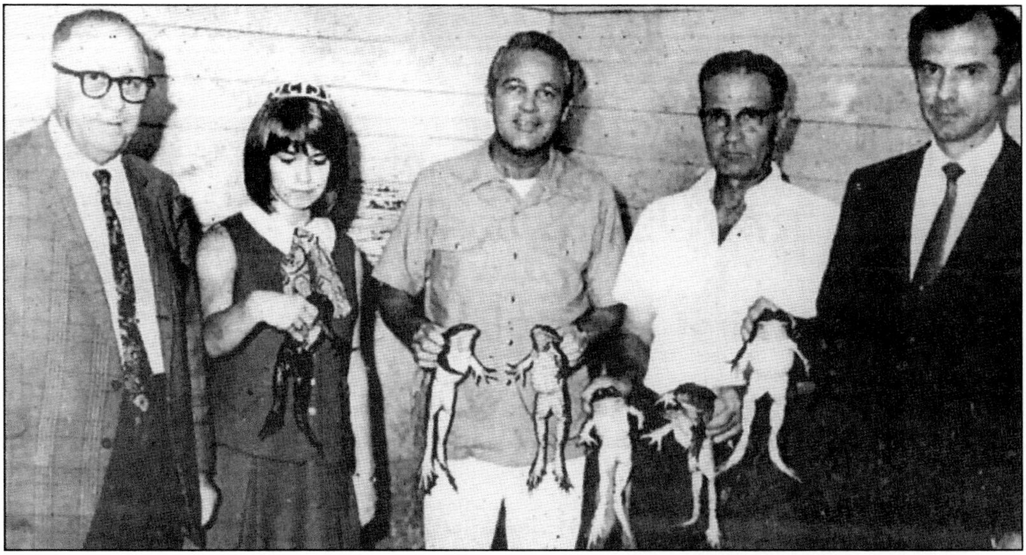

Rayne's giant "oua-oua-rons" can truly claim the title of the "jumpingest frogs in the world" as these big fellows go into orbit around the world as part of NASA's program for research for future space projects. Space-bound frogs attract the special attention of Rayne Mayor Bill Gossen, Frog Queen Sue Guidry, Congressman Edwin W. Edwards, David "Pete" Babineaux, and Ralph Stutes (Rayne councilman). These were some of the frogs selected by NASA for the OFO Program in the early 1970s. (Courtesy Fair Craig Hash.)

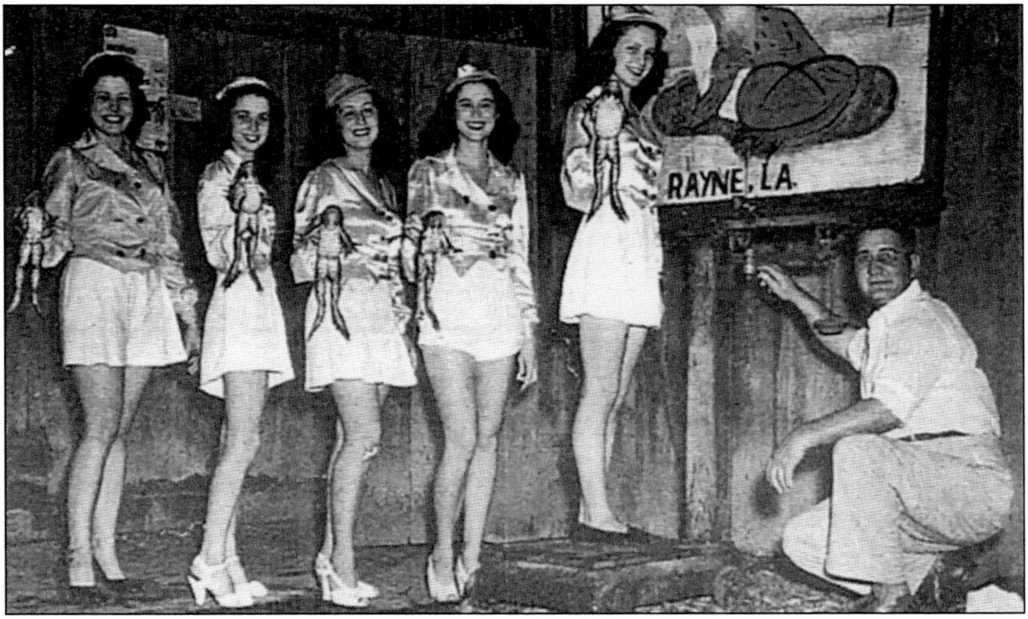

The young ladies named each year to serve as "Frog Jockeys" for Rayne's famous Frog Derby, staged by the Rayne Lions Club each year were selected based on looks, charm, and personality. This cover photo shows Betty Lou Babineaux (Mrs. Will Robert Kennedy), Joyce Zaunbrecher (Mrs. Stanley Faulk), Henrietta Gossen (Mrs. Julian Didier), Ethelyene Comeaux (Mrs. C.B. Jones,Jr.), and Sybil Hains (Mrs. Joel Deville). Officially weighing the girls and their frogs in before the Derby is Lionel Babineaux, member of the Babineaux Bros. firm, who was an avid "Frog Derby" enthusiast. (Courtesy Fair Craig Hash.)

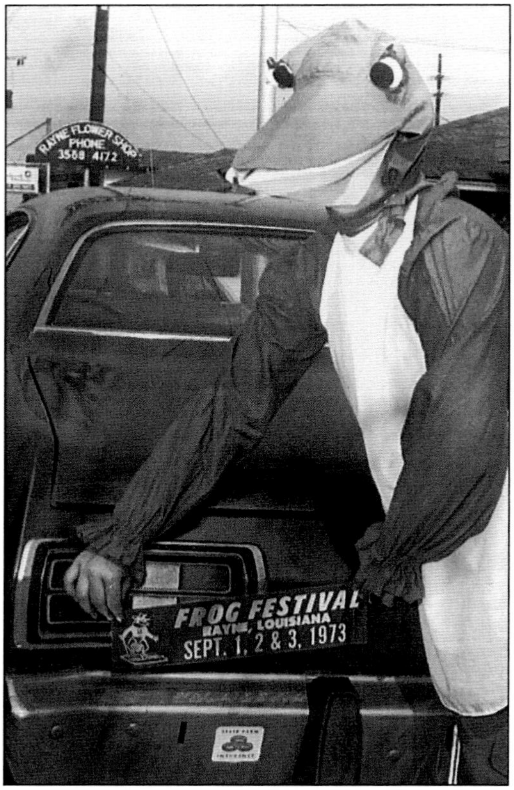

M'sier Le Oua Oua Ron is shown putting on a bumper sticker for the first Frog Festival held on September 1, 2, and 3, 1973. (Courtesy Fair Craig Hash.)

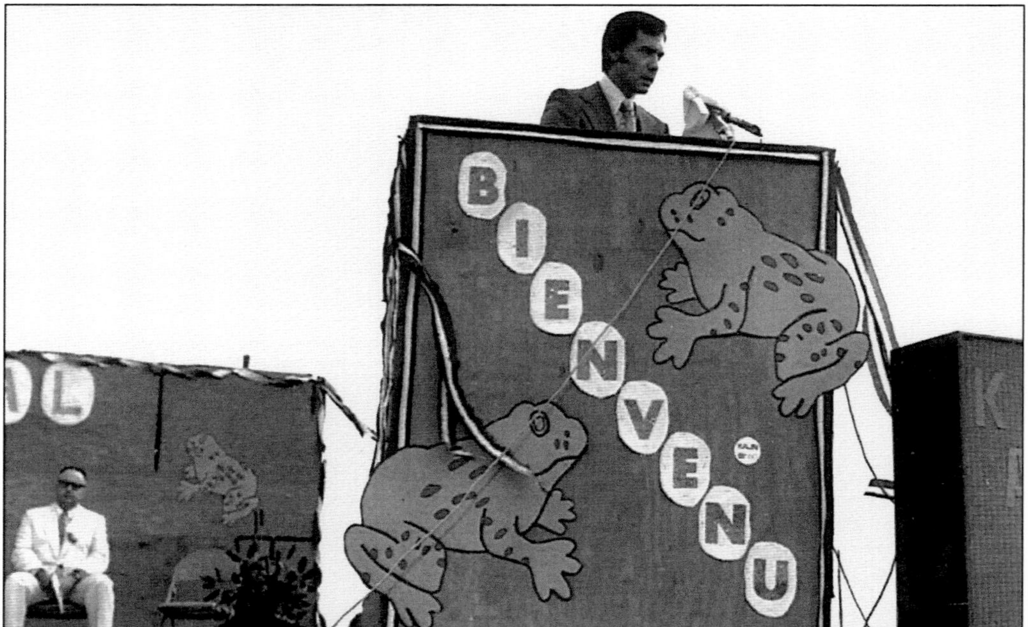

Mayor Pro Tem Ralph Stutes opens the yearly Frog Festival during its kickoff ceremonies. He later opened many of the festivals while serving the City of Rayne as mayor. (Courtesy Fair Craig Hash.)

Frog Jockey Connie Arabie is shown jumping her frog Antoine with Lions Club Frog Derby chairman Hilary Olinger looking on. (Courtesy Fair Craig Hash.)

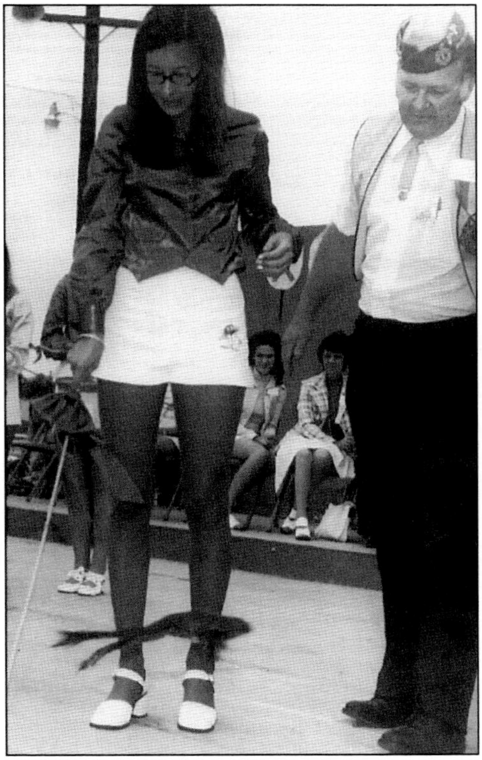

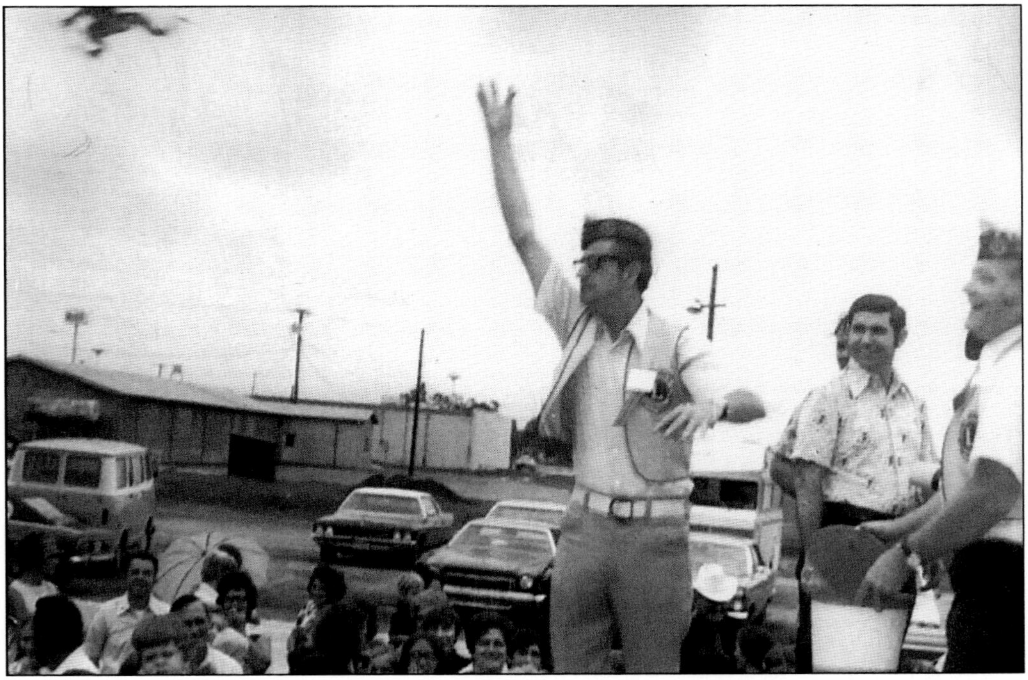

Lion Robert Cart happens to let a big bullfrog get into the crowd at the first Frog Festival, a popular part of the Rayne Lions Club Frog Jockey contest. Note the buildings in the background. The first festival was held on the first part of Gossen Drive and later moved to the back where it is presently held. (Courtesy Fair Craig Hash.)

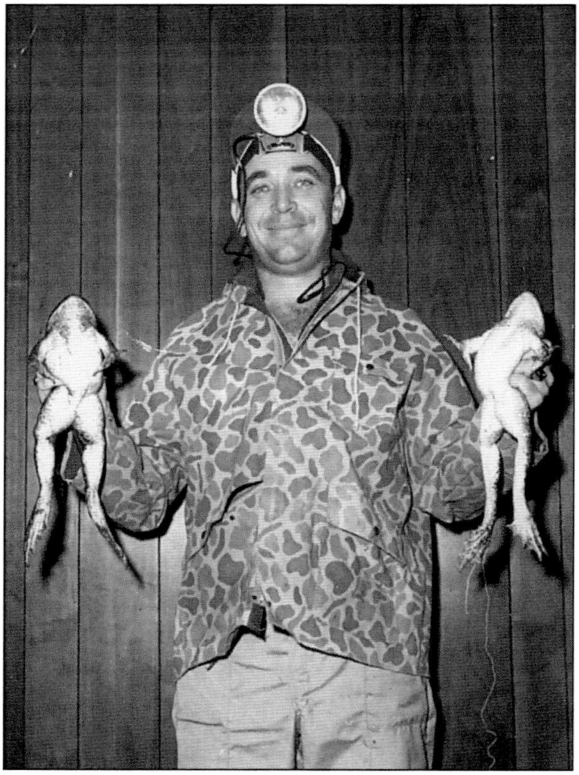

Horace Thibodeaux, a known catcher of frogs, shows the product of a successful trip he had into the rice fields. Like most successful hunts, he uses a lamp to temporarily blind the frog so they can be captured. (Courtesy Horace Thibodeaux.)

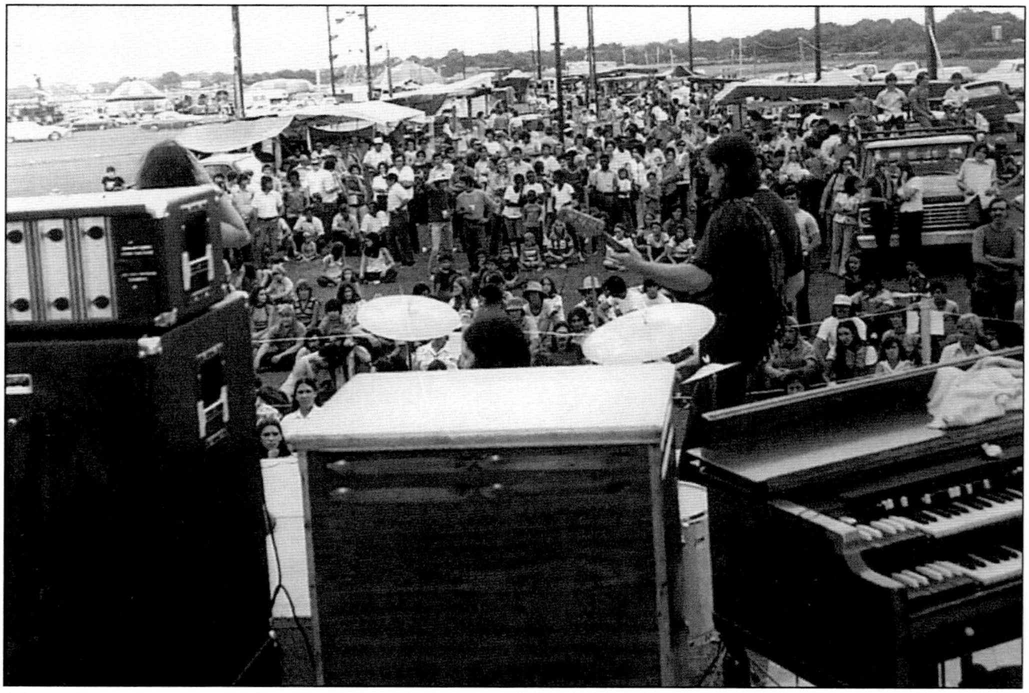

Musical entertainment has been a main focus of the annual Frog Festival, which celebrates the culture of the community. Shown here is a large crowd gathered for a performance by Shepard, from Jennings. (Courtesy Fair Craig Hash.)

Five

STREETSCAPES

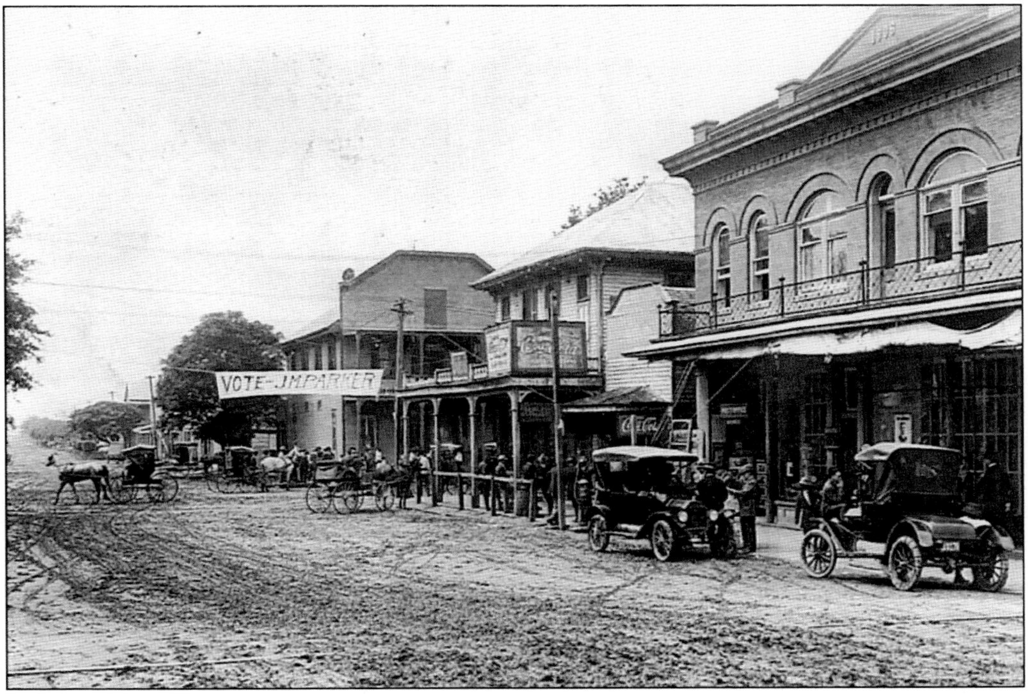

This is an early view of South Adams looking south from the railroad track. From the right is Broussard's Drug Store, the Rayne Post Office, and a restaurant. The election banner is for J.M. Parker who ran for Louisiana governor in 1916 and won in 1920. Right behind the second car you can see a gasoline pump, one of Rayne first gas stations. (Courtesy Marguerite Kahn Hoskin.)

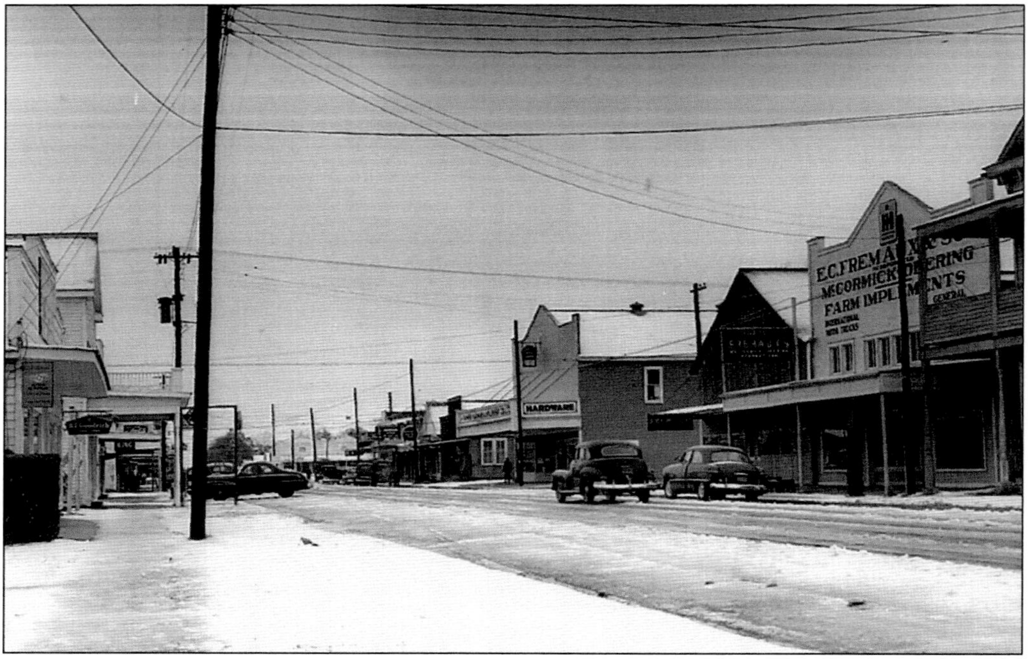

This 1940s view of South Adams is looking north with an unusual sight—snow on the ground. To the right, the business landmark of E.C. Fremaux can be seen and further down is the first location of Sim Babineaux's Western Auto Store. (Courtesy Jo Cart.)

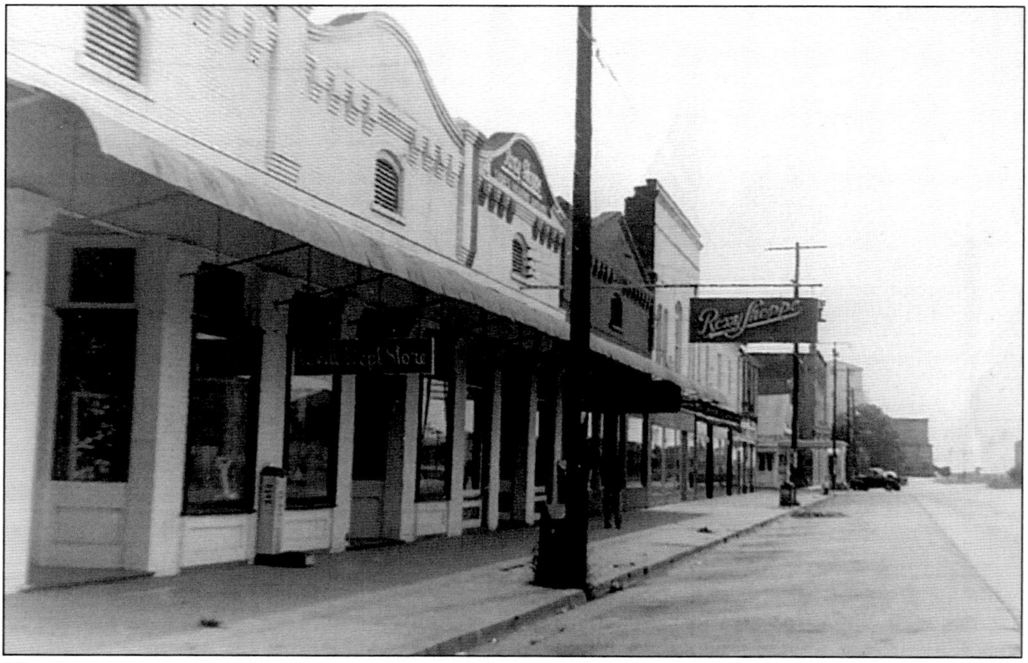

This business scene of Louisiana Avenue shows Weill's Department Store, which was opened in 1948 and run by the Jimmie Orillion family, and the Roxy Dress Shop, which was operated by Polly Gilbert. The picture is absent of vehicles, a sight which is not common for this busy business area. (Courtesy Jo Cart.)

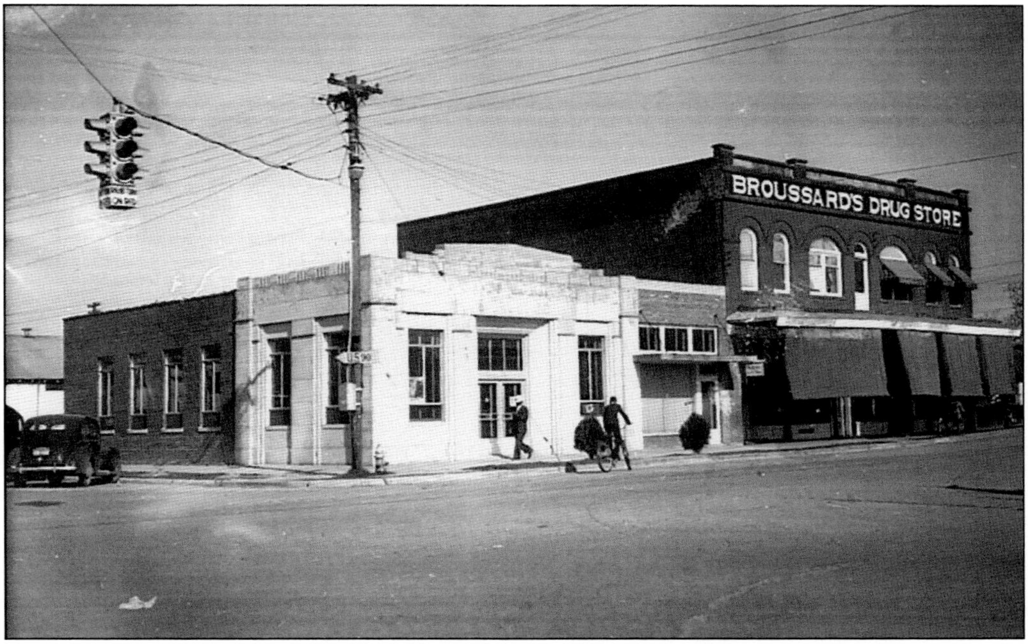

The intersection of South Adams and Texas Avenue in the 1950s shows, from left to right, the Bank of Commerce, Austin's Coffee Shop, and Broussard's Drugstore with cloth curtains blocking the sun. Notice the red light had a sign stating "right turn on red," apparently a new law for drivers. (Courtesy Andrus Fontenot.)

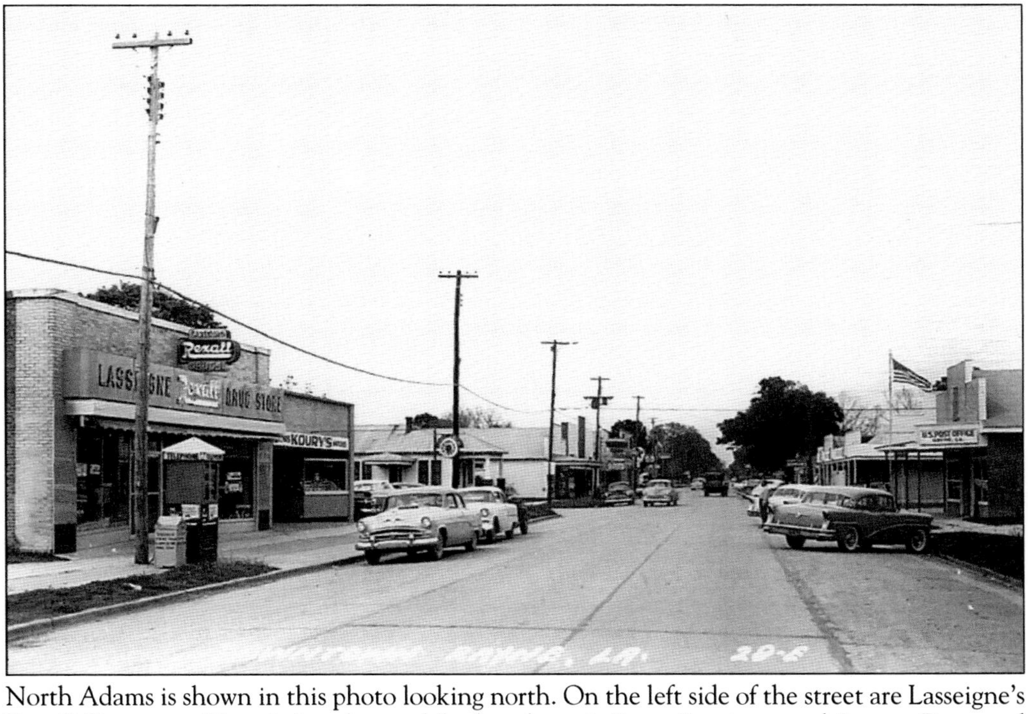

North Adams is shown in this photo looking north. On the left side of the street are Lasseigne's Rexall Pharmacy, Koury's Jewelry, and further down is Besse Furniture and Stamm Raymond Motors. The right side of the street shows the Rayne Post Office, Batson Richards Grocery, and other businesses on the block. (Courtesy Steve Leblanc.)

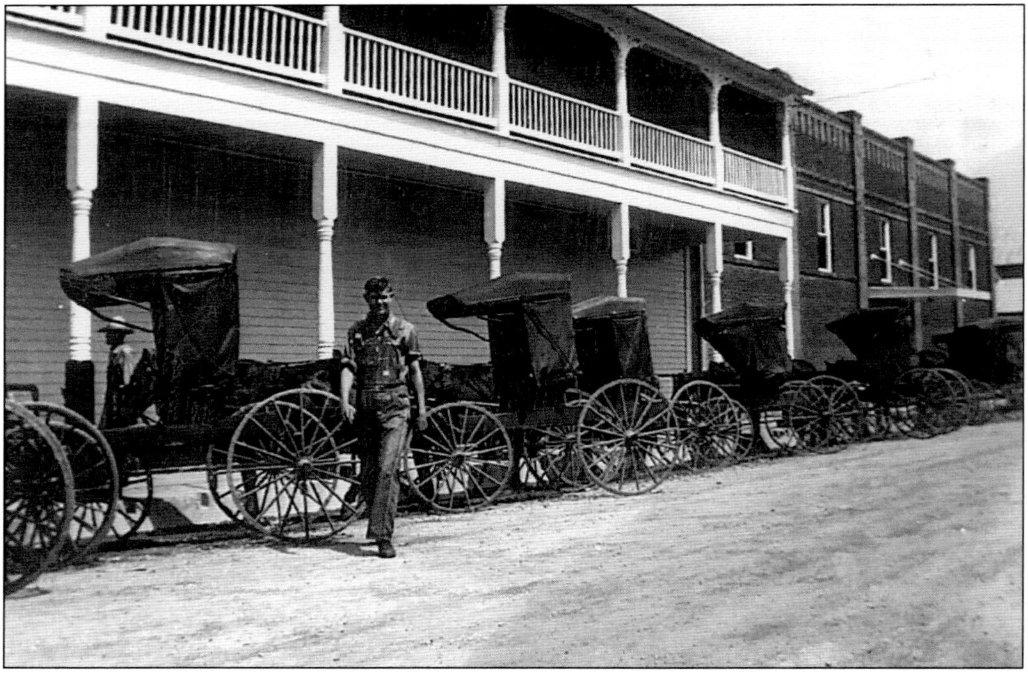

This eastside view of Mervine Kahn's taken in 1923 shows the original building with the porch and the addition to the building. The buggies are apparently for shoppers inside the store. (Courtesy Fair Craig Hash.)

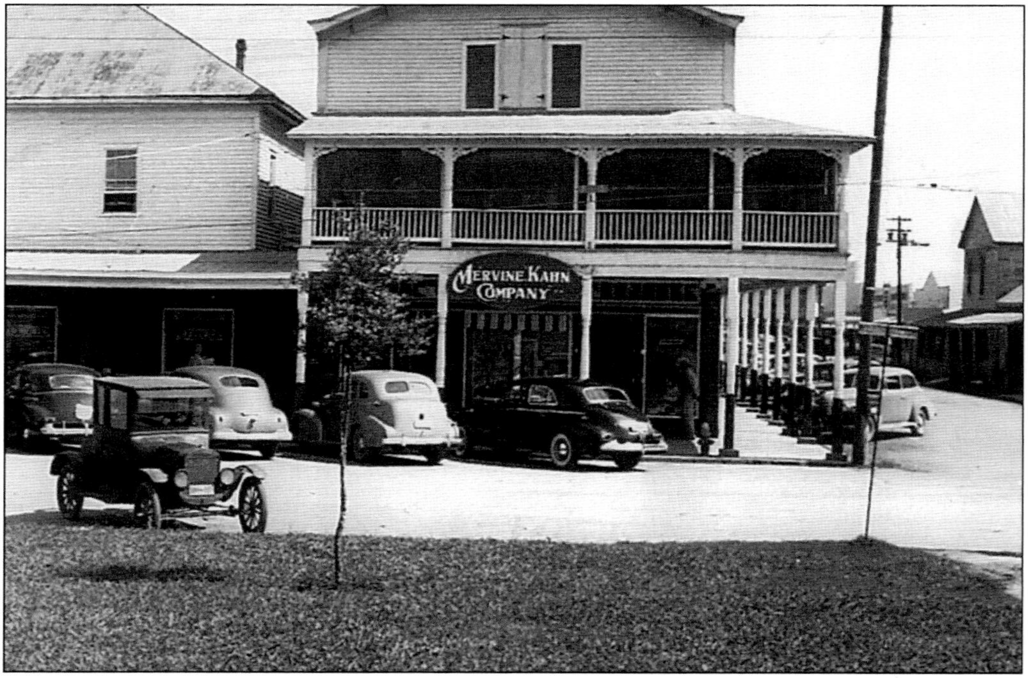

A classic view of Mervine Kahn's Co. from the railroad tracks show that the east side of the building now has cars parked there, a sign of the changing times. (Courtesy Fair Craig Hash.)

This shot of the intersection of South Adams and Texas Avenue shows the popular corner housing Hank's Bar and Robichaux's Meat Market. The building also housed a restaurant and had boarding rooms on the top floor. Later Hank's Bar moved across the street. (Courtesy Tom Johnson.)

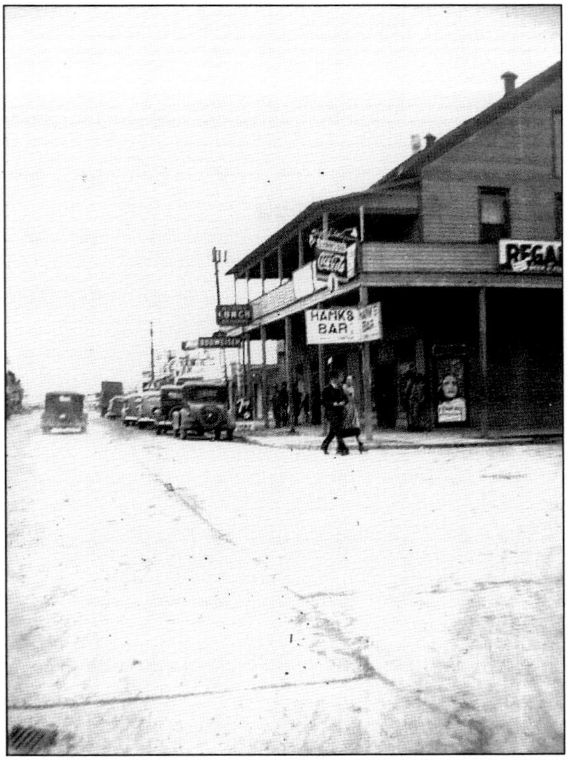

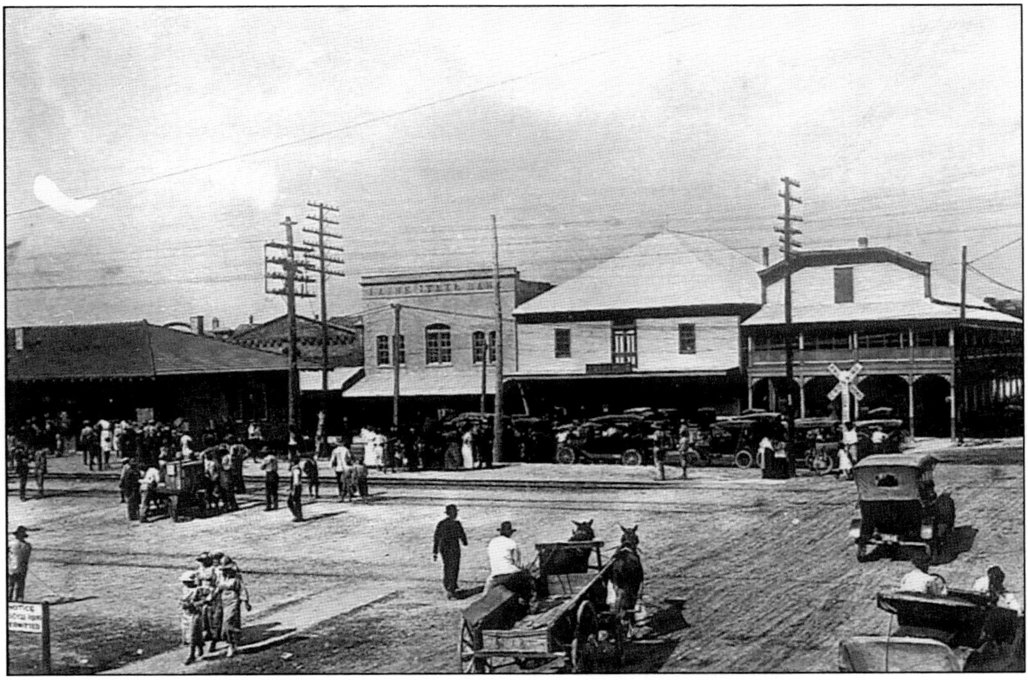

This is an upper view of the depot area, probably taken from Jacques Weil, Boudreaux, and Leger's second floor. Modes of transportation include walking, horse-drawn wagons, and motorized vehicles. Note the sign on the lower left side of the picture stating "Notice—No Bicycle Riding Permitted." (Courtesy Charles S. Stutes.)

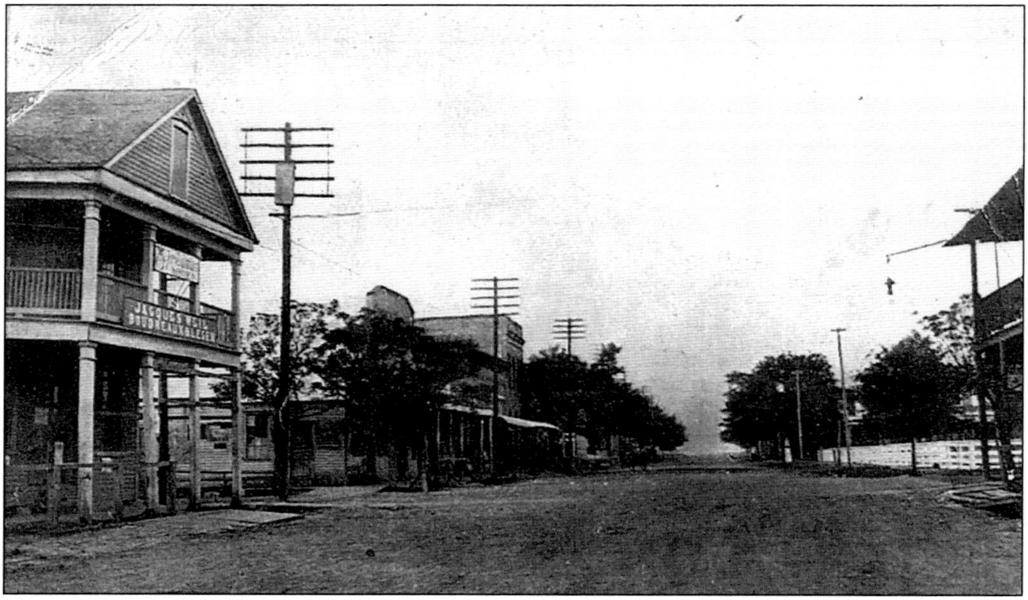

A westward view of Texas Avenue shows Jacques Weil, Boudreaux, and Leger on the left. The two-story building further down on the left is the Commercial Bank. The right side shows the corner of the Cumberland Telephone and Telegraph Co. Notice the white fence surrounding the freight depot, apparently to keep livestock corralled. Also note the street light hanging from the second floor of the Cumberland building. (Courtesy Dr. Ed Moody.)

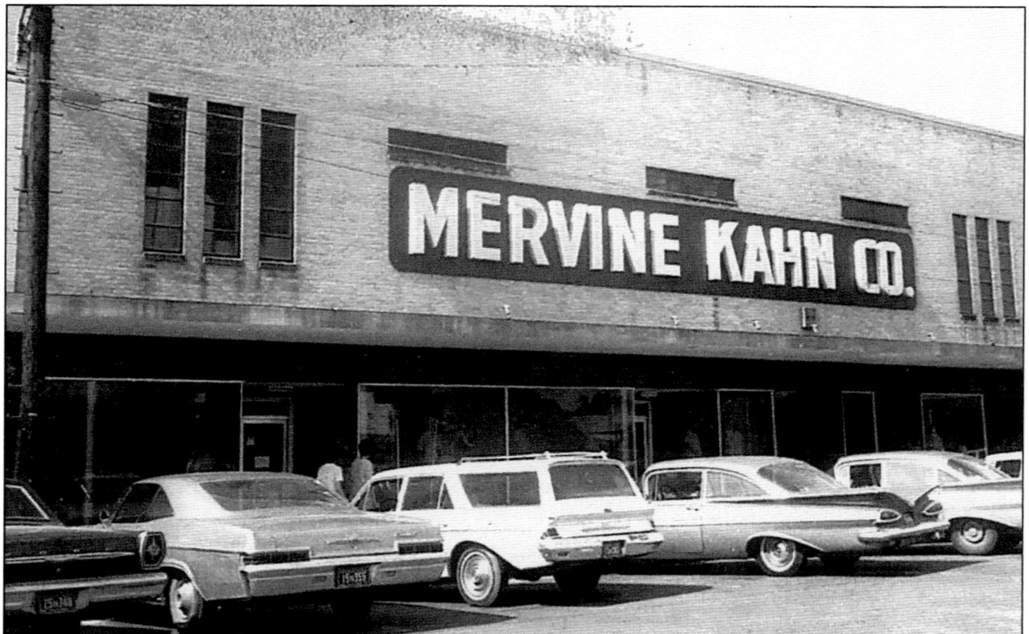

A common sight even today is the large sign of the Mervine Kahn building. At one time the business almost consumed the entire block with a department for men's and women's clothing, hardware, and many other household items. (Courtesy Jo Cart.)

Six

Planes, Trains, and Automobiles

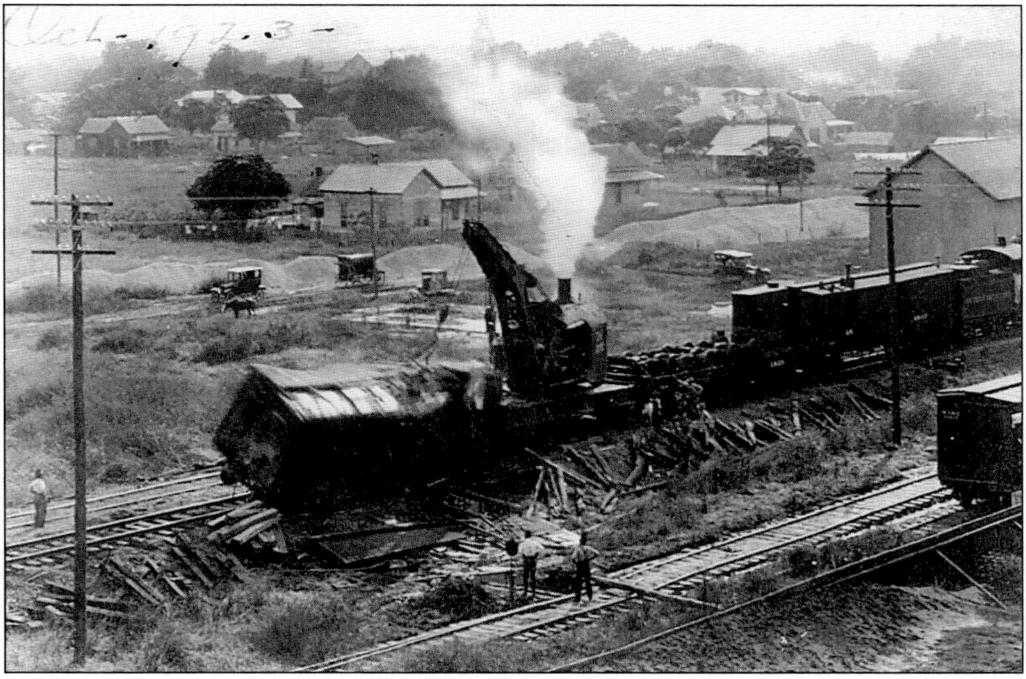

Rayne was a victim of two known train derailments, this being the first in 1923 near the Louisiana State Rice Mill. You can see the crane righting an overturned car and the axles on the car in the front. In the background you can see what is now Highway 90. Note the piles of gravel on the side of the road waiting to be spread for the new horseless carriages. (Courtesy Annette Gossen.)

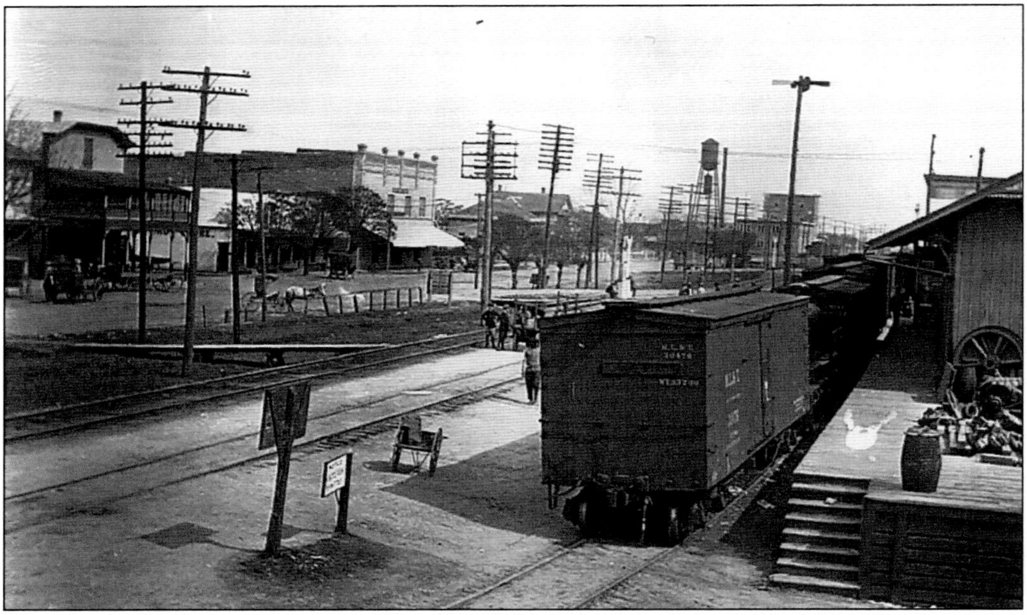

The Southern Pacific Freight depot is shown in 1916. To the left of the railroad tracks, a plank crosses over the ditch where the passenger depot will be later built. The loading dock on the depot was built at the same height as the train cars to allow easy loading and unloading. (Courtesy Charles S. Stutes.)

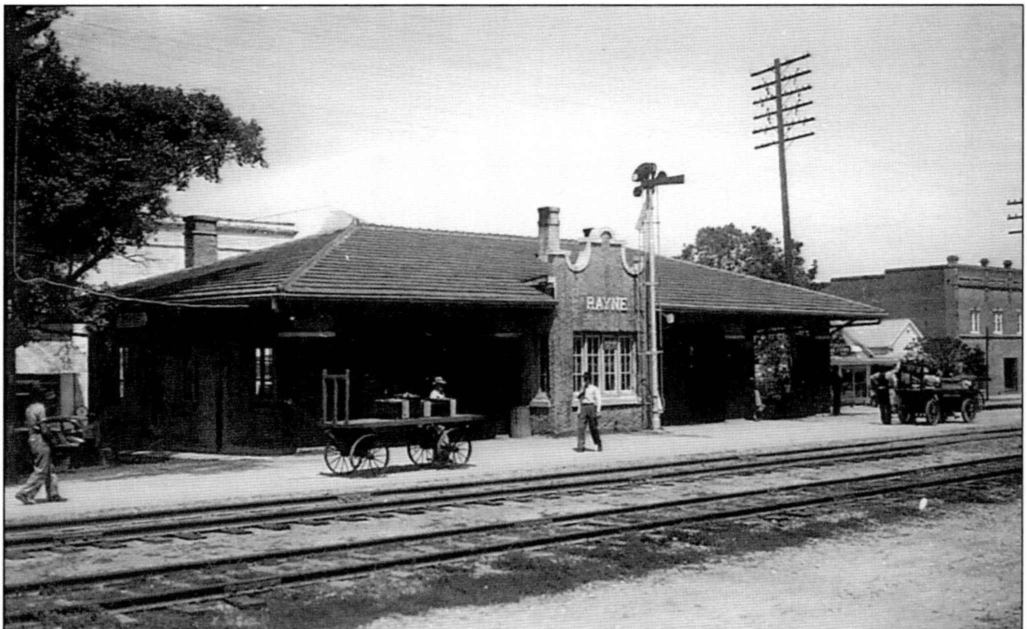

The Southern Pacific Passenger depot is shown in 1920 with two carts located in front to load luggage or supplies. The station included a seating area and Western Union clerk. (Courtesy Charles S. Stutes.)

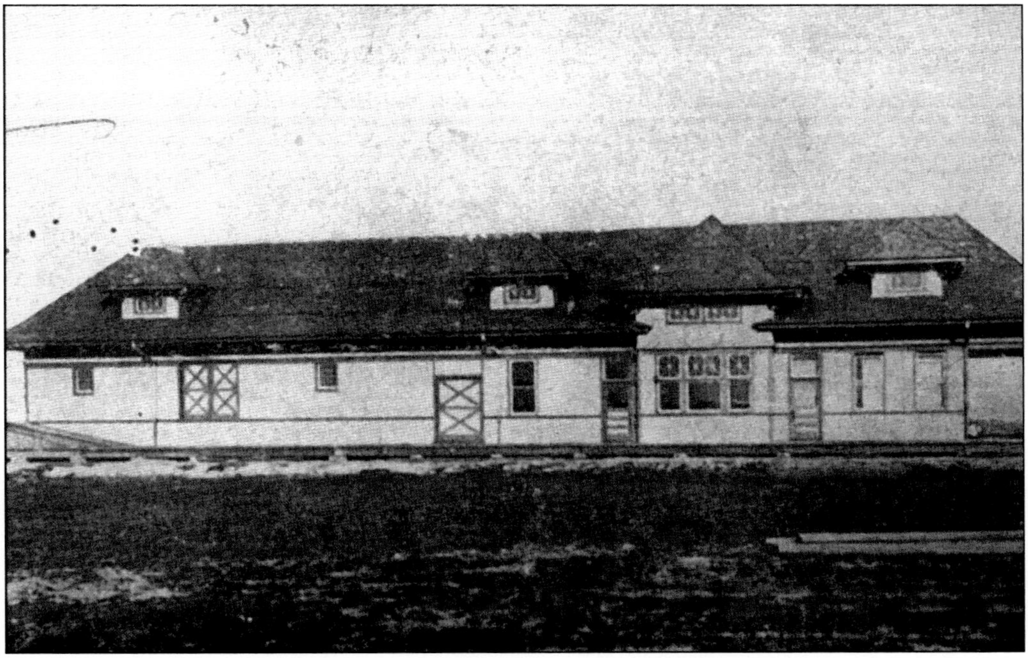

The depot for the "OG", Opelousas, Gulf, and Northeastern Railroad was photographed as it made its way to Rayne in 1907 from Church Point and continued to the south. Notice the German influenced design on the building. (Courtesy Charles S. Stutes.)

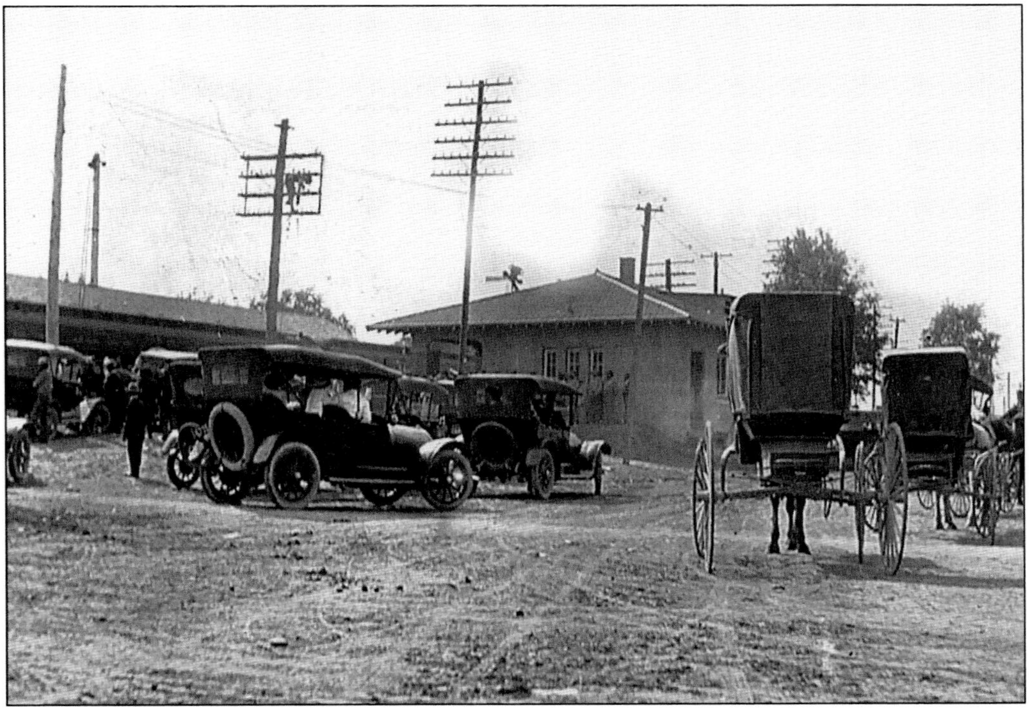

Both horse-drawn wagons and horseless carriages are shown at the Passenger Depot. Note the man up on the utility pole—he was apparently hanging up a mail bag to picked up by a train passing through. (Courtesy Albert Owers.)

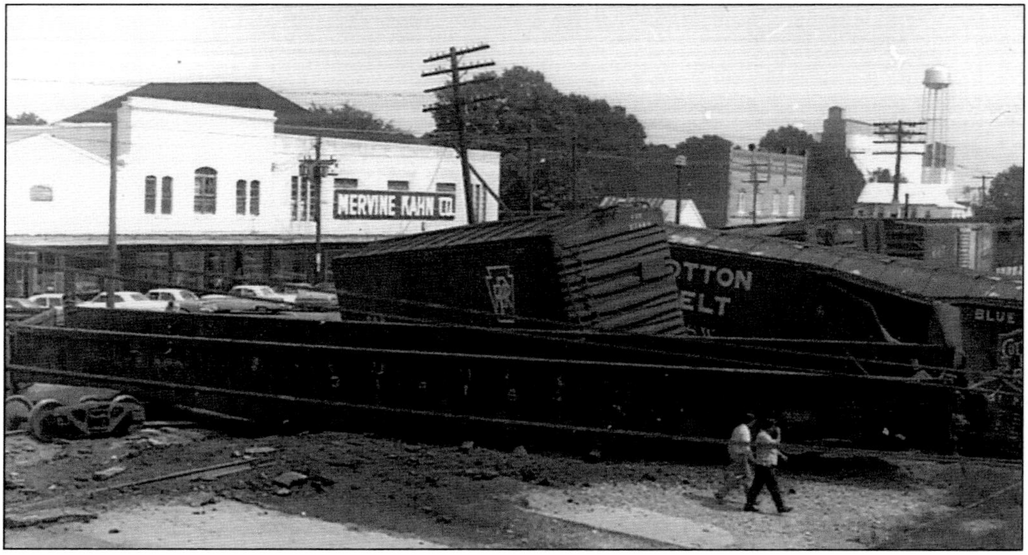

On October 3, 1970, Rayne miraculously escaped tragedy when Southern Pacific freight train No. 242, traveling from Houston to New Orleans, was derailed in the center of the business section of the city at 12:10 p.m. The derailment forced seven freight cars into tumbling, twisted masses of wreckage and tore up almost a block of railroad right-of-way and tracks, while derailing two of the four engine units and two more box cars. Jo Cart witnessed the derailment and captured this catastrophe on film. (Courtesy Jo Cart.)

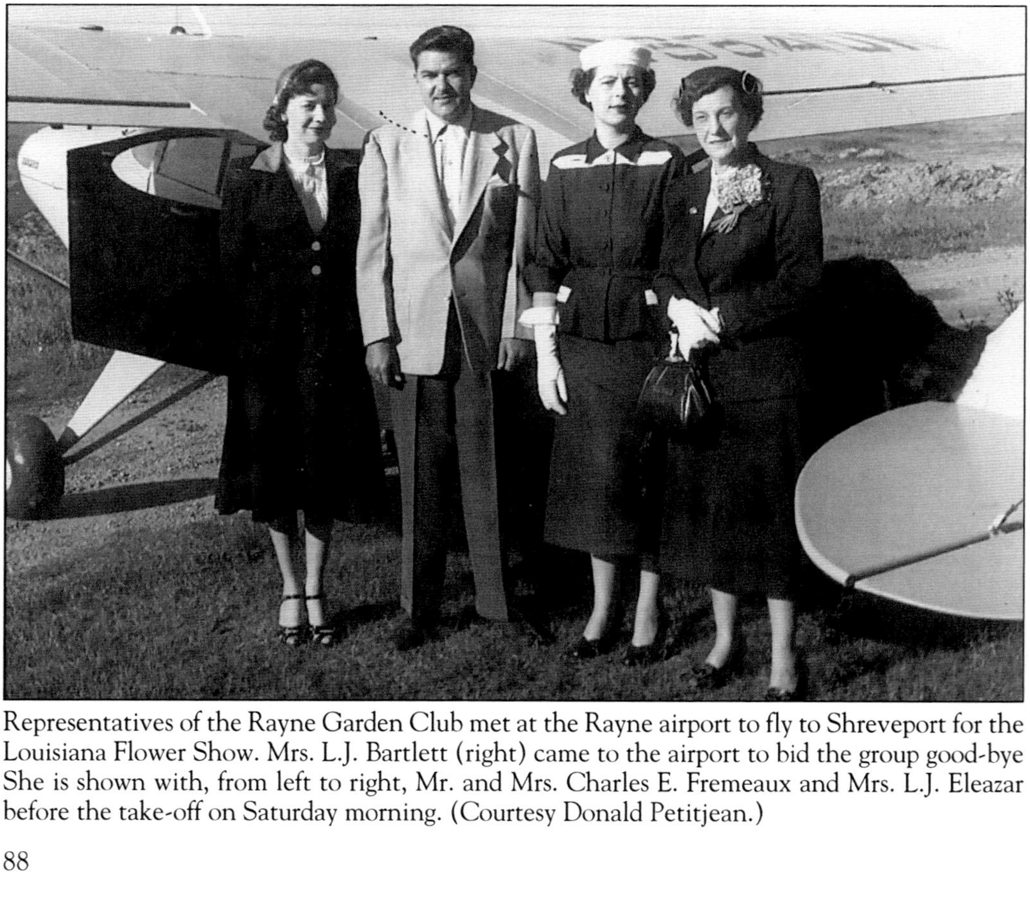

Representatives of the Rayne Garden Club met at the Rayne airport to fly to Shreveport for the Louisiana Flower Show. Mrs. L.J. Bartlett (right) came to the airport to bid the group good-bye She is shown with, from left to right, Mr. and Mrs. Charles E. Fremeaux and Mrs. L.J. Eleazar before the take-off on Saturday morning. (Courtesy Donald Petitjean.)

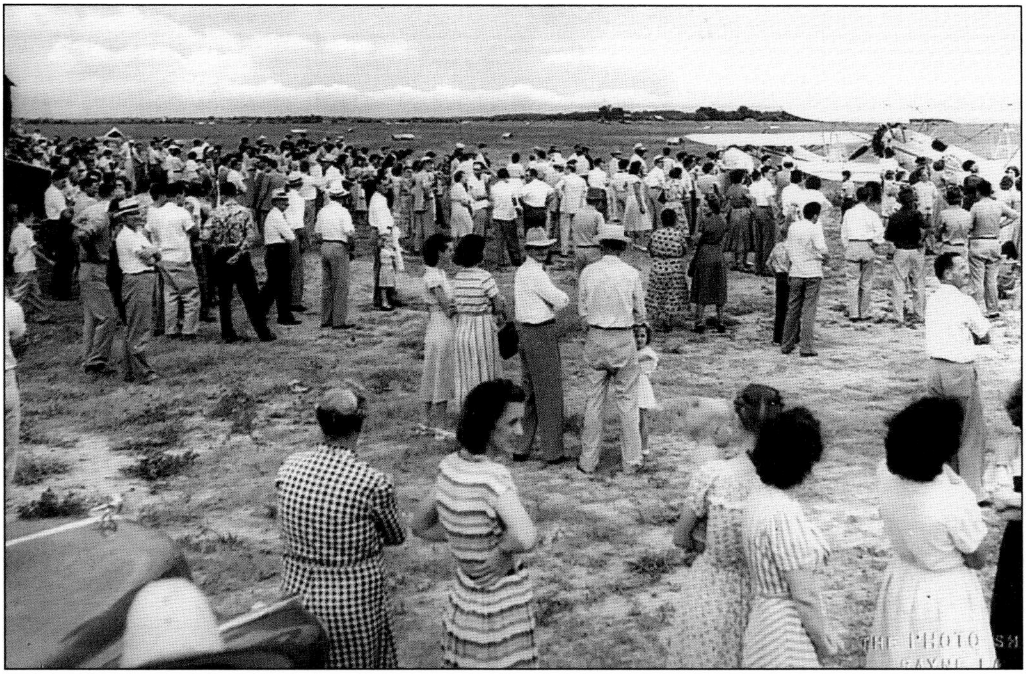

Rayne's airport was the scene of an interesting gathering, which marked the official visit to Rayne of the annual Louisiana Air Tour, sponsored by the New Orleans Jaycees. The top photo shows the crowd enjoying the show. A crop duster from Hains-Leger is parked. The bottom picture shows among the crowd, Mayor Pro Tem Barney S. Foreman, his little son "Doodie" Foreman, and Mayor Lionel Babineaux. (Courtesy Donald Petitjean.)

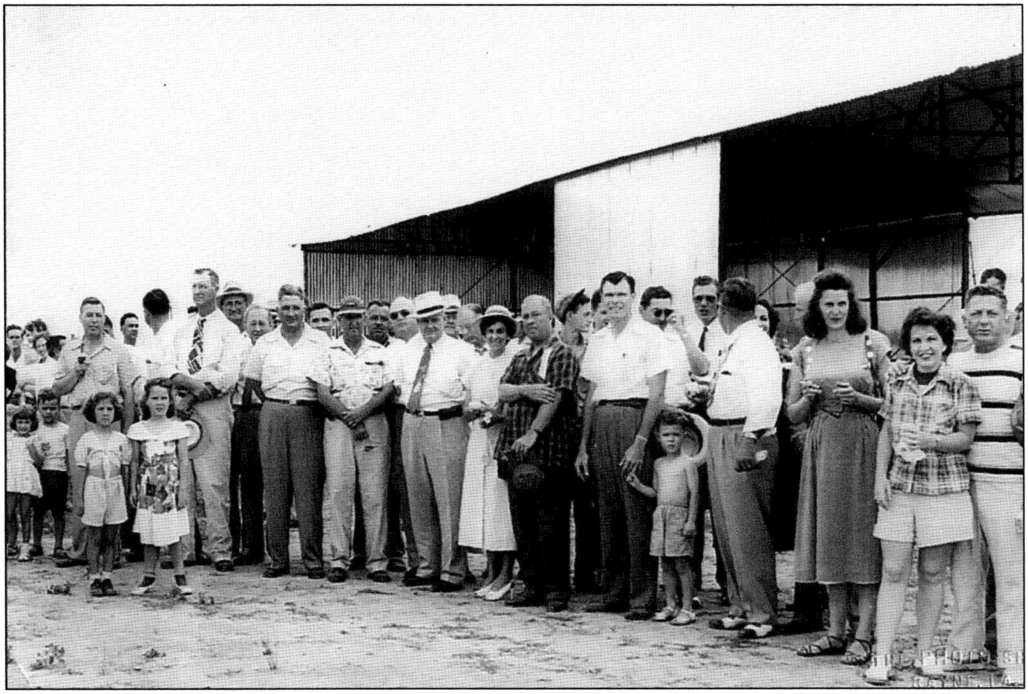

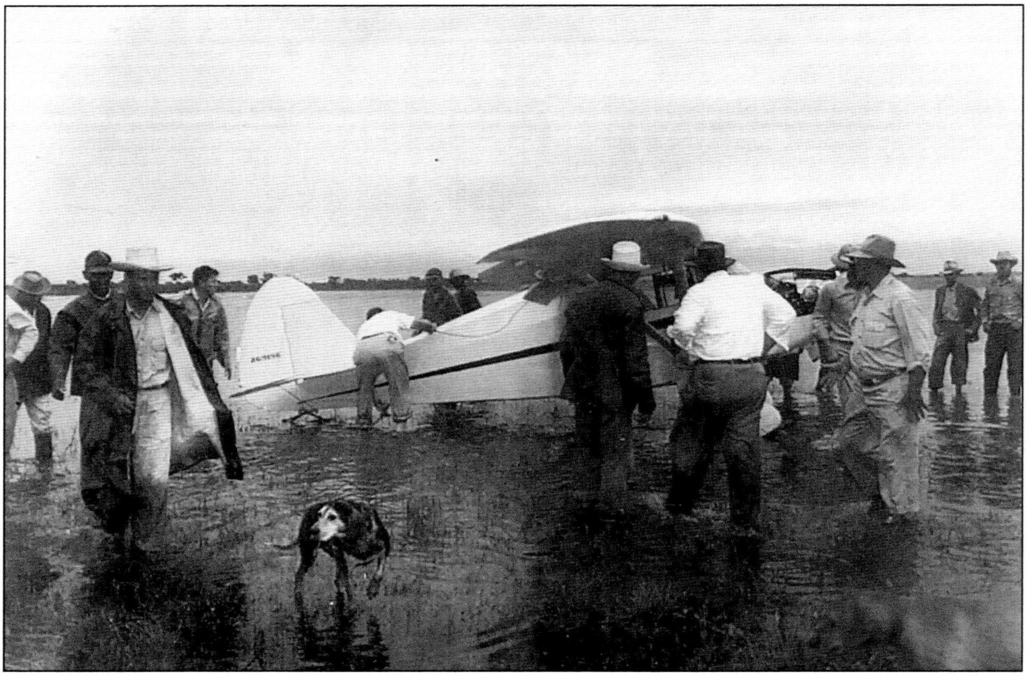

A Cub plane nosed over while coming in for a forced landing at the Rayne airport during a heavy rain. The pilot was unhurt but estimated damage to the plane was nearly $100. A large crowd turned out on the double to help the pilot right the plane. (Courtesy Donald Petitjean.)

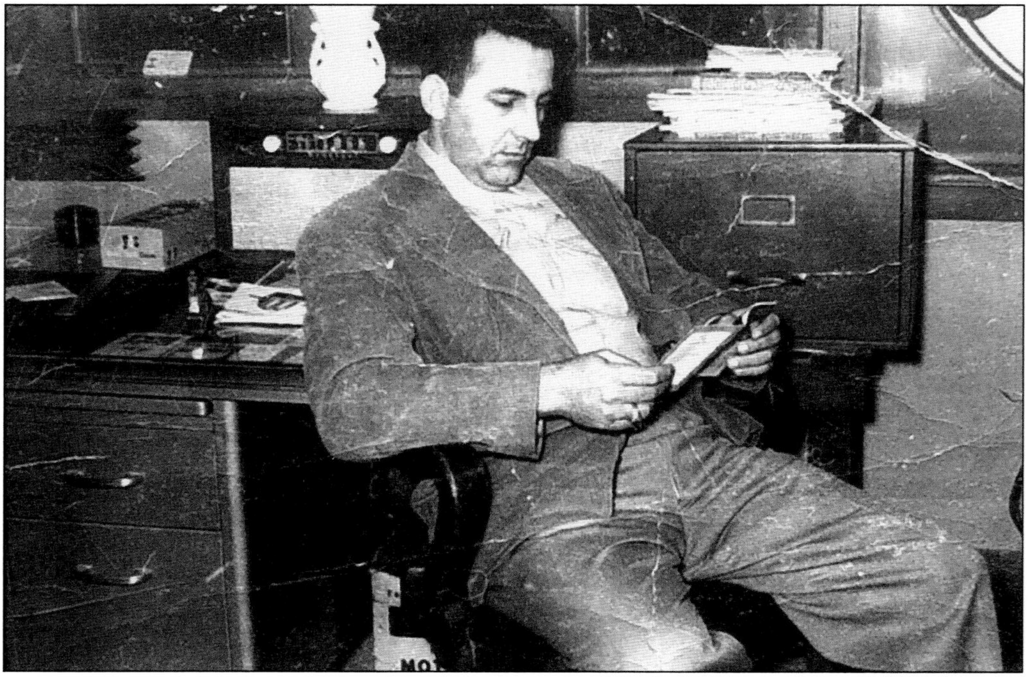

Lewis Cook founded Rayne Motors, which sold GMC trucks and later, Studebaker and Packard cars. He is pictured seated at his desk. The business was later sold to Bickham Motors of Lafayette. (Courtesy Josie Cook.)

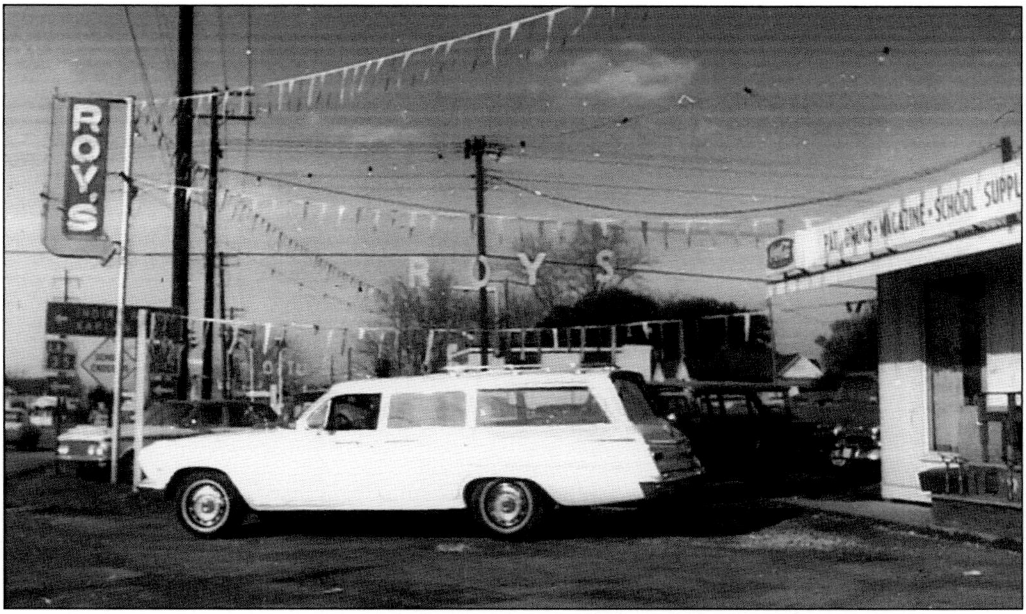

A local landmark was the used car dealership of Roy Ancelet located at the intersection of South Adams and Hwy 90, the original location of the OST club. The business also sold snack and school supplies due to its location across the street from South Rayne Elementary. Note the shoeshine stand located in front of the business. The pennant flags flying over the cars was a familiar sight on the lot. (Courtesy Fair Craig Hash.)

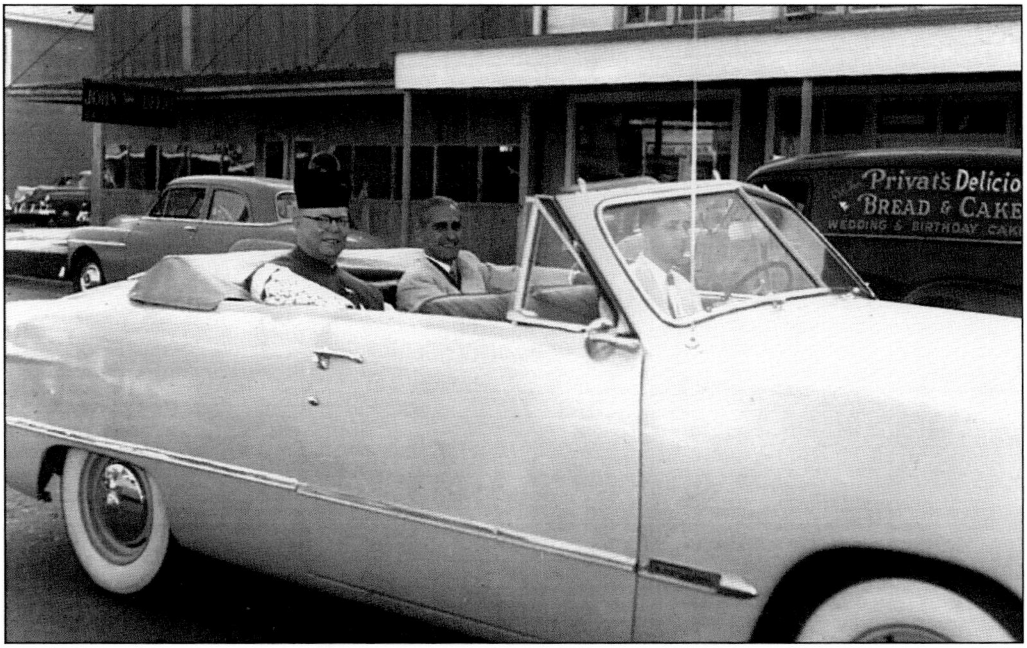

In 1953, The Rt. Rev. Msgr. Hubert A. Lerschen was recognized by the Rayne Acadian Council 1897 Knights of Columbus at the first initiation the council had held since 1948 to honor him for having served as their chaplain for 30 years along with his duties as pastor of St. Joseph Catholic Church. He rode in the parade with Emile Reggie of Crowley, the KC state deputy. (Courtesy Fair Craig Hash.)

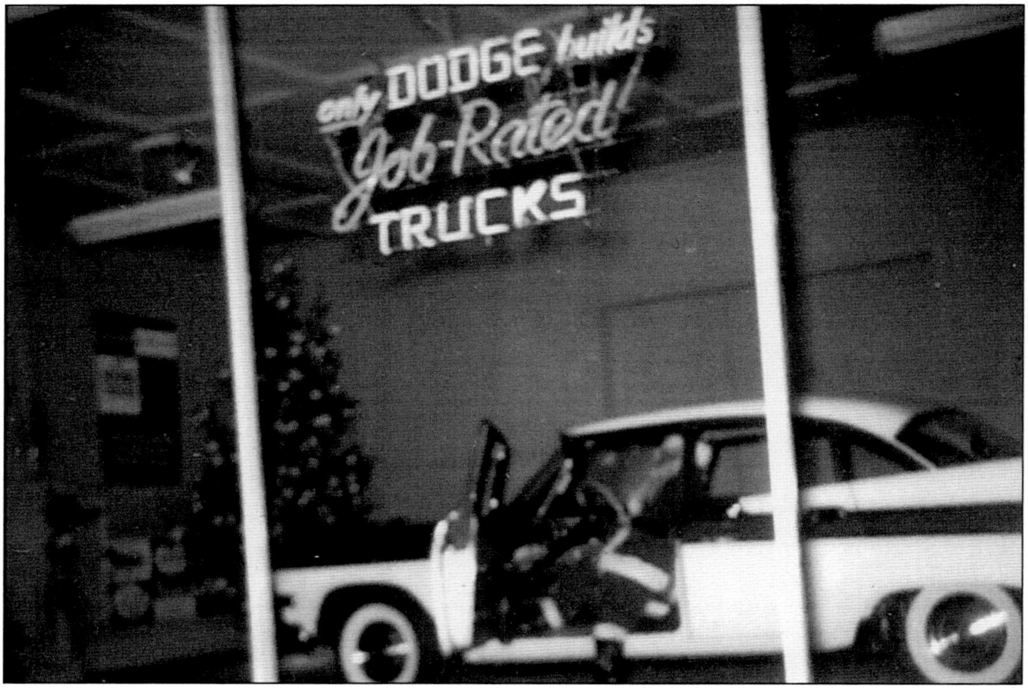

Santa Claus is shown in the latest model car at the Stamm-Raymond Car Dealership at Christmas in 1957. The car was featured in the large plate glass showroom window. (Courtesy Jim and Mary Ann Bush.)

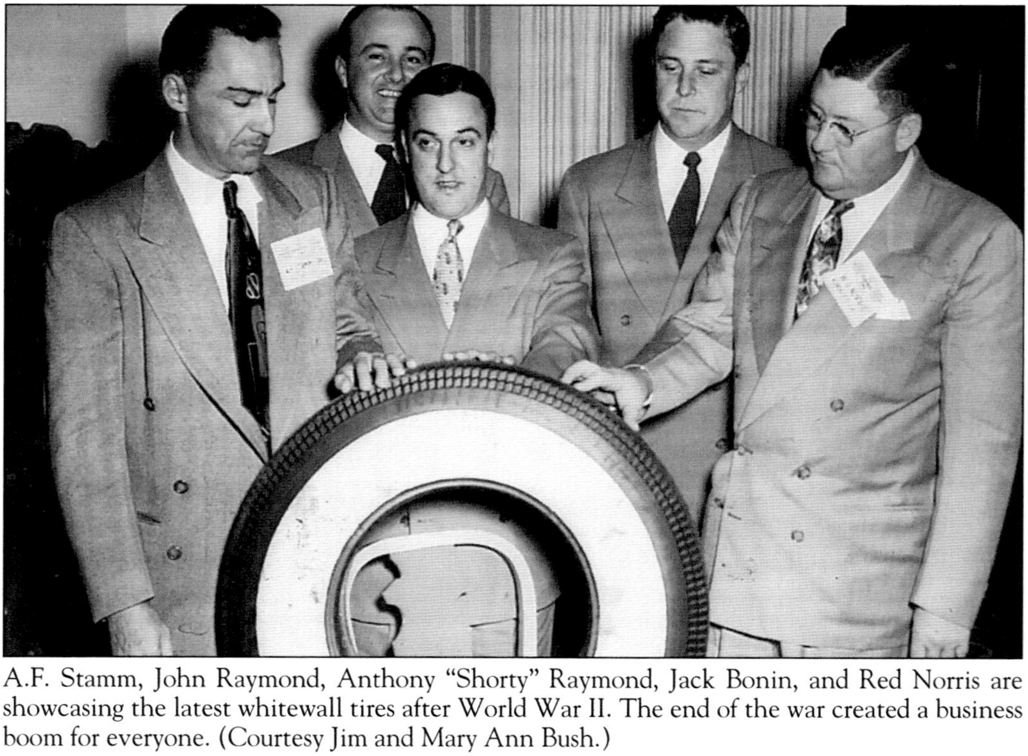

A.F. Stamm, John Raymond, Anthony "Shorty" Raymond, Jack Bonin, and Red Norris are showcasing the latest whitewall tires after World War II. The end of the war created a business boom for everyone. (Courtesy Jim and Mary Ann Bush.)

Seven

BUILDING BLOCKS

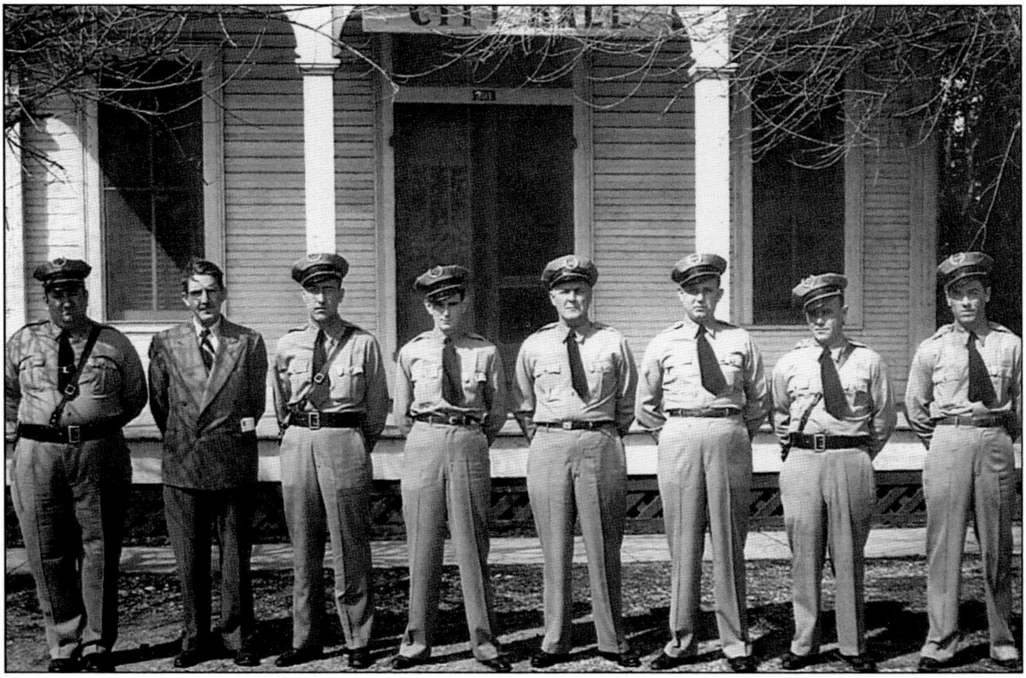

Looking mighty fine in their new uniforms are members of the 1947 Rayne Police Force shown with Mayor N. Curtiss Petitjean. Pictured are, from left to right, Lozen Baronet, Mayor Petitjean, Chief Clyde Lacroix, Preston Daigle, Odell Meche, Frank Bergeron, Ophie Boudreaux, and Asa Touchet. The picture was taken in front of the old wood city hall, which was sold and moved off to make room for the new modern brick building. The building is still standing and is being used as a rent house. (Courtesy Martin Petitjean II.)

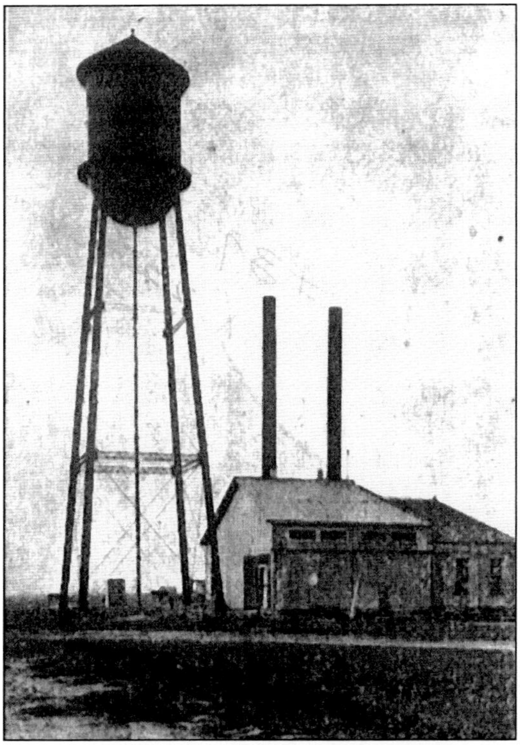

The Rayne Water and Power plant was built in 1902. A well was dug and the water was held in a reservoir until the water tower was built. The familiar water tower can be seen in many pictures throughout the book. (Courtesy Charles S. Stutes.)

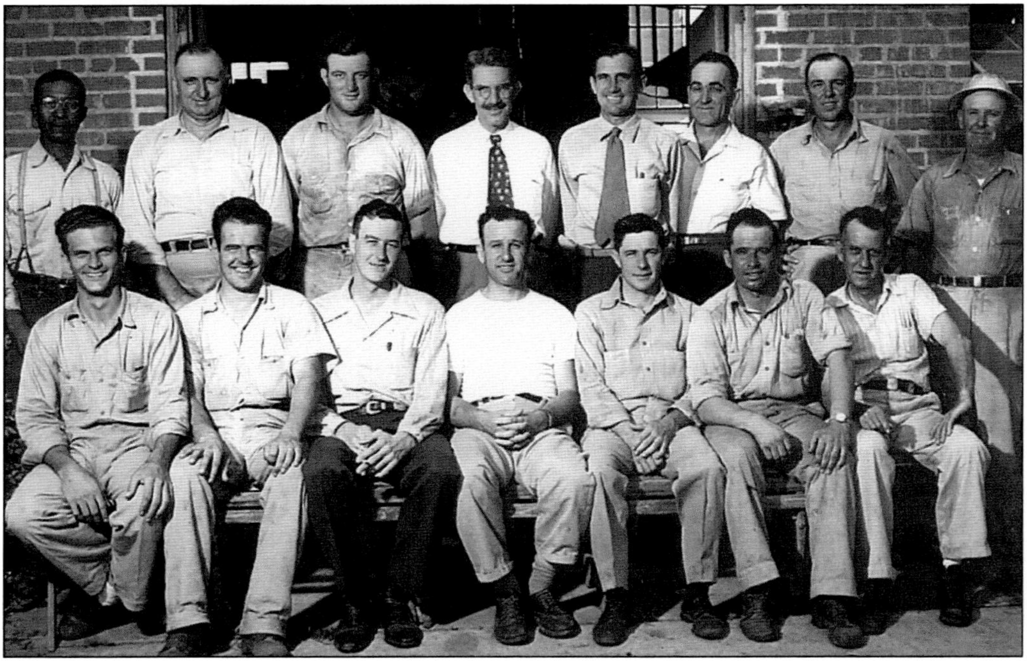

City of Rayne workers from different departments are pictured here. Seated are Claude Gary, Leo Melancon, Paul Prevost, Harold "Boone" Molbert, Curley Dupuis, Louis Boulet, and C.D. Hoffpauir. Standing are John Murphy, Eugene Boullion, Peanut Trahan, Mayor Curtiss Petitjean, Superintendant D.L. Ousse, Bennett Caioullet, Blaise Arsement, and Tonis "Tony" Faulk. (Courtesy Martin Petitjean II.)

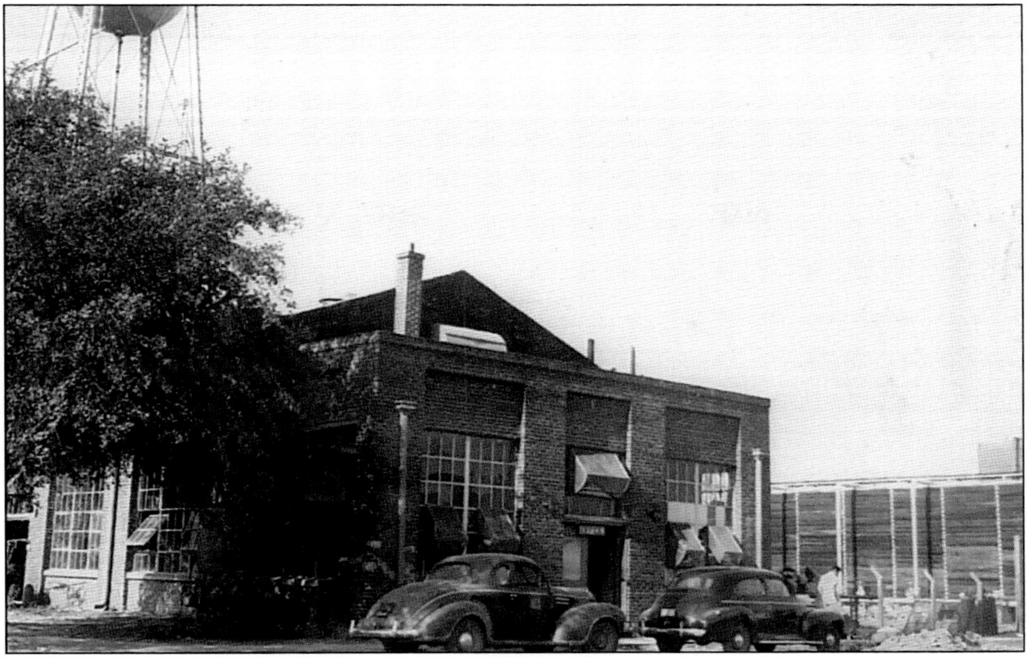

This 1940s picture shows the Rayne Power and Water plant on West Texas Avenue. The water tower is the second one built. A larger tank replaced it years later and is still in use today. The plant was renovated and updated in the 1960s and is at its original location. (Courtesy Andrus Fontenot.)

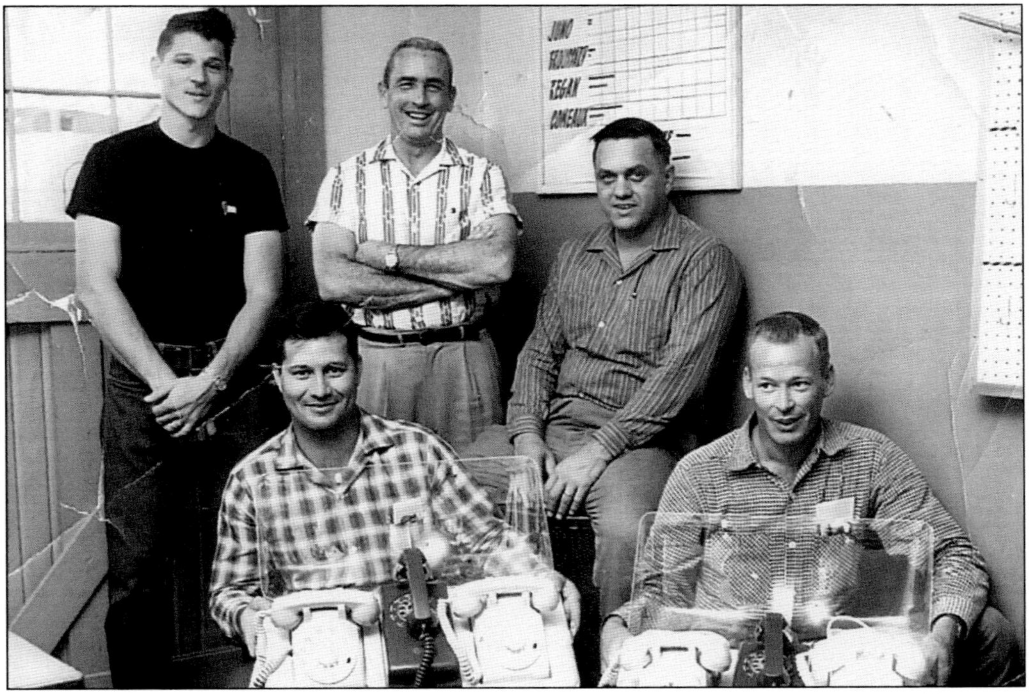

Employees of South Central Bell pictured are (seated) Leewood Junot and Donald Regan. Standing are Clyde Comeaux, Bill Mooney, and Bertel Broussard. These men were showing off new phones. (Courtesy Tom and Rhonda Broussard.)

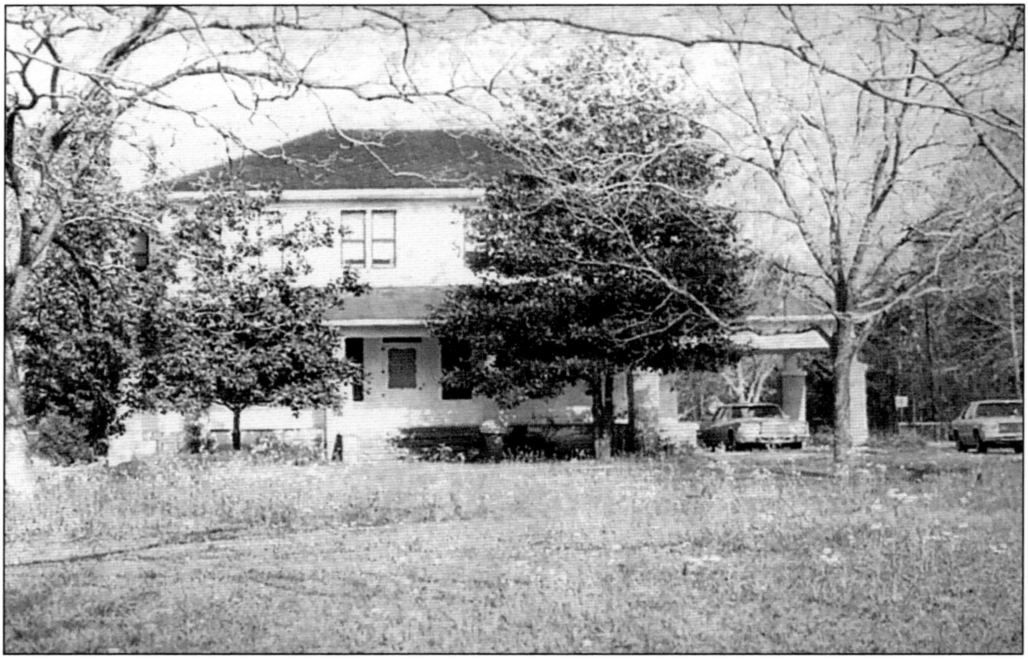

Several families owned this residence that was bought by R.C. Webb and became the Rayne Sanitarium, Rayne's first hospital. In 1917 it became the Zaunbrecher family home. (Courtesy Charles S. Stutes.)

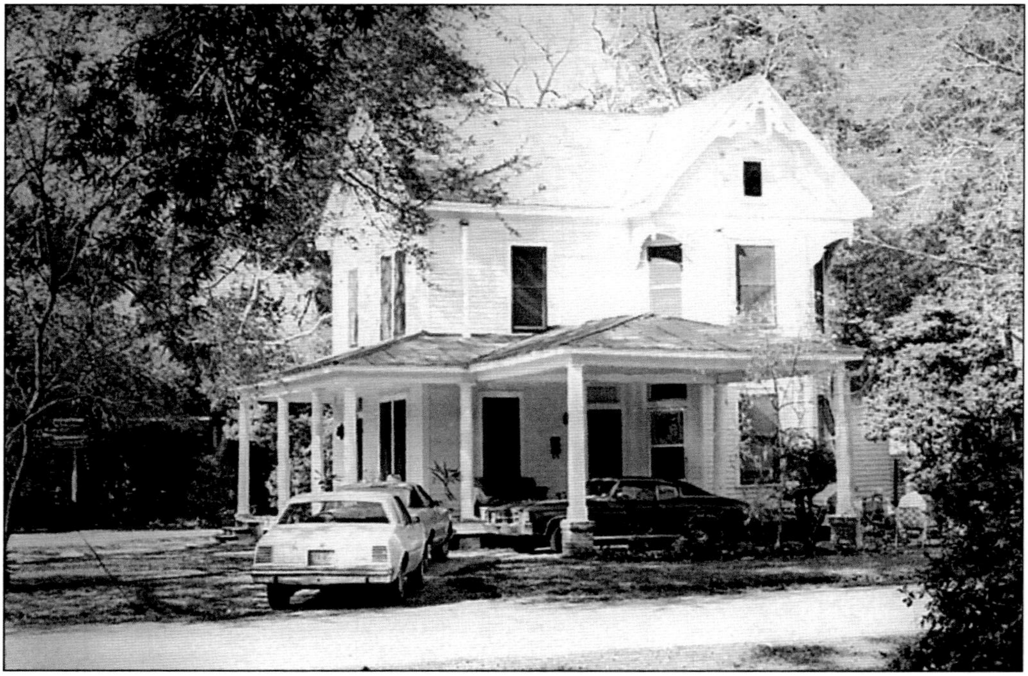

Dr. Bruner's St. Mary's Hospital, pictured here, was in use until the new modern hospital was built. It was located on the 500 block of North Parkerson and was lost in a fire in 2000. (Courtesy Charles S. Stutes.)

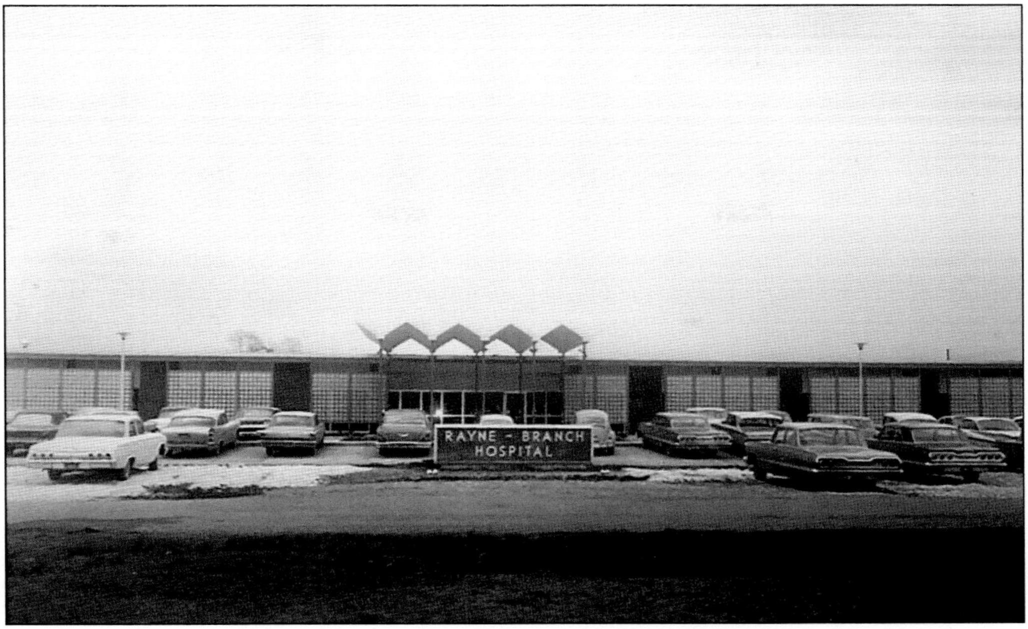

The newly remodeled Rayne-Branch Hospital was a facility offering private and semiprivate rooms, an emergency room, and an operating room. Several employees worked there including Dallas and Gloria Domingue from the beginning in February 1958 until it closed in 1990. (Courtesy Fair Craig Hash.)

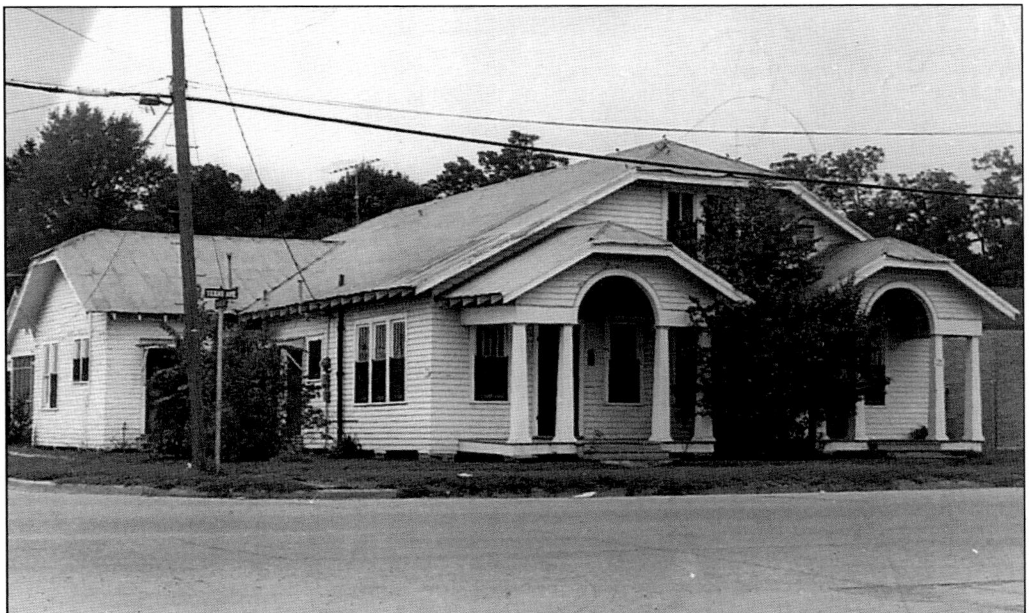

This building was one of the structures moved from Poupeville to Rayne. It was operated by Francois Crouchet as a rooming house for people and salesmen who would come in on the train. Later, Wilbur and Hilda Ardoin used it as Ardoin Funeral Home, the first funeral home in Rayne. The funeral home was on the left and they resided on the right. It was later sold to American Legion Post #77 for expansion. (Courtesy Fair Craig Hash.)

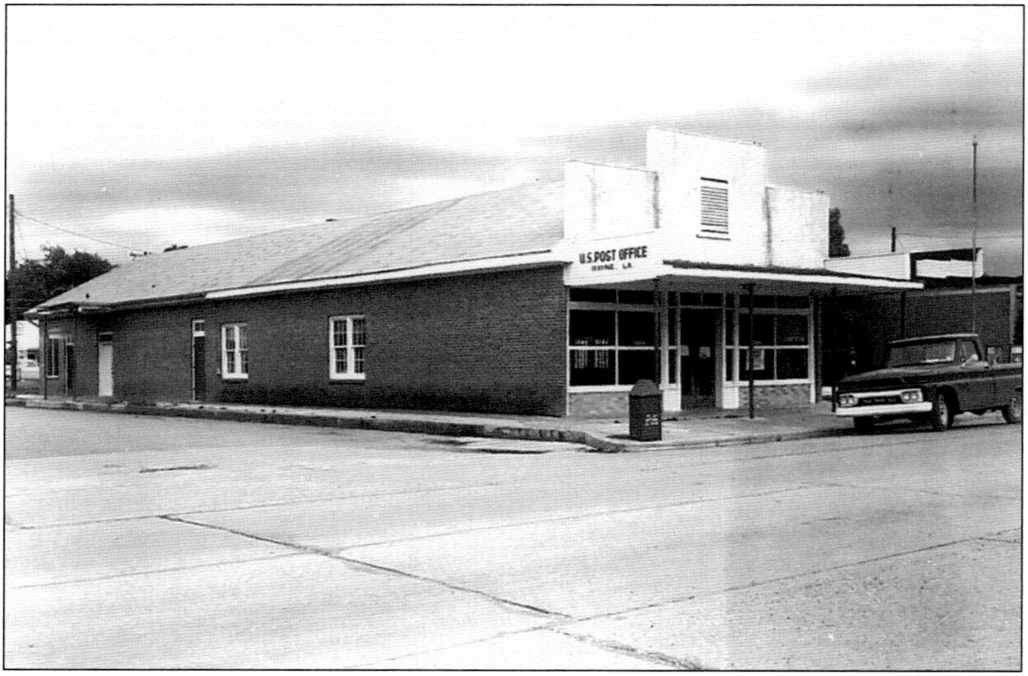

This is the United States Post Office located on North Adams. This was the location until the new post office was built in 1967 on East Texas. August Chappuis was the postmaster for many years. (Courtesy Fair Craig Hash.)

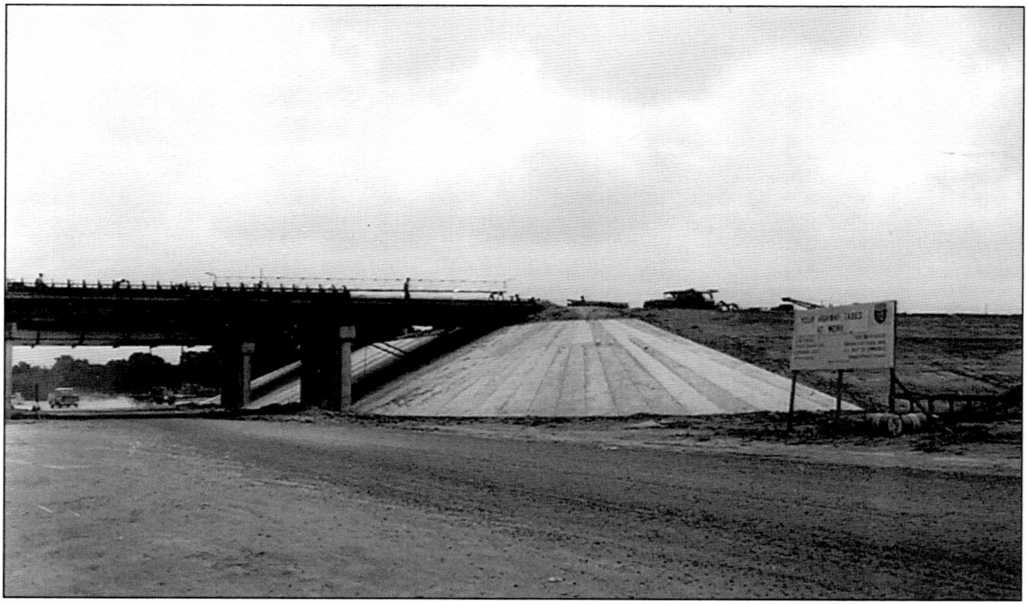

The construction of Interstate 10 in the 1960s is a major factor in the continuing growth of Rayne as we know it today. This phase of completion allowed travelers to journey between Crowley and Duson. (Courtesy Fair Craig Hash.)

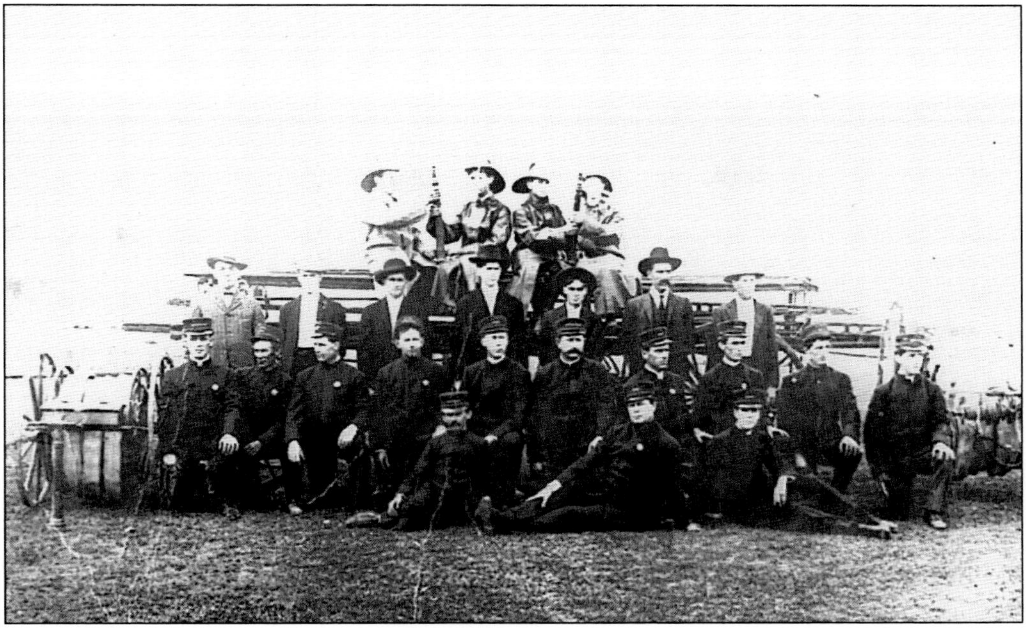

The Hook and Ladder Co. was established by O'Neil Comeaux in 1903, who is shown on the second row, third from left. (Courtesy Andrus Fontenot.)

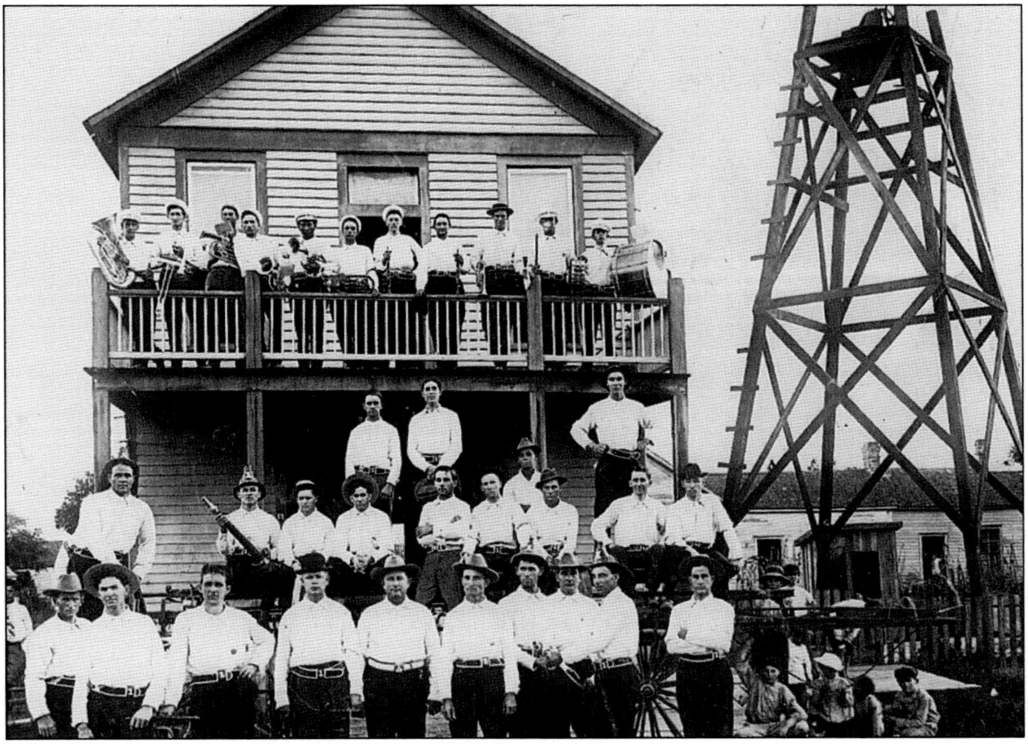

This picture shows the fire department at the turn of the century. Whoever got to the fire bell (top of photo) and rang it first got paid. Forrest Arceneaux had the old bell at his camp for many years. (Courtesy Charles S. Stutes.)

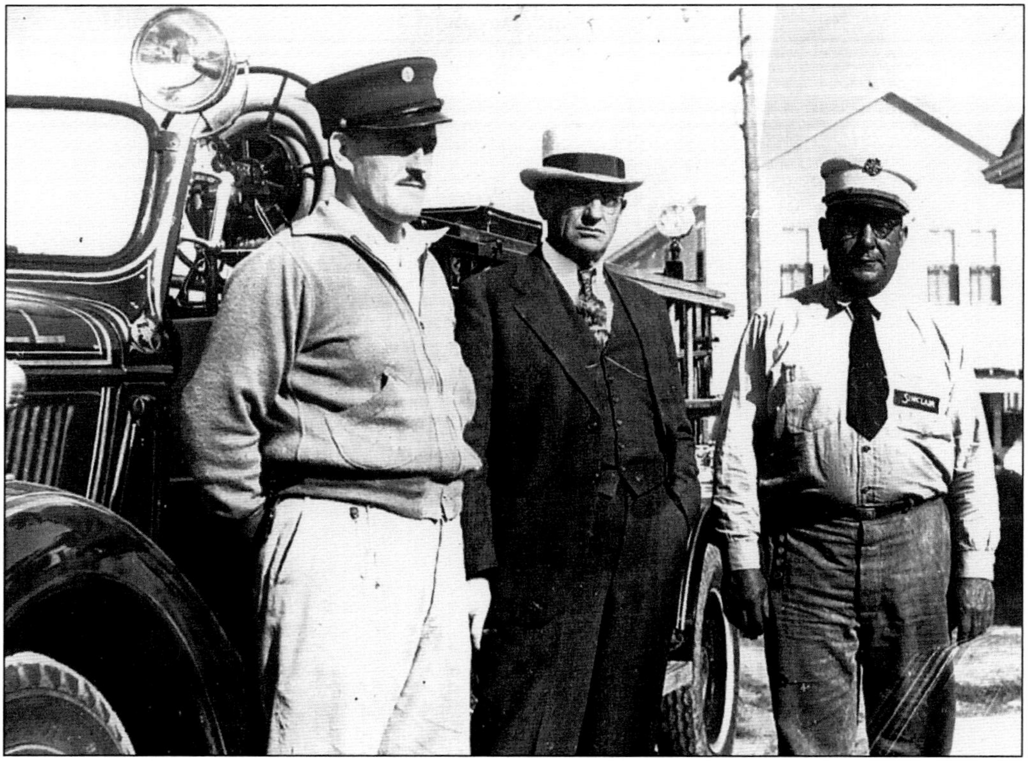

This new fire truck was purchased with proceeds from the Rayne Rice Birds ballgames. The truck had the words "Play Ball" on the hood. Pictured are Fernand Privat, Lozon Leger (owner of the Ricebirds), and Felix Peres. (Courtesy Rayne Fire Department.)

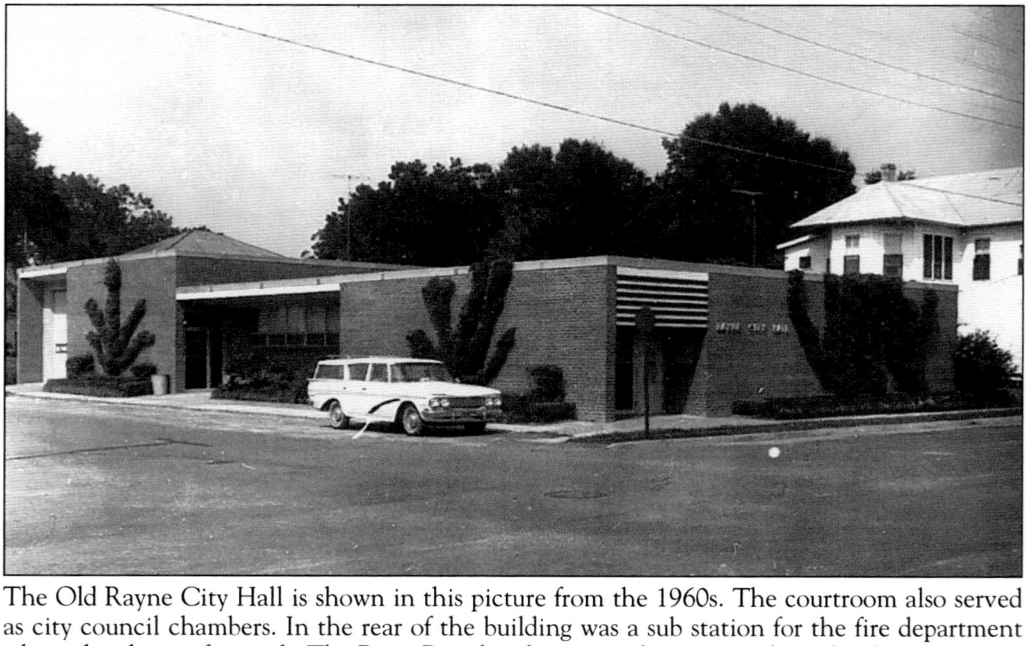

The Old Rayne City Hall is shown in this picture from the 1960s. The courtroom also served as city council chambers. In the rear of the building was a sub station for the fire department where they kept a firetruck. The Besse Boarding house can be seen on the right. (Courtesy Fair Craig Hash.)

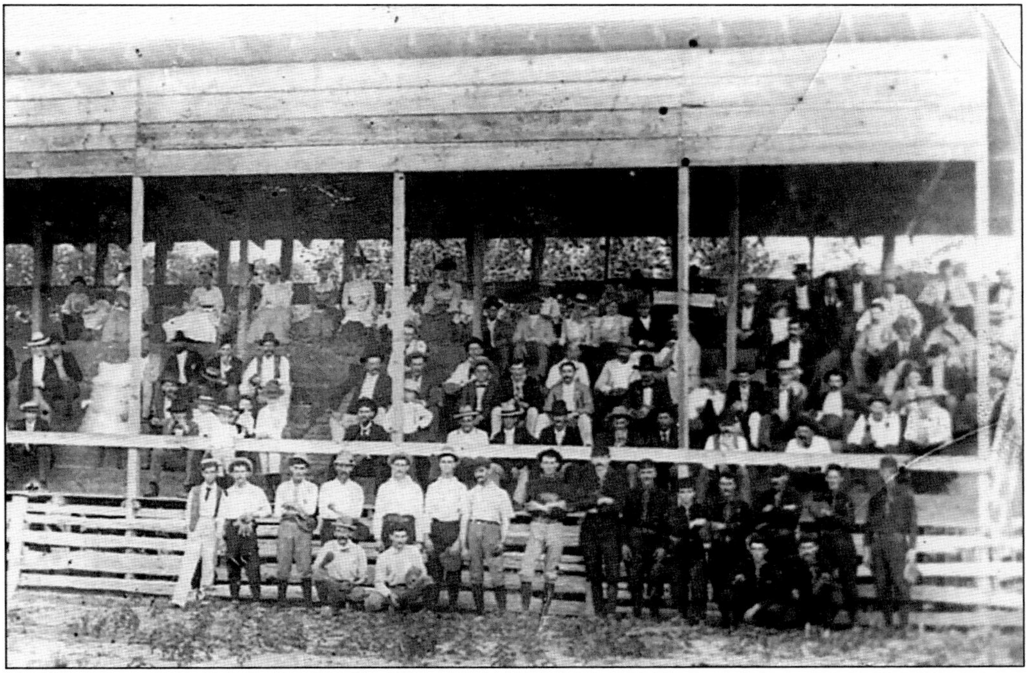

The Rayne and Jennings baseball clubs are shown at the old ballpark located on Fourth Street where the City Park is now. The Rayne team is identified, from left to right, as (kneeling) Leon Labbe and Ove Comeaux; (standing) Frank Denais, Newt Kershaw, Calice Leblanc, Roy Windsor, ? Broussard, and Ed Wimberly. (Courtesy Fair Craig Hash.)

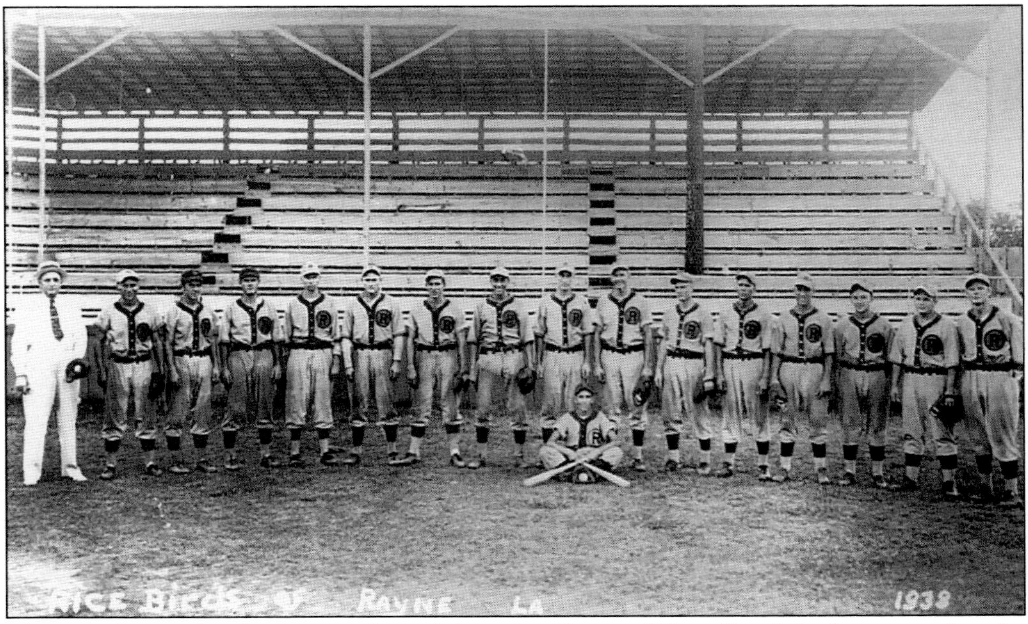

The 1938 Rayne Ricebirds was a farm club to the Chicago White Sox. They're pictured at the stadium on the Abbeville Highway south of the South Rayne School. Lozon Leger owned the team. (Courtesy Fair Craig Hash.)

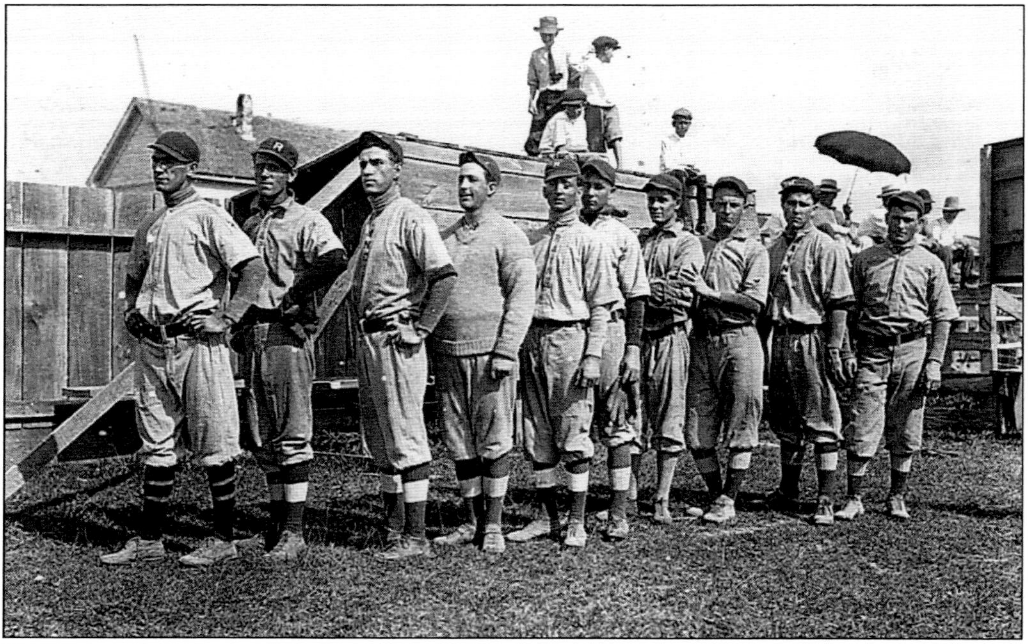

The Rayne Ball Team shown are, from left to right, Riley Boudreaux, Newe Hebert, Joseph Duclos, Stoney Bonvilla, Wallace Ousse, Winfred Plattsmier, Wilber Hains, Top Vitter, Neg Vance, and Bobby Hains. (Courtesy Margo Goertz.)

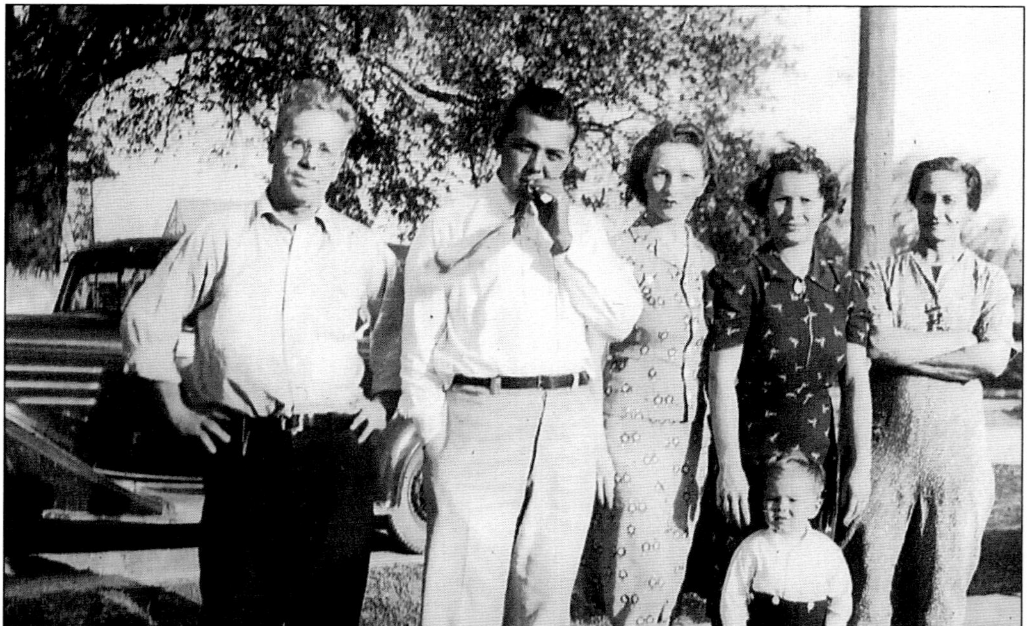

This pictures shows, from left to right, L.J. "Let Me Pitch" Maloz, who was a popular comic relief as a heckler at ball games, Wade Guilliot, Hazel Maloz Guilliot, Violet Maloz Domingue, and Elodie Broussard. Kneeling is Alex Babineaux. "Let Me Pitch" was known as the Rice Birds biggest fan. He would heckle the opposing pitcher by asking to let him pitch or tell batters after they swung and missed "don't wave at me, I don't have a skirt on." (Courtesy Tom Johnson.)

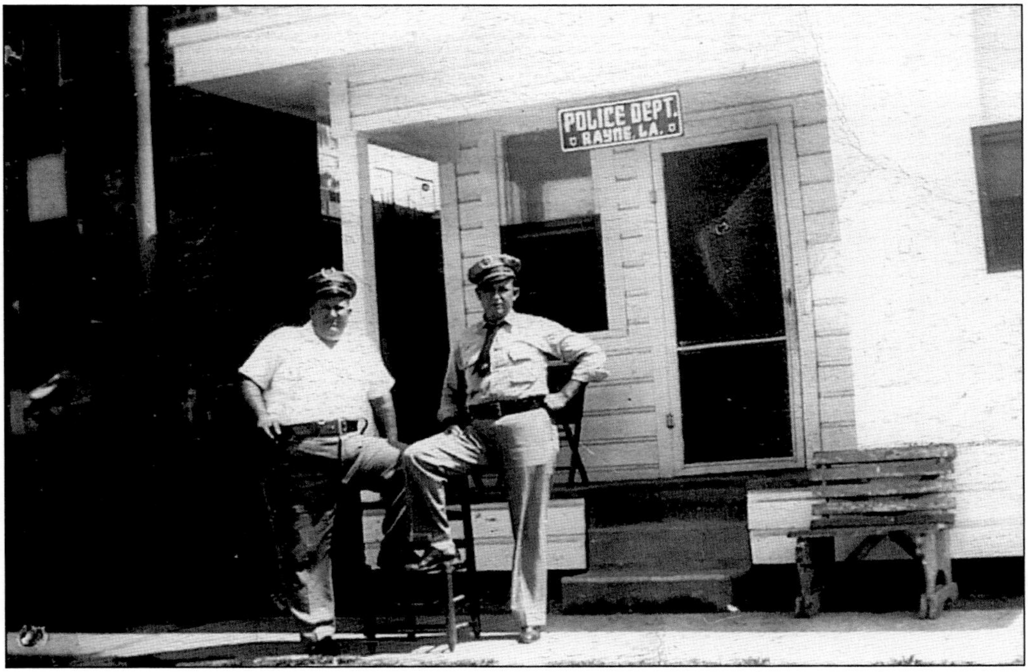

The first separate Rayne Police Station building was located next to the power plant on Texas Avenue. Before this building, the police department was based in the City Hall. Pictured is Lozan Baronet and Rodney Leblanc. (Courtesy Martin Petitjean II.)

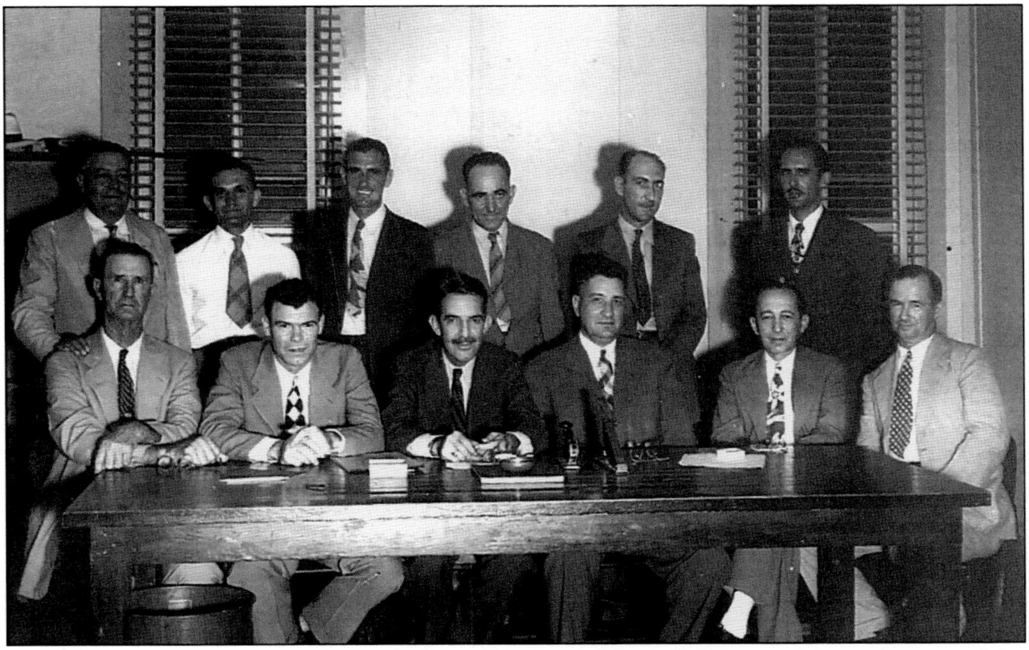

Shown is Rayne's new city administration, shortly after this group took over operation of the city's affairs in 1946. Pictured, from left to right, are (standing) O.U. Landry, Weston Aube, D.L. Ousse, Bennett Caillouet, Clyde Lacroix, and James C. Arceneaux; (seated) Adam R. Trahan, Barney S. Foreman, Mayor N. Curtiss Petitjean, Lionel Babineaux, Walter J. McBride, and Mickeal Fields. (Courtesy Martin Petitjean II.)

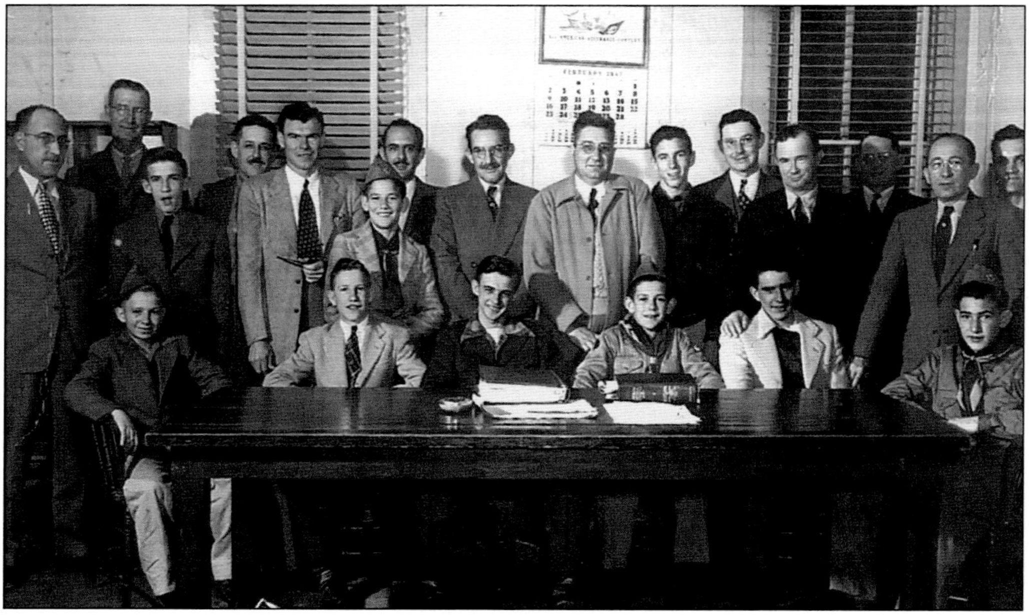

Rayne's Boy Scout Troops took an active part in city administration, when, in observance of National Boy Scout Week, Mayor N. Curtiss Petitjean, members of the city council, Chief of Police Clyde A. Lacroix, his force, and other city employees and officials relinquished the duties of the town to the Scouts for this one-day governmental program. (Courtesy Martin Petitjean II.)

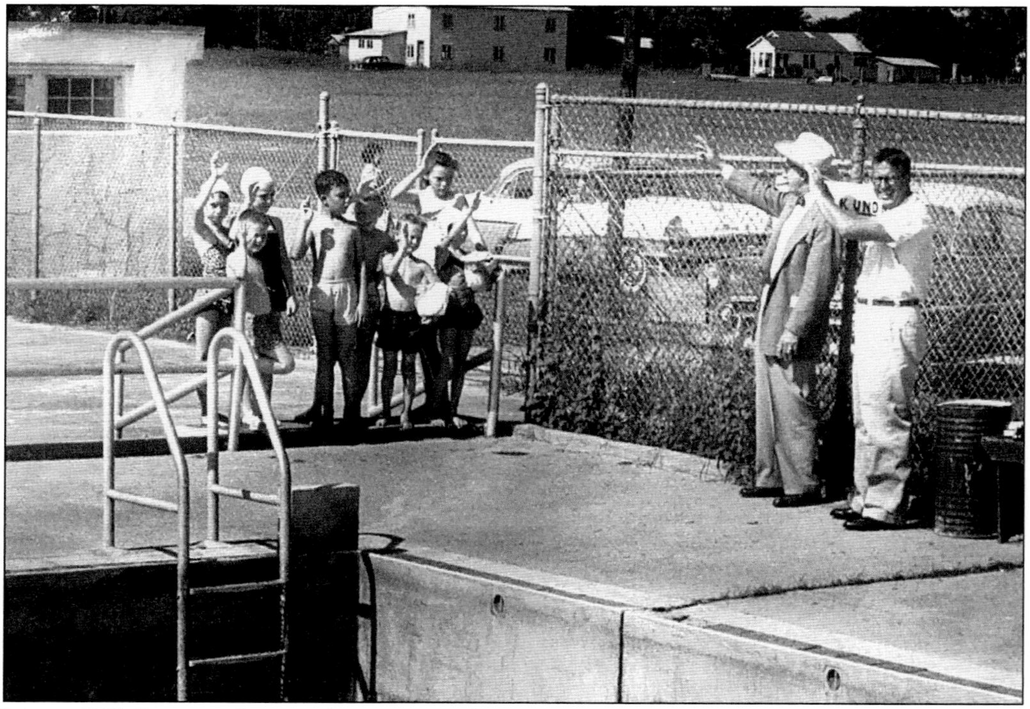

Mayor Bill Gossen, along with Vincent Chappus, greets future swimmers at the sight of the Rayne Municipal pool in this photo taken to encourage the passing of a bond issue to fund the pool refurbishment for its re-opening. (Courtesy Donald Petitjean.)

Eight

Famous Faces

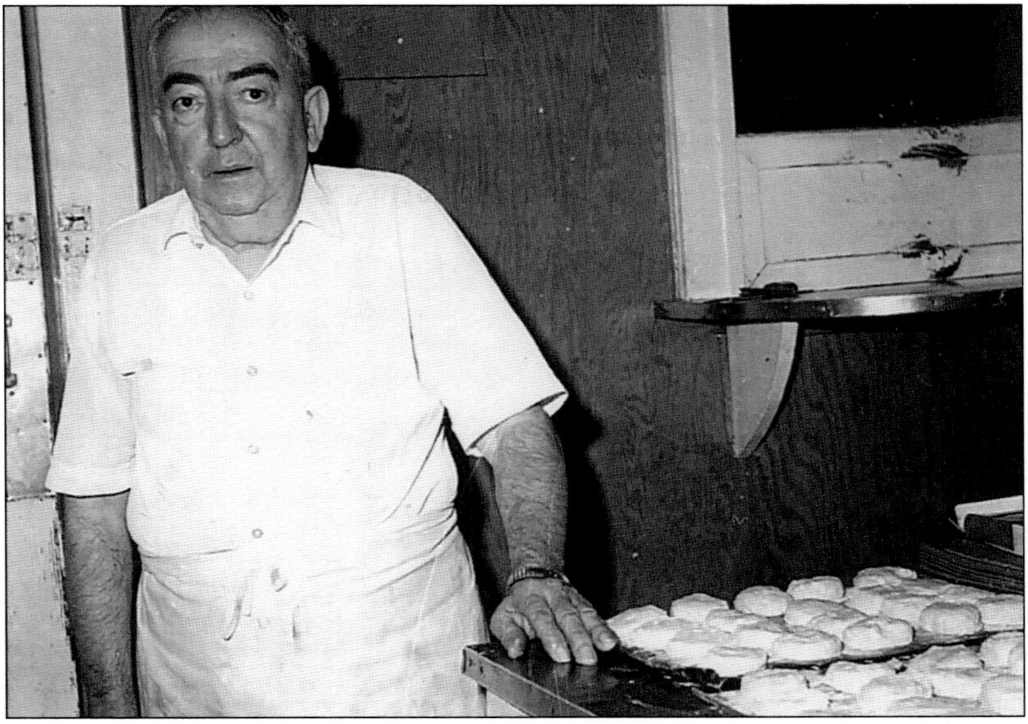

Paco Borne of the People's Café is shown with his famous biscuits, the recipe for which he took to his death. Note in the background, the hole in the wall which was connected to the dining room. He used a Campbell's soup can to cut his biscuits and would make the first batches of the day until his employees showed up. (Courtesy Rayne State Bank.)

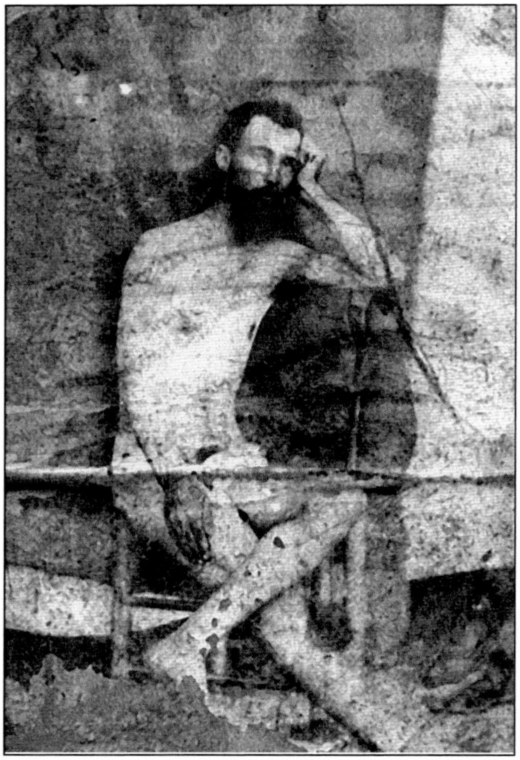

This picture taken from a tintype picture shows Jean Mouton wearing just a towel as a prisoner of the Civil War in New Orleans. He later escaped from jail and returned to Rayne. (Courtesy Clarence Cahanin.)

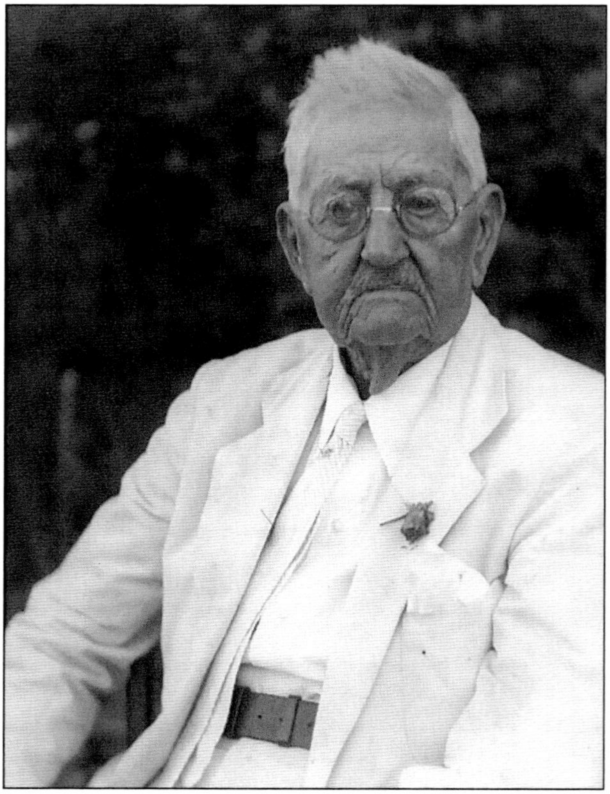

Martin Guidry Sr., a native of Rayne, rode his horse "Snap" to Mansfield and fought in the Civil War. Both he and the horse survived the battle and he rode his horse back to Rayne. Upon his arrival in Rayne, he discovered the railroad was built next to his house. In an ironic turn of events, Snap the horse, who survived the Civil War, was killed by a train. Guidry lived in the small house on North Eastern between the railroad tracks and Mauboules Park. (Courtesy Annette Gossen.)

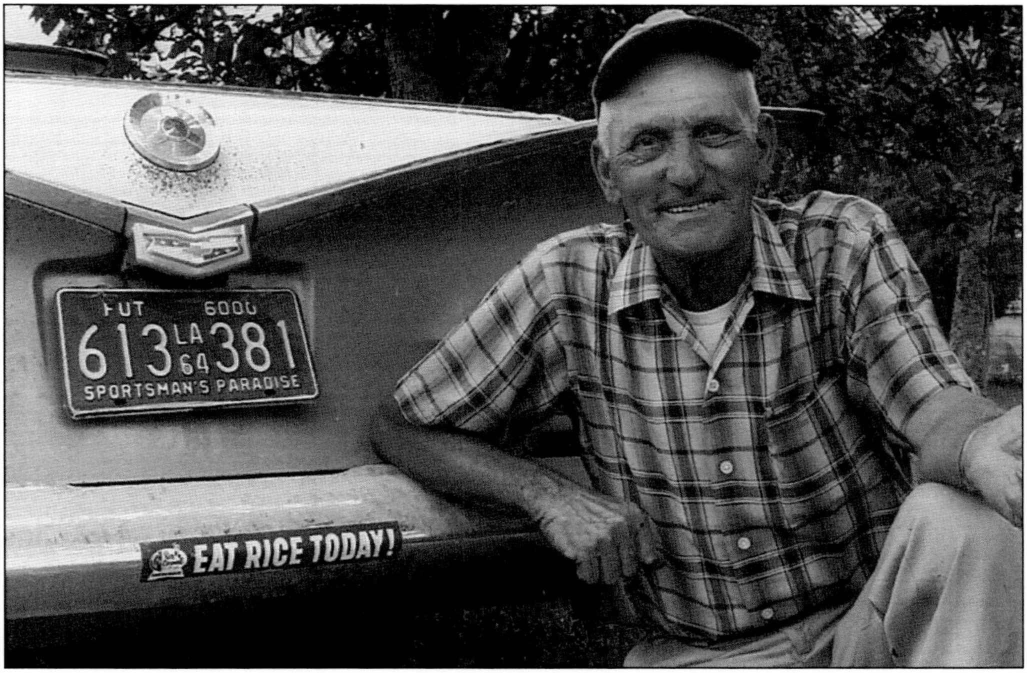

Joseph "Jack" Gilford Hains Sr. was a lifelong rice farmer south of Rayne. He is shown promoting the rice industry with a bumper sticker in this 1964 photo. (Courtesy Marjorie Hains McCarty.)

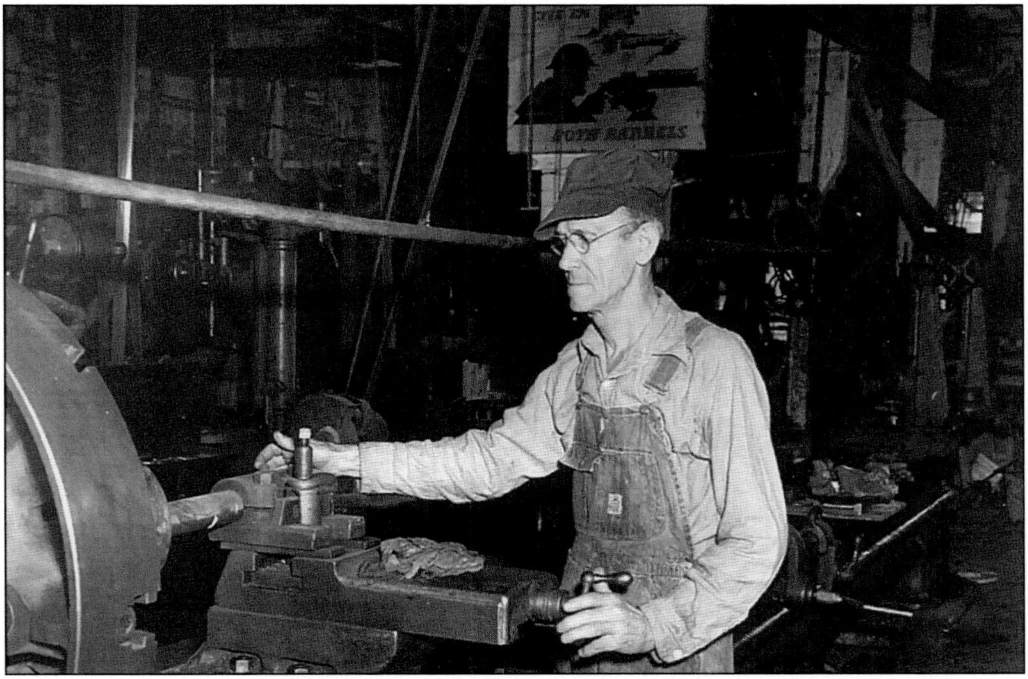

This is a 1948 picture of Newt Hebert at work on a lathe at Stamm-Scheele, from where he retired after 40 years of service. Notice the poster proclaiming "Give them both Barrels." This was a popular sight during World War II to promote patriotism and support the war. (Courtesy Donald Petitjean.)

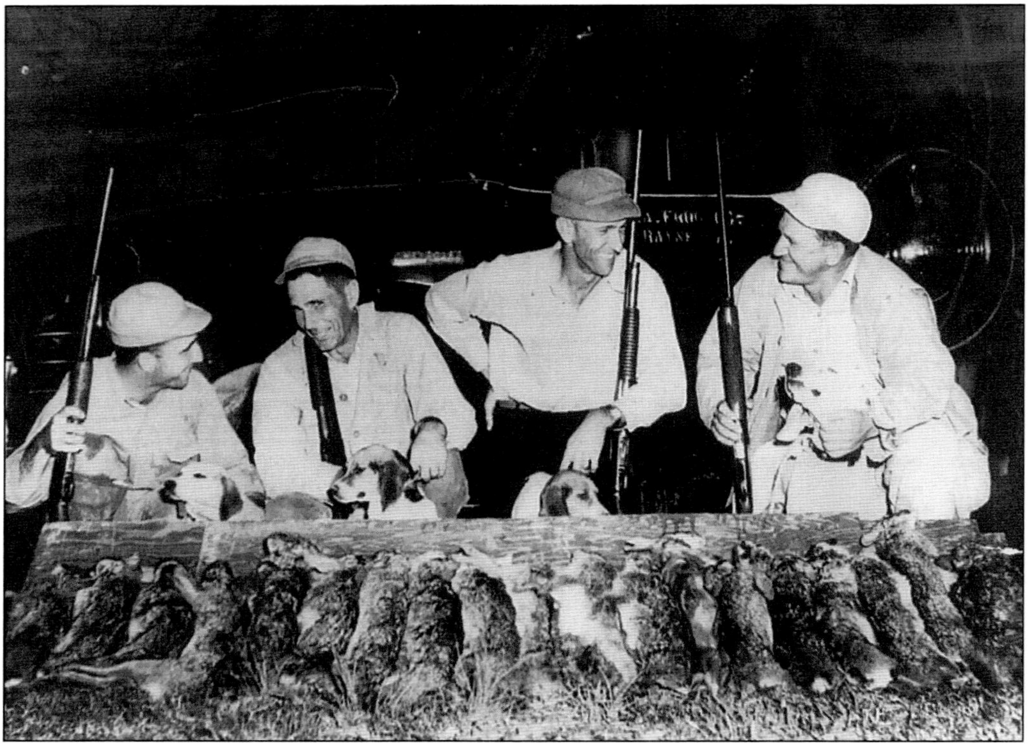

A successful rabbit hunt is photographed in the late 1940s. From left to right are Junior Wright, Pete Babineaux, Leland Hebert, and Aaron Arceneaux. Pete Babineaux's Louisiana Frog Co. truck can be seen in the background. (Courtesy Ray Hebert.)

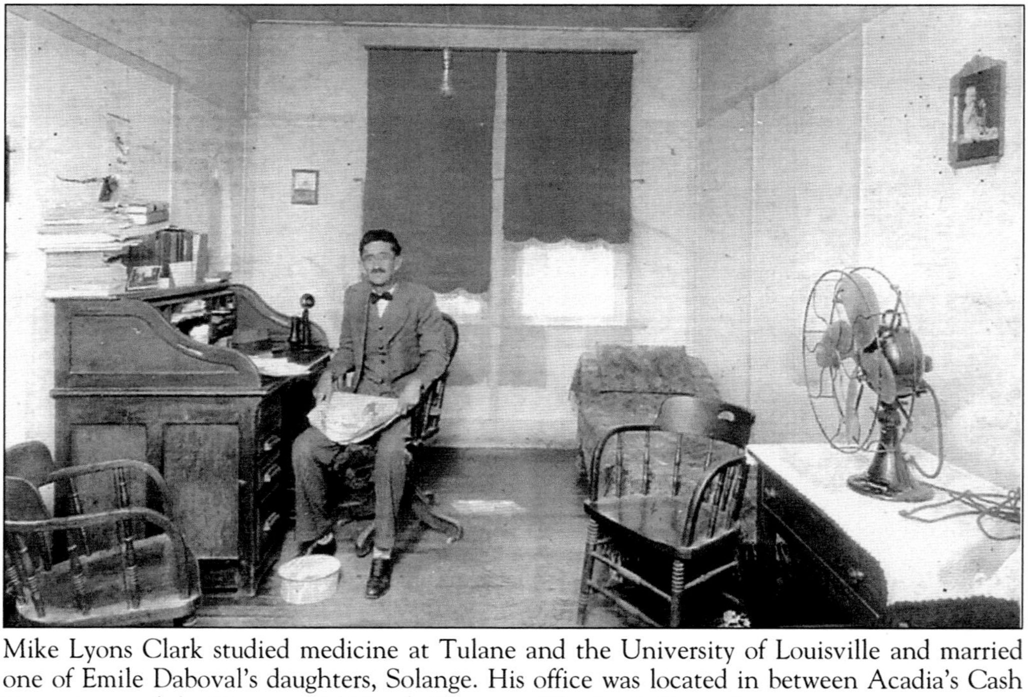

Mike Lyons Clark studied medicine at Tulane and the University of Louisville and married one of Emile Daboval's daughters, Solange. His office was located in between Acadia's Cash Emporium and the Commercial Hotel. (Courtesy Charles S. Stutes.)

Dad Robinson had a store with the best hamburgers in town and could often be seen walking around town with a basket of peanuts for sale. His peanuts were a must-have for anyone going to the movies. (Courtesy of Charles S. Stutes.)

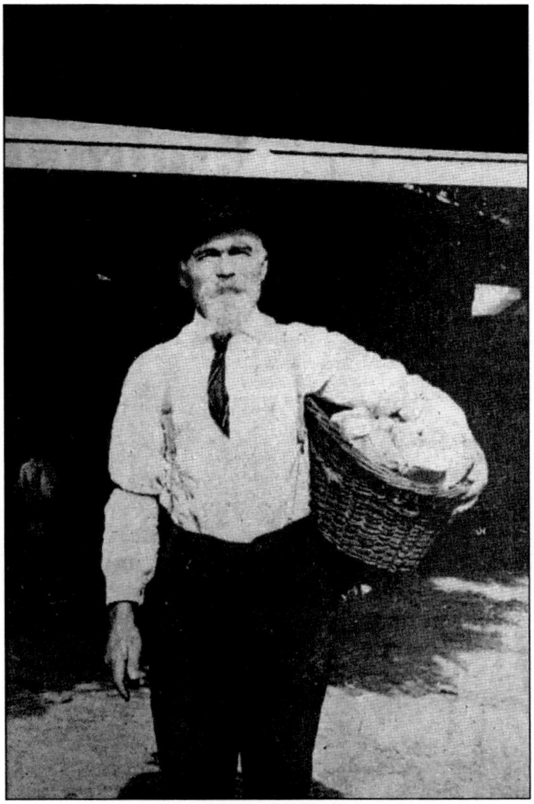

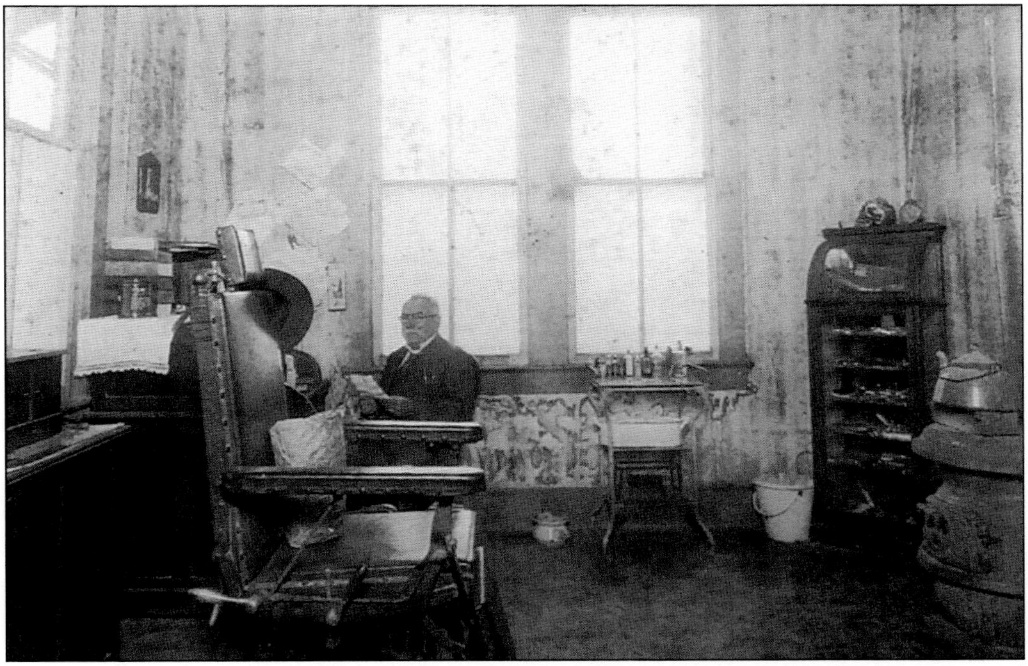

This is a rare look into the medical office of Dr. J.P. Mauboules between People's Drugstore and the Mervine Kahn Warehouse. Note the old pot-belly, wood-burning stove and the bookshelves. (Courtesy Annette Gossen.)

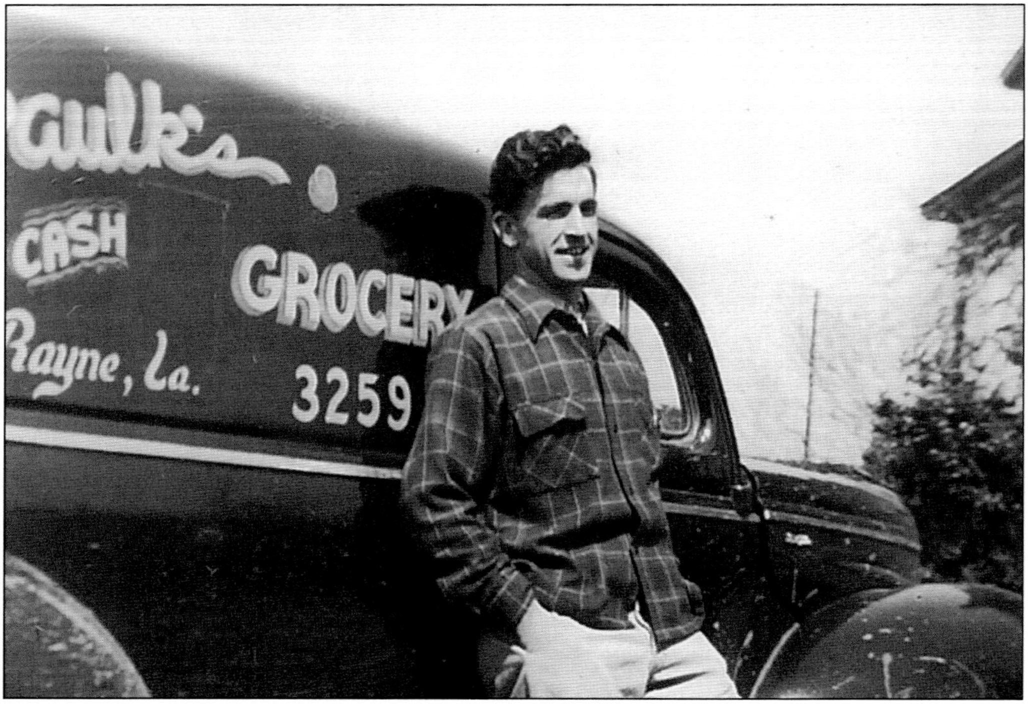

Stan "The Man" Faulk is shown next to his delivery truck for Faulk's Ideal Cash Grocery, which was located on South Adams in front of St. Joseph's Church. Stan "The Man" was known in his later years for his insurance business. (Courtesy Joyce Faulk.)

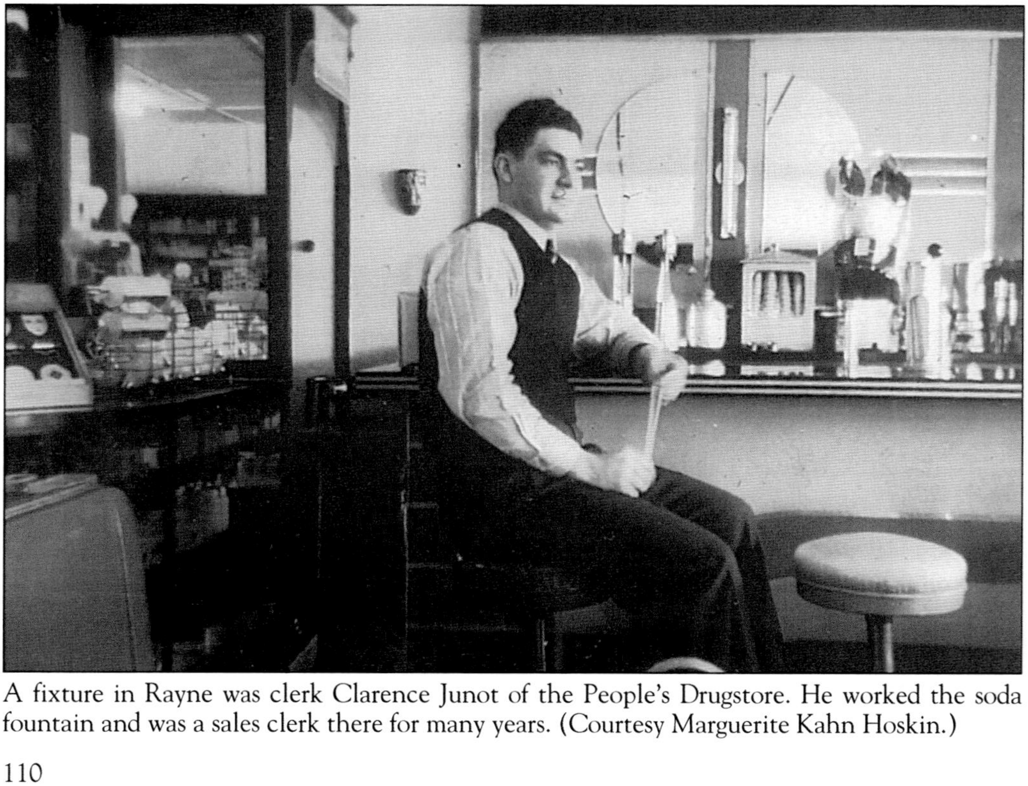

A fixture in Rayne was clerk Clarence Junot of the People's Drugstore. He worked the soda fountain and was a sales clerk there for many years. (Courtesy Marguerite Kahn Hoskin.)

Bertha Doty was the first female town clerk. All minutes of council meetings were handwritten up until the time Doty began typing them, thereby moving into a new technological age. After her tenure as clerk, she opened an accounting and income tax business. (Courtesy Charles S. Stutes.)

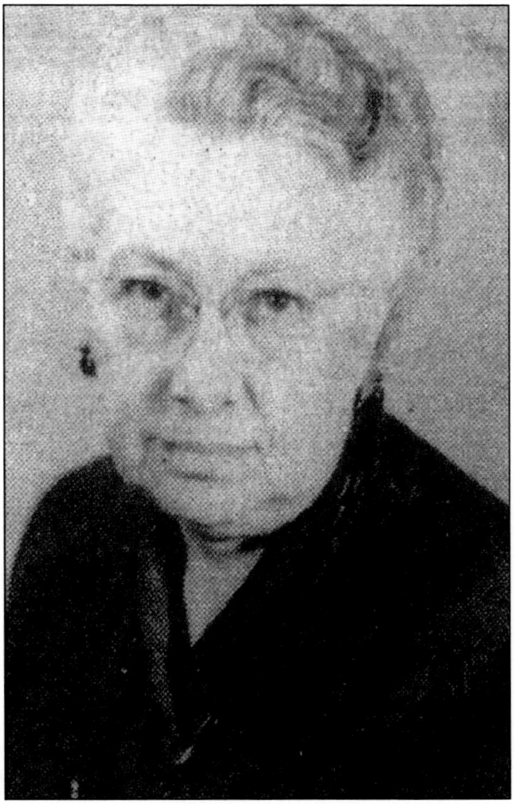

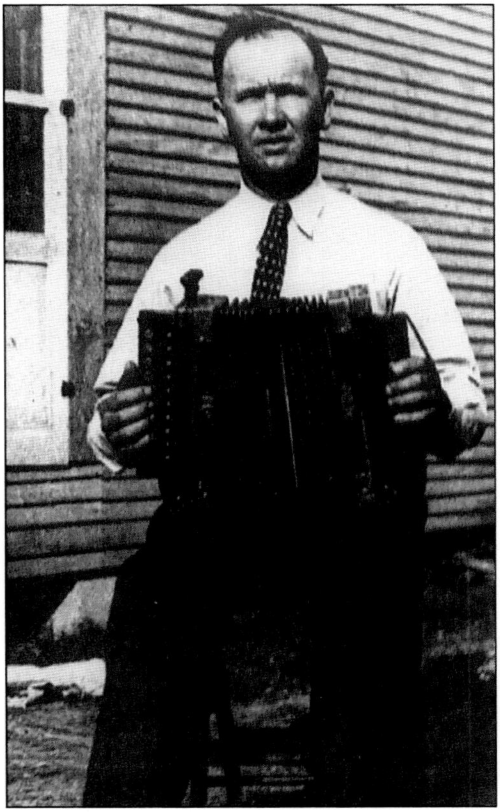

Joe Falcon is pictured playing his accordion. He was the first inductee into the Cajun Music Hall of Fame and was the first artist to record a Cajun song. He played for over a half century and recorded hundreds of folk songs in Cajun French. (Courtesy Fair Craig Hash.)

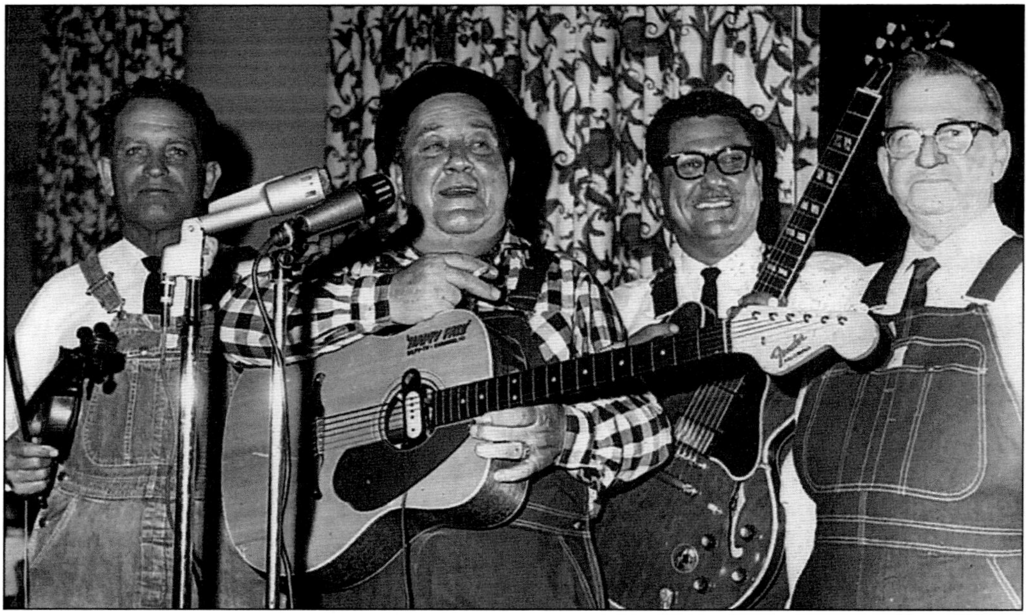

Rayne is known to produce some of the best musical talent in South Louisiana. Pictured from left to right are Uncle Ambrose Thibodeaux, Happy Fats Leblanc, Duless Landry, and Curley Lefleur. Happy Fats had several bands throughout the years including the Rayne-Bo Ramblers. He played the Louisiana Hayride and helped write "Jambalaya" with Hank Williams Sr. (Courtesy Charles S. Stutes.)

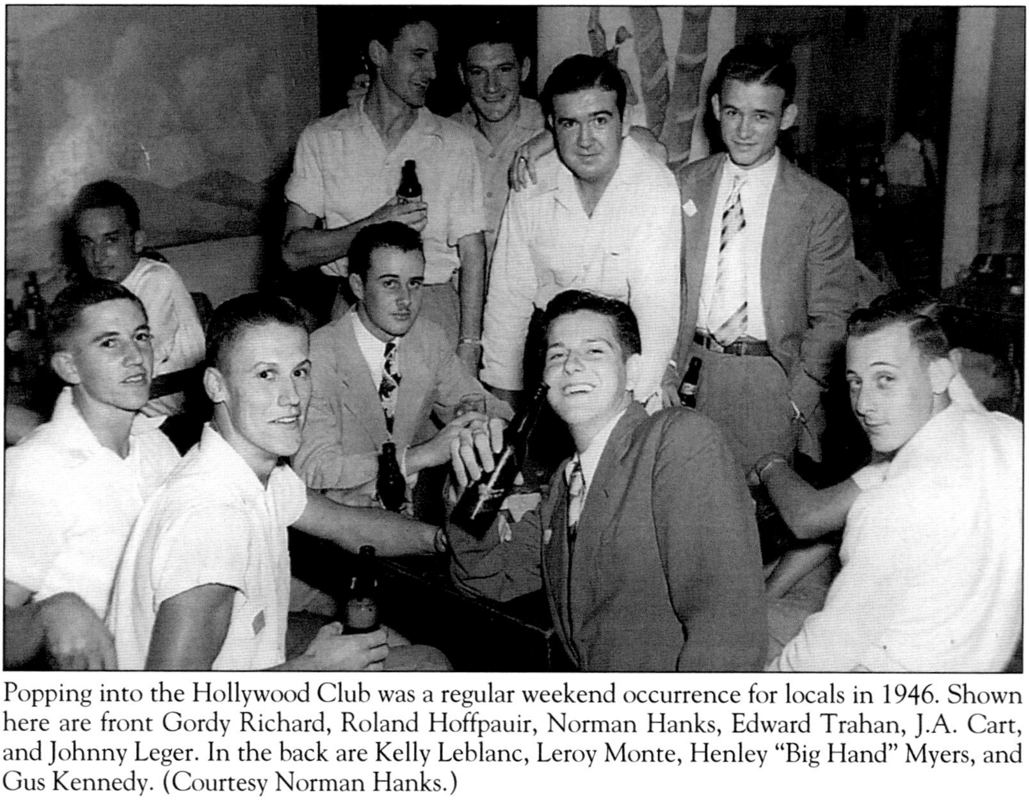

Popping into the Hollywood Club was a regular weekend occurrence for locals in 1946. Shown here are front Gordy Richard, Roland Hoffpauir, Norman Hanks, Edward Trahan, J.A. Cart, and Johnny Leger. In the back are Kelly Leblanc, Leroy Monte, Henley "Big Hand" Myers, and Gus Kennedy. (Courtesy Norman Hanks.)

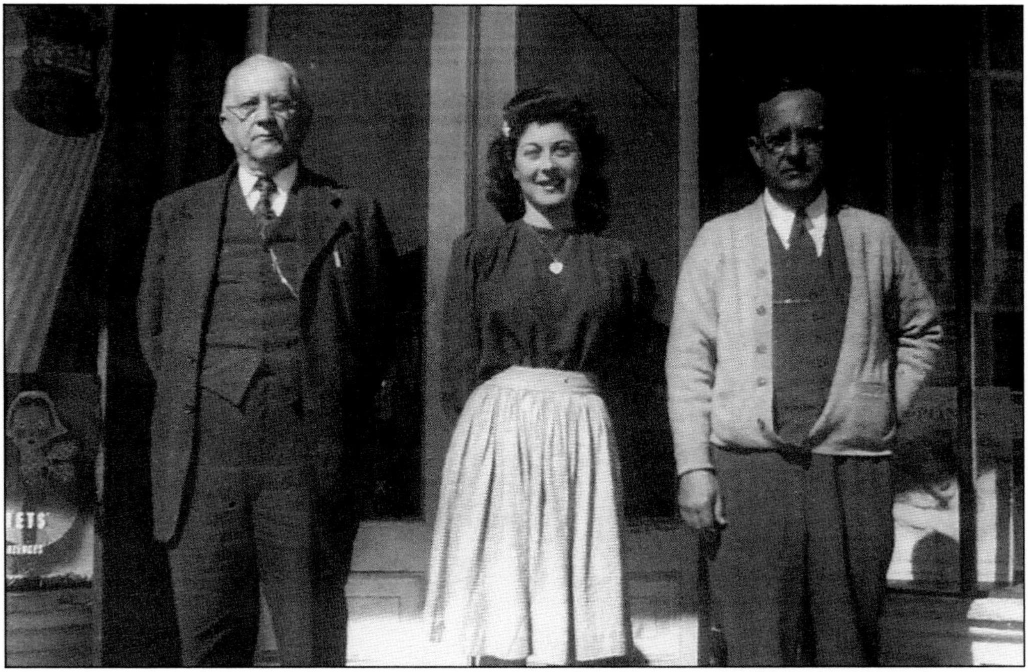

Olivier Broussard Sr., Faye Stutes Harrington, and Olivier Broussard Jr., are pictured in the front veranda of Broussard's Drugstore. (Courtesy Faye Harrington.)

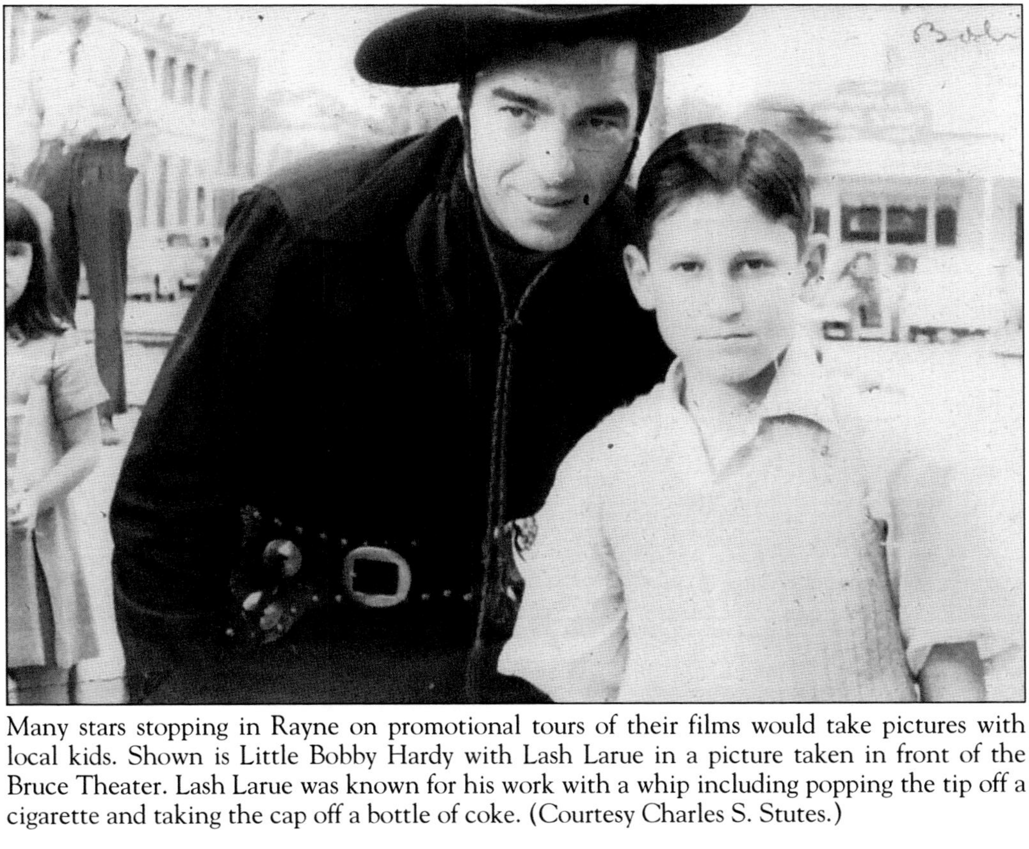

Many stars stopping in Rayne on promotional tours of their films would take pictures with local kids. Shown is Little Bobby Hardy with Lash Larue in a picture taken in front of the Bruce Theater. Lash Larue was known for his work with a whip including popping the tip off a cigarette and taking the cap off a bottle of coke. (Courtesy Charles S. Stutes.)

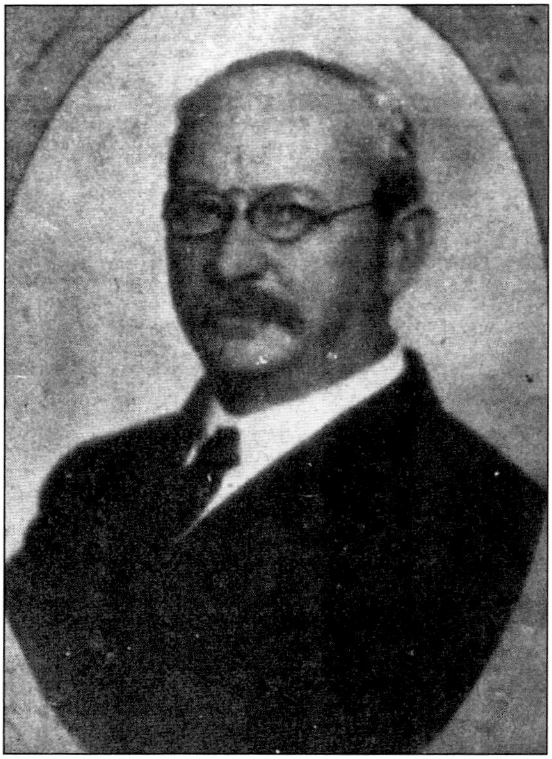

Mervine Kahn was born in Plaquemine before making Rayne his home. His name is perhaps the most familiar one associated with successful businesses in the community, and his signature store became the largest in town, remaining so throughout his life. (Courtesy Charles S. Stutes.)

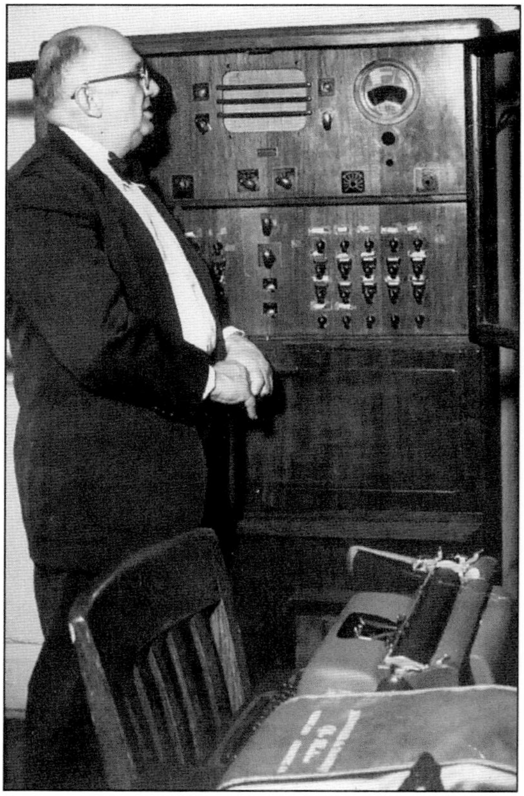

In 1924, William Sonnier, shown here in front of the school PA system, became principal of Rayne High, a post he would hold until 1964, except for the time he spent serving in World War II. (Courtesy Charles S. Stutes.)

Nine

EVENTS AND CULTURAL CELEBRATIONS

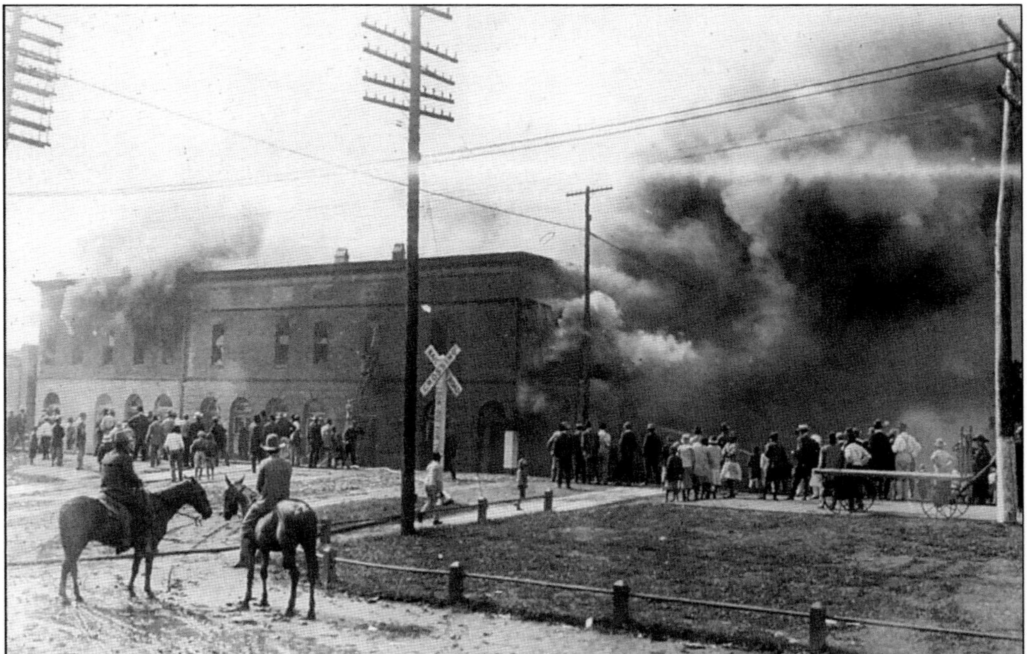

A gasoline explosion in 1916 started the fire that destroyed a Rayne landmark, the Valverde Hotel. The large brick structure, located near the railroad tracks, housed a hotel on the second floor and a restaurant and a tailor shop on the ground floor. Mrs. Theo Mire and her daughter, managers of the hotel, were trapped in a second floor bedroom and are shown being rescued by ladder by a fireman, who happened to be a nephew to Mrs. Mire. It is rumored that none other than Mervine Kahn snapped this photo. (Courtesy Charles S. Stutes.)

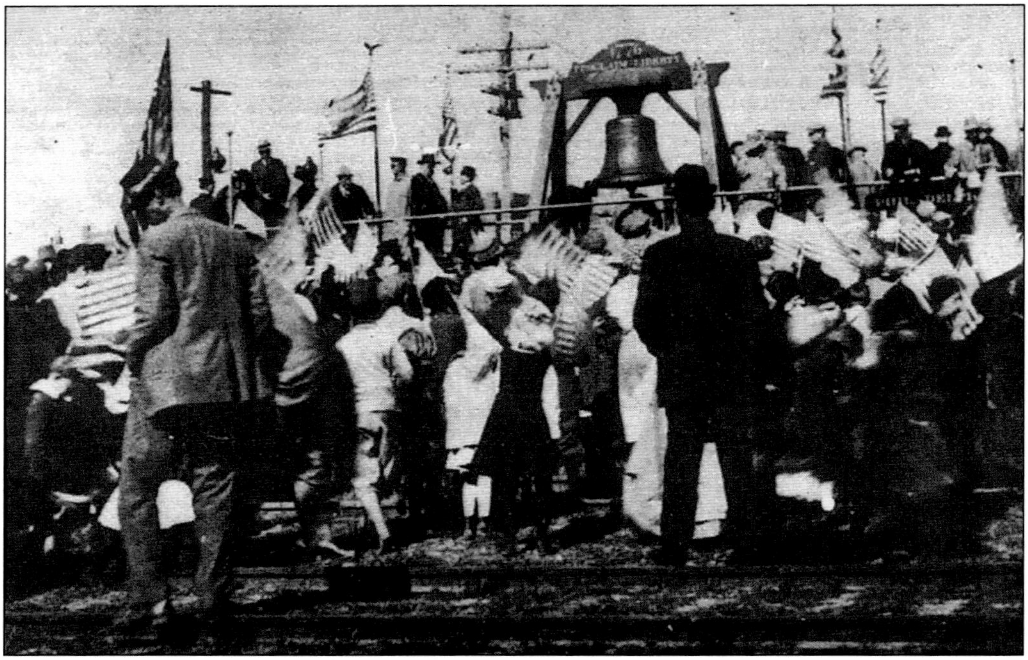

In November 1915, the Liberty Bell made a visit to Rayne on a cross country railroad tour. (Courtesy Charles S. Stutes.)

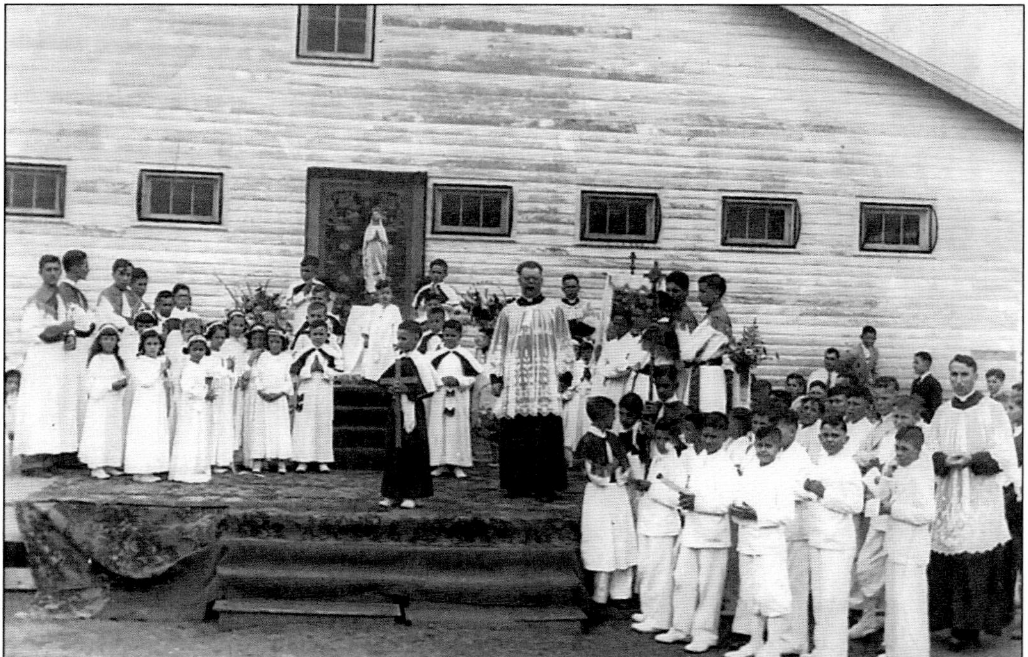

Msgr. Hubert Lerschen is photographs at a May Day celebration at St. Joseph's High School. (Courtesy Louis Privat.)

Snow is an unusual occurrence in Rayne, as shown in this 1934 picture taken in front of Pop and Herb's Bar on West Texas Avenue. The unidentified people are enjoying making snowballs. (Courtesy Fair Craig Hash.)

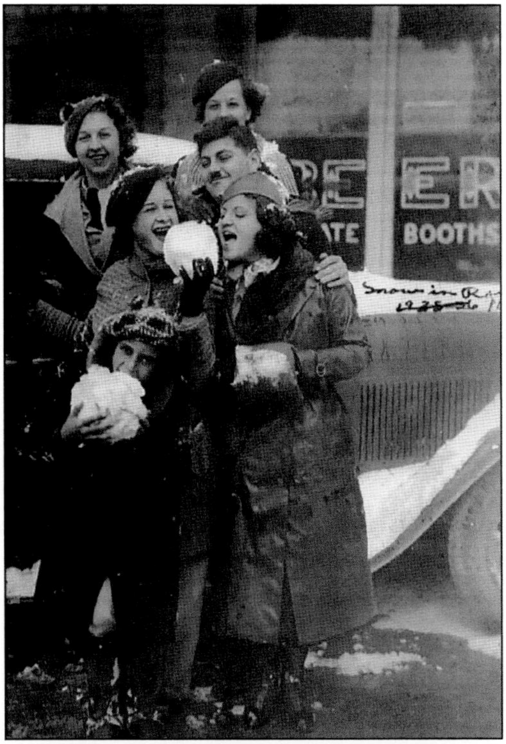

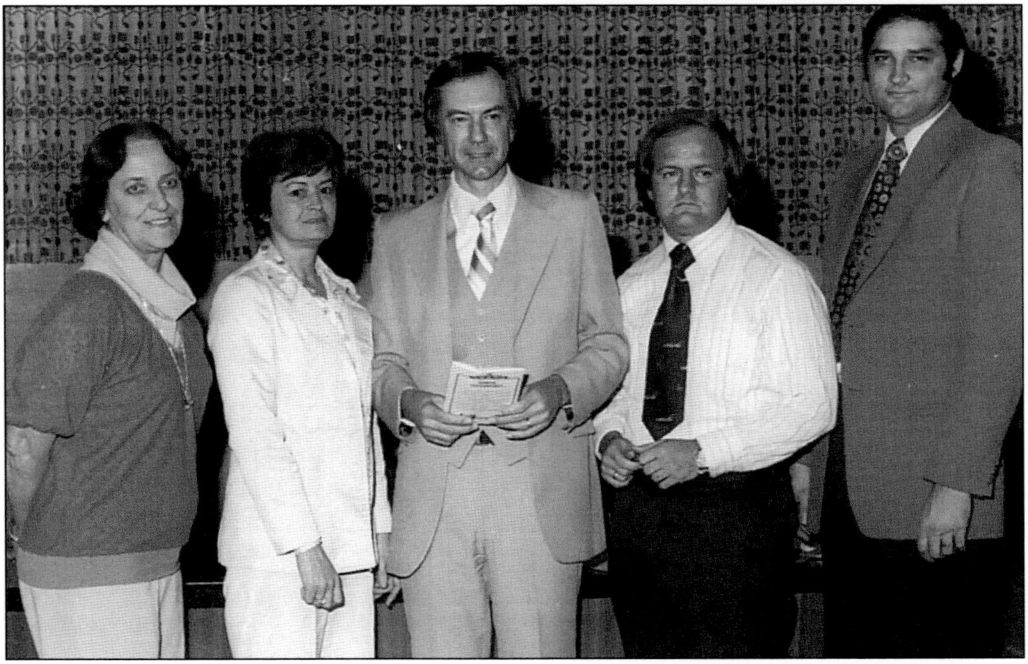

Members of the Rayne Garden Club are shown at Rayne City Hall signing up Rayne for the Cleanest City Contest in 1973. Pictured are Jo Cart, incoming president; Melba Olinger, president; Mayor Ralph Stutes, Chamber of Commerce Beautification Chairman; Chris Zaunbrecher; and Roland Guidry, vice president of the Chamber of Commerce. (Courtesy Melba Olinger.)

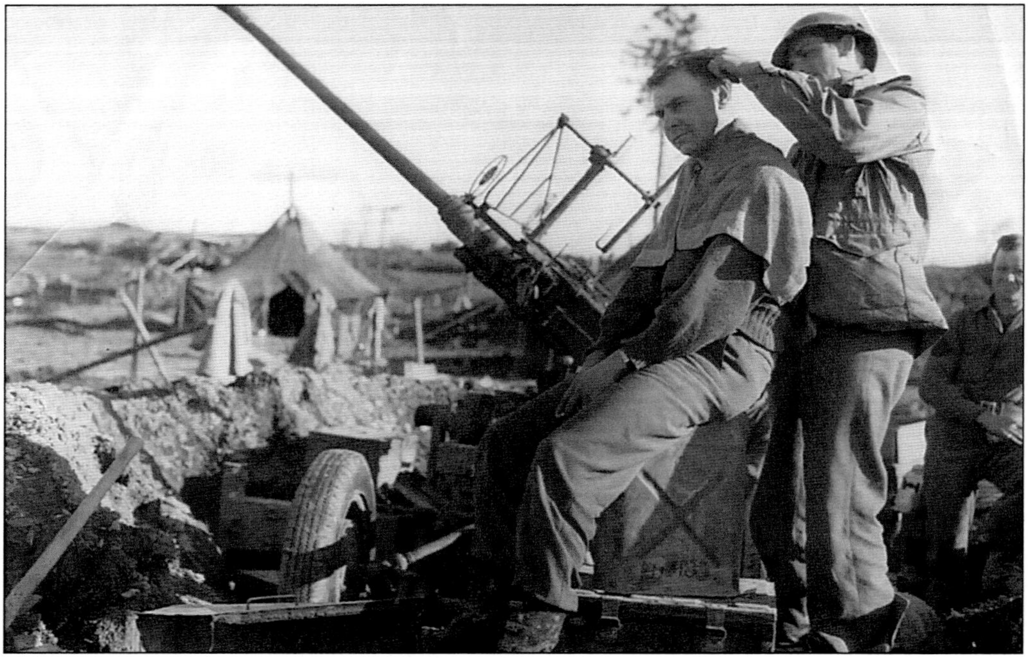

With the skies over Germany controlled by Allied planes, PFC Nelson Stelly took time out for a haircut. Stelly was a 4th Division anti-aircraftman. (Courtesy Donald Petitjean.)

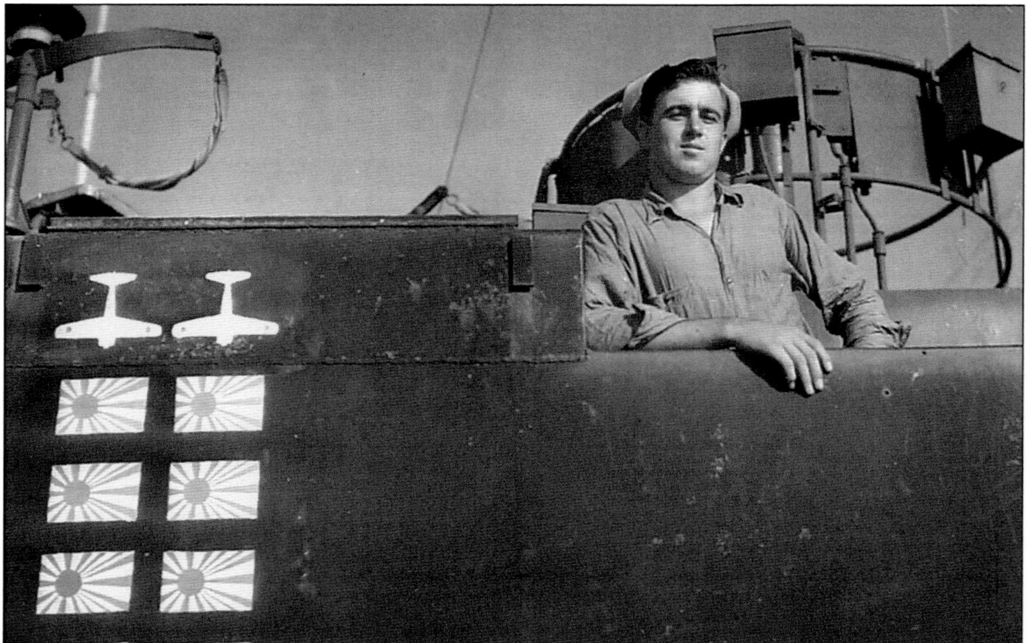

Lenis J. Domingue, 19, Seaman First Class, is pictured at a lookout station aboard the Navy support carrier USS *Steamer Bay*, on which he saw action at Iwo Jima and Okinawa. Domingue entered the Navy in 1943. (Courtesy Donald Petitjean.)

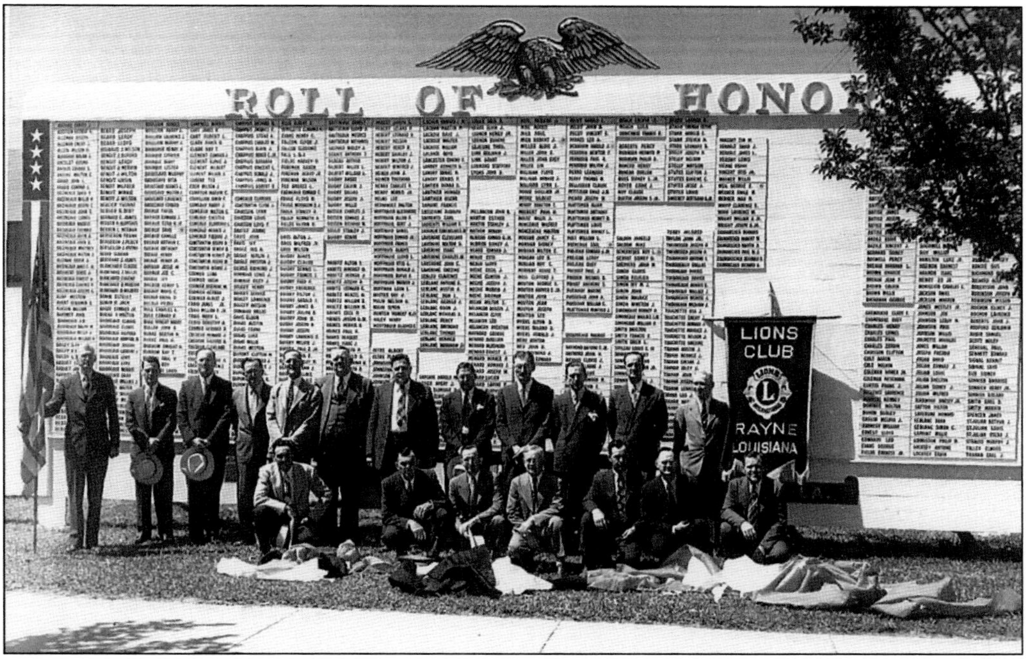

The Rayne Lions Club established a Roll of Honor for the World War II veterans in the late 1940s at the Rayne Depot. Pictured are, from left to right, (front) Walter Bruner, Marcus Bordelon, Otis Lalande, Cliff Besse, Romain Navarre, Thomas Johnson Sr., and Willie Gilbert; (top) Emile Daboval, Louis Butaud, an unidentified person, Orton Besse, Paul Breaux, Waddy Arceneaux, Adolph Sommer, Red Norris, Ed Allen, Edel Jankower, August Chappuis, and Earle Craig. (Courtesy Tom Johnson.)

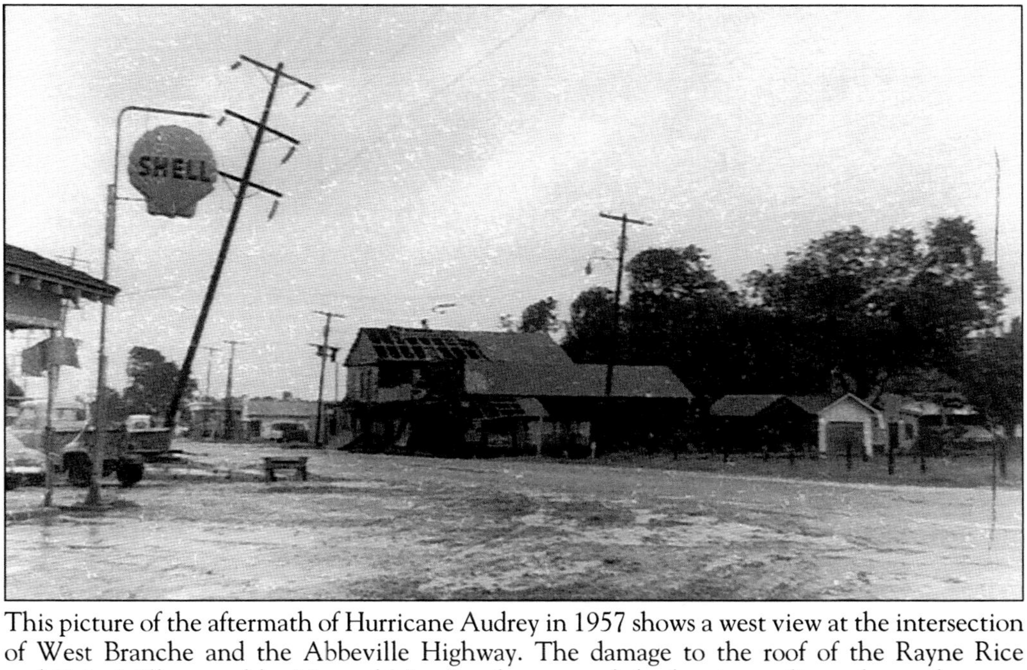

This picture of the aftermath of Hurricane Audrey in 1957 shows a west view at the intersection of West Branche and the Abbeville Highway. The damage to the roof of the Rayne Rice and Grist Mill, owned by Mr. and Mrs. Boudreaux, and the leaning utility pole can be seen. (Courtesy Michael "Pickle" Besse.)

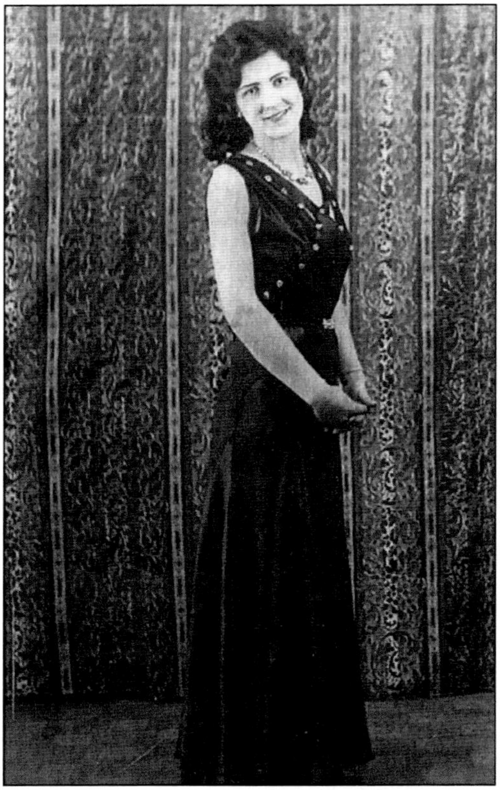

Loida Hulin (Mrs. Clet Leblanc) was crowned the first Miss Rayne in 1931. She won her title representing the Acadia Bakery. (Courtesy Edwin and Julie Ousse.)

Mayor Bill Gossen is presenting a key to the city to Miss Rayne 1957, Rose Marie Robichaux, who is being crowned by Connie Butaud. (Courtesy Rose Marie Stelly.)

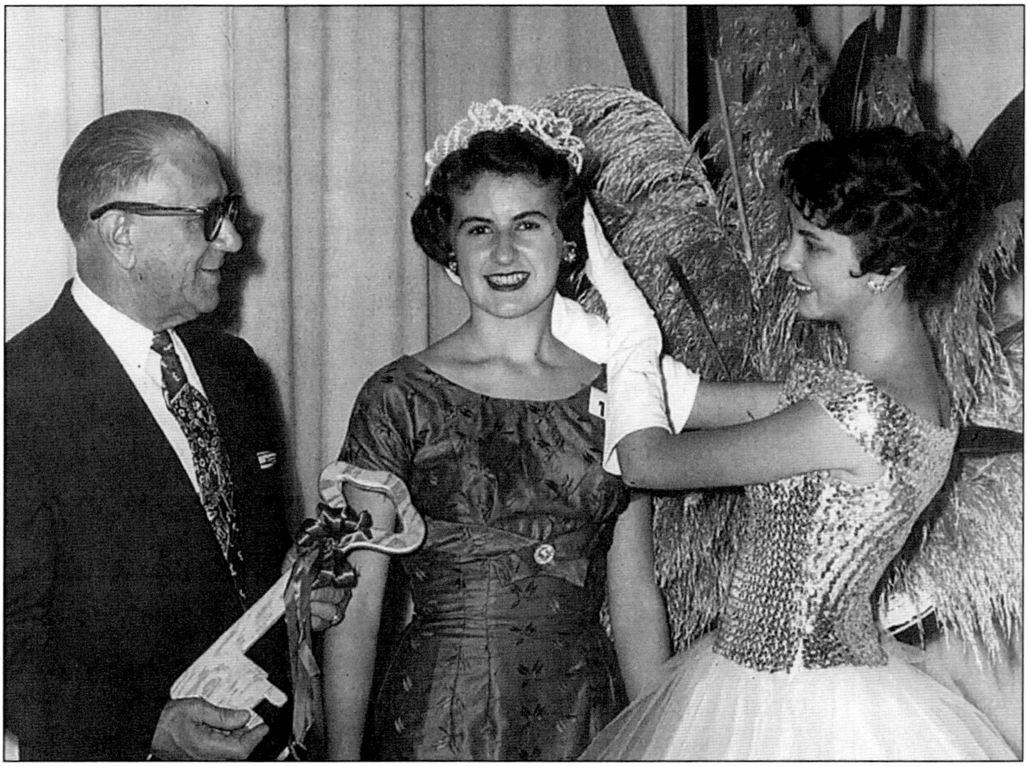

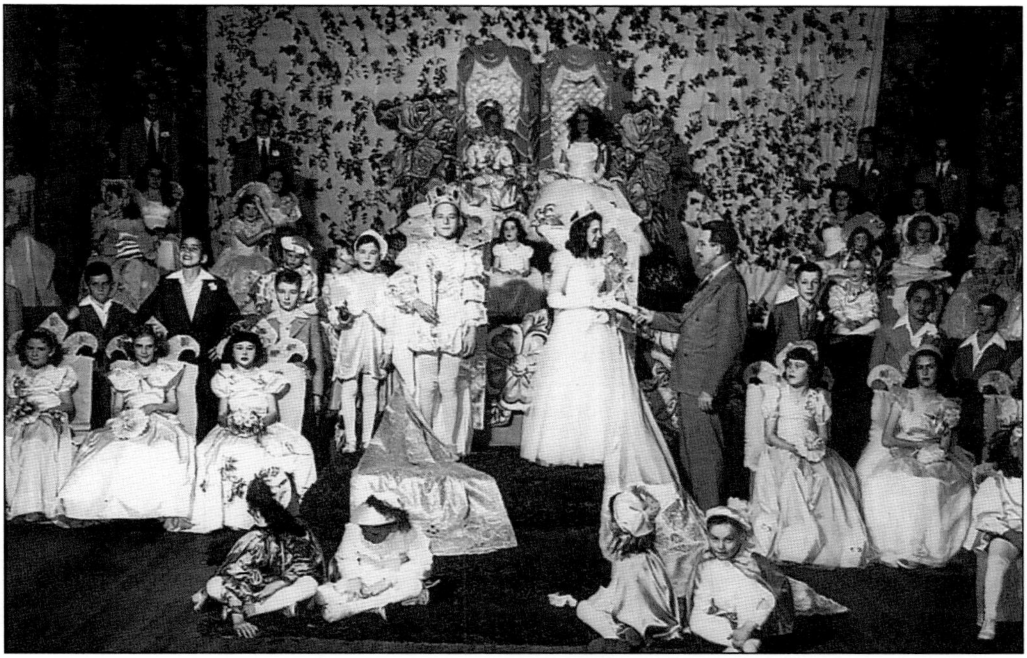

This photo shows the court for one of the glittering Mardi Gras Festivals that was produced by the former St. Joseph Catholic School. The mayor at that time was N. Curtiss Petitjean. He is shown here as he makes a special presentation to the new Queen of the Hearts, Helen Larriviere Foreman. (Courtesy Rose Marie Stelly.)

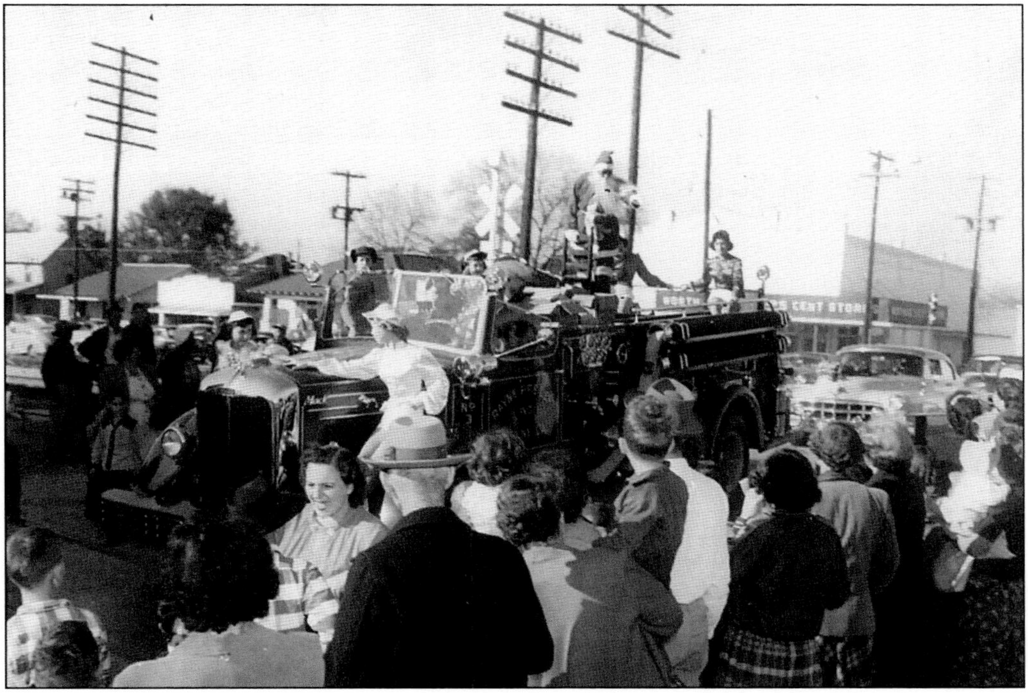

The Rayne Christmas parade crosses the railroad track on Adams Street and shows Santa Claus riding on the firetruck with the Rayne Lions Frog Jockeys in the late 1950s. (Courtesy Donald Petitjean.)

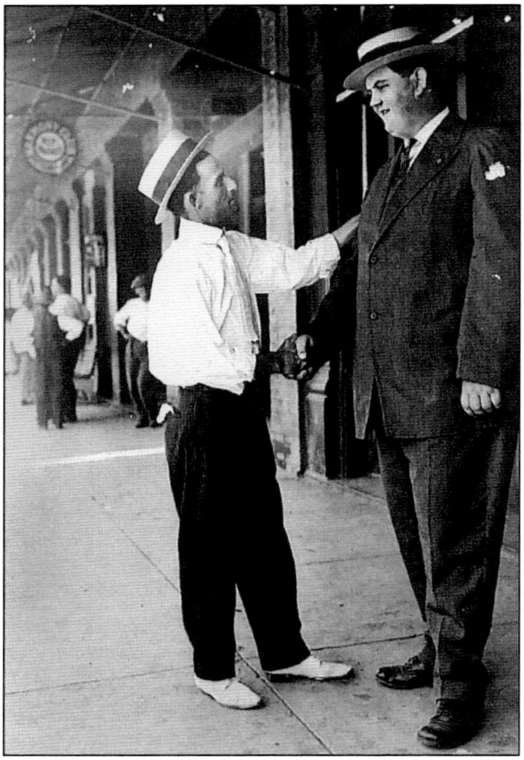

Mervine Kahn had a unique promotion. They had a "Very Big and Tall" suit designed and promised to give it to whoever it would fit. Pictured is the winner of this interesting promotion who walked off the train and back on with his new suit. (Courtesy Charles S. Stutes.)

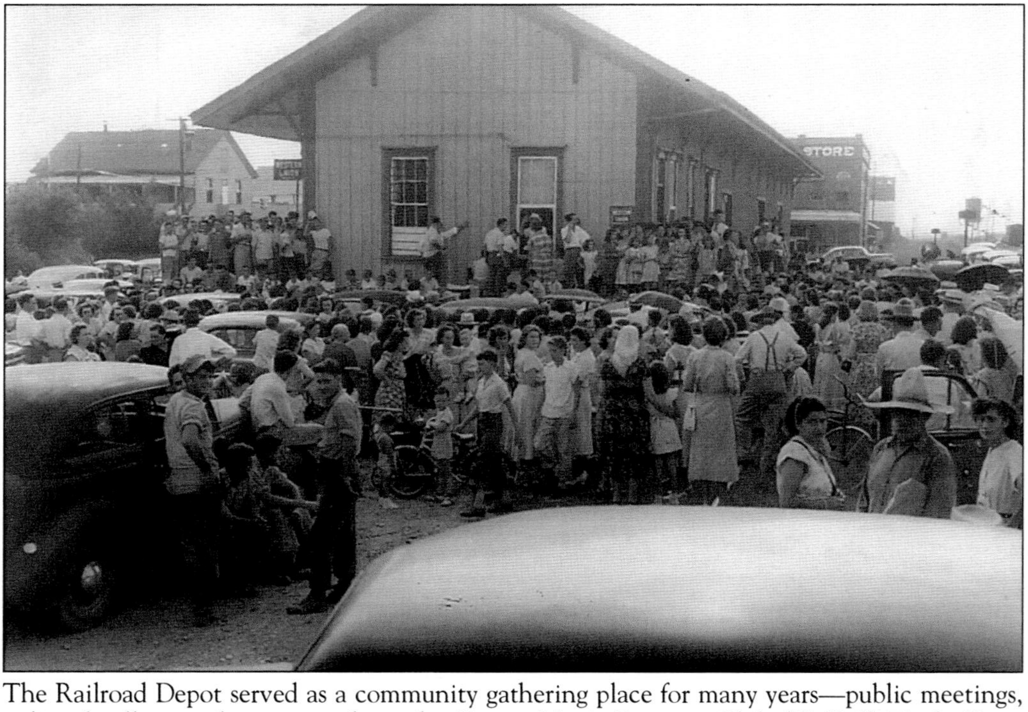

The Railroad Depot served as a community gathering place for many years—public meetings, political rallies, and events such as the Young Men's Business Club (YMBC) Trade Days. Valuable gifts and cash prizes were awarded during ceremonies, which highlighted the day's event. (Courtesy Donald Petitjean.)

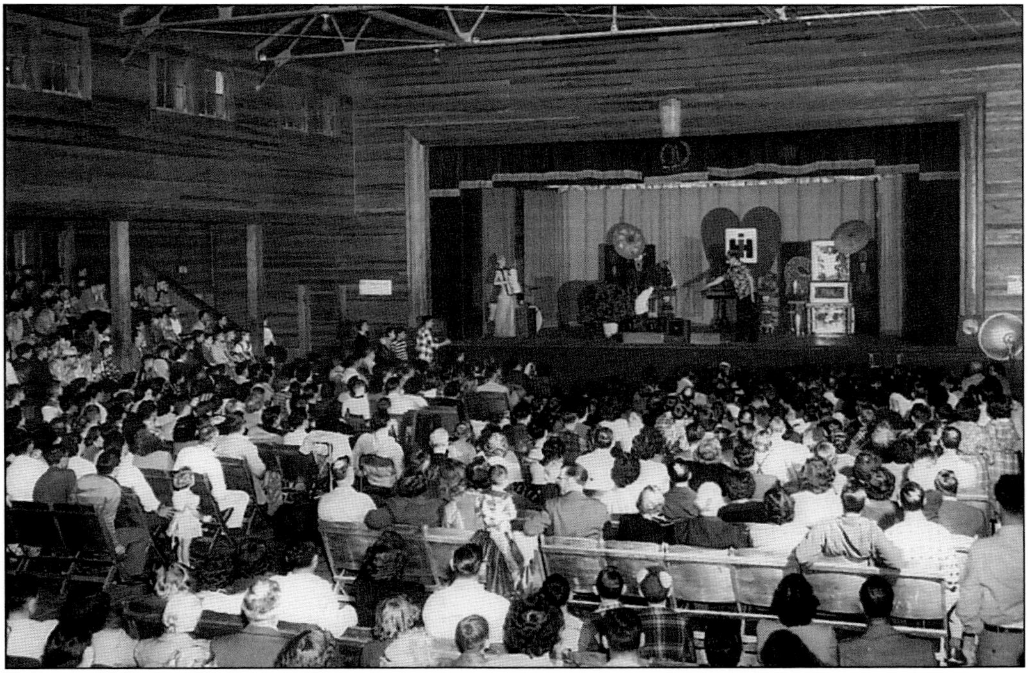

The International Harvester Family Party was hosted by E.C. Fremaux and Son, Inc. The annual party was a free performance given each year to help promote International Harvester products and was held at South Rayne Gym. (Courtesy Donald Petitjean.)

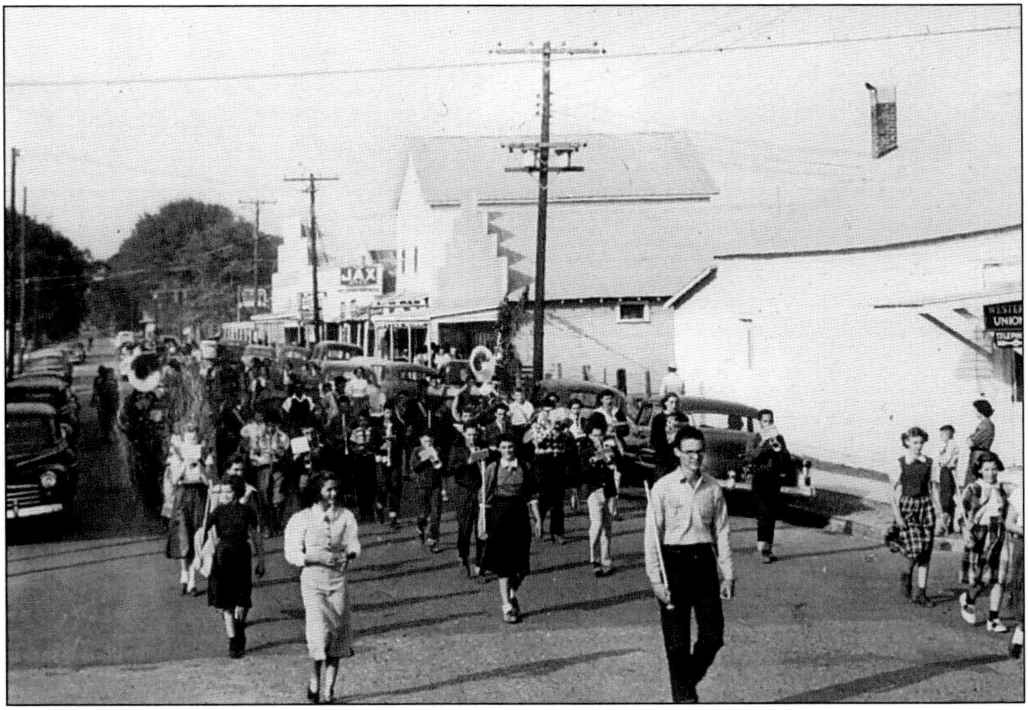

The Rayne High School Marching Band is led by drum major Archie Andrus in the Homecoming Parade in the early 1950s on North Polk Street next to People's Drugstore. The parade began at Rayne High and culminated at the Depot Square. (Courtesy Charles S. Stutes.)

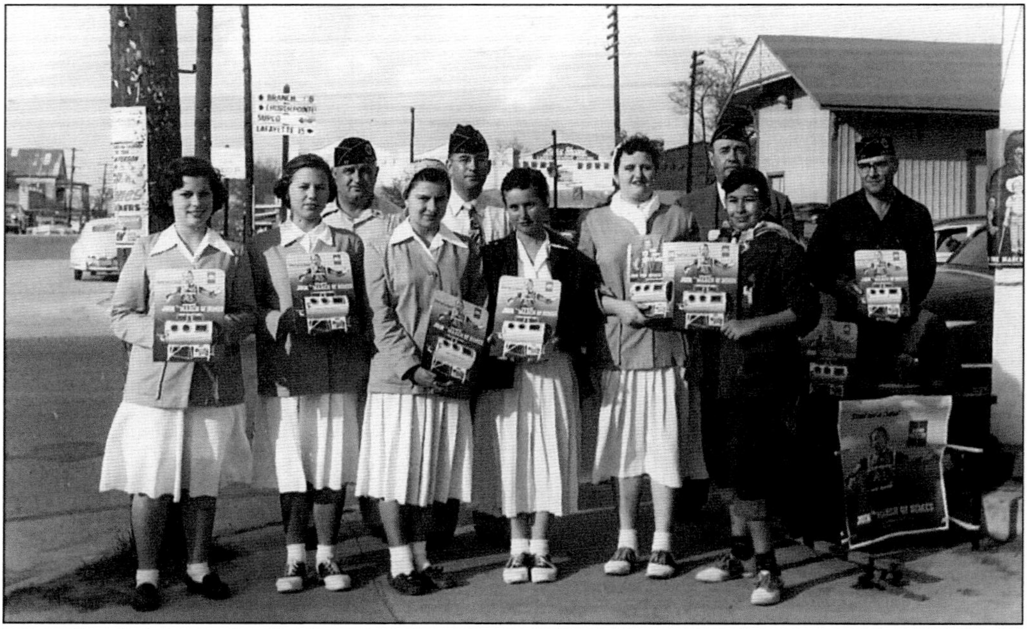

These lovely lassies, the Wolfettes, did much toward aiding the American Legion in their street collection for polio. The attractive workers were on the streets the entire day. Shown, from left to right, are (front row) Myrtle Simpson, Margie Richard, Nettie Trahan, Mildred Perrodin, Betty Lou Boudreaux, and Ann Bienvenu; (back row) Legionnaires Geo. Addison, Willie Arceneaux, Cmdr. J. Duclos, and Lester Richard. (Courtesy Donald Petitjean.)

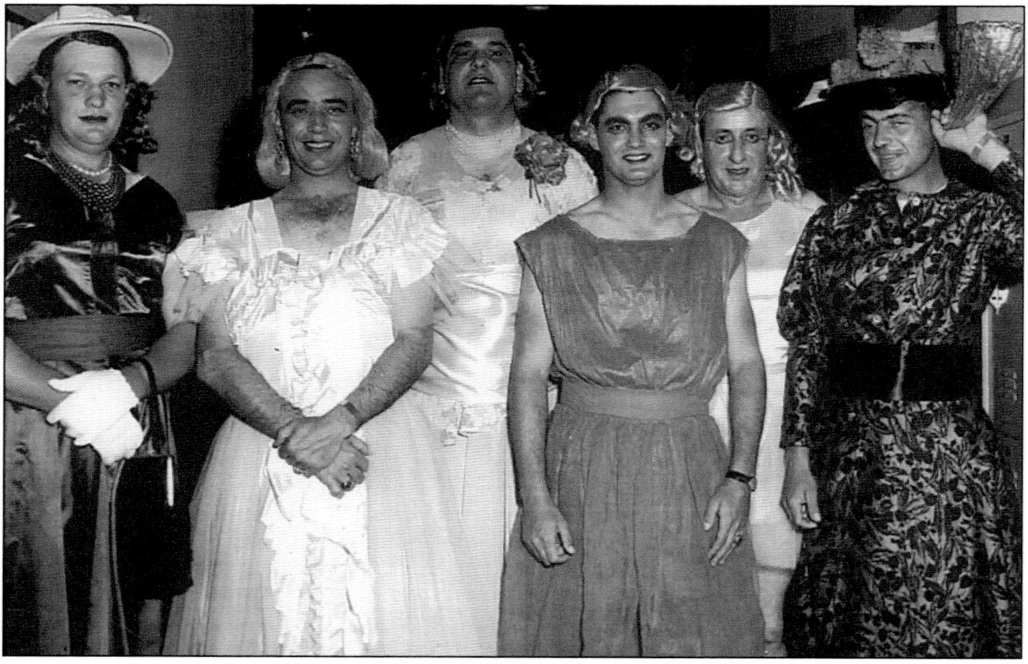

For many years the Rayne Lions Club was known for entertaining city residents with their Minstrel shows and plays. Shown in their evening attire are Raymond Gossen, Horace Thibodeaux, Charles "Moon" Chappuis, Gerald Harrington, Edwin "Son" Bercier, and Dave Besse. (Courtesy Horace Thibodeaux.)

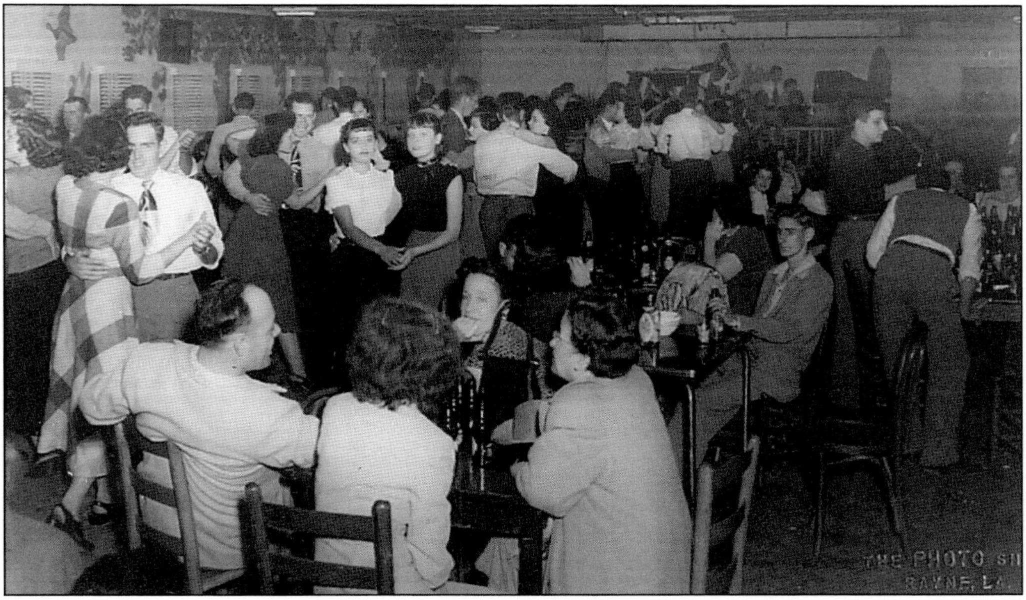

This picture depicts the popularity of the Hollywood Club in Rayne. This was a scene repeated many weekend nights. This picture was reportedly taken during the Grand Opening. (Courtesy Donald Petitjean.)

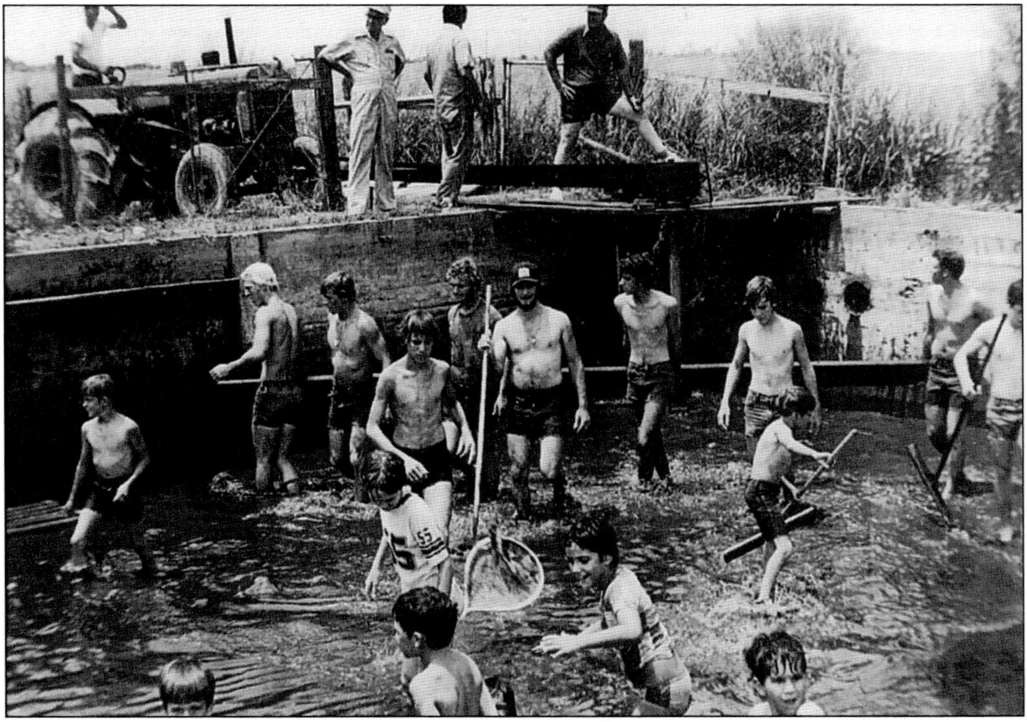

This pool, built by Henry Zaumbrecher in 1926, stored water in case of a fire. The pool had two water wells, one to pump water into the pool and the other to pump water into the fields. It is one of the first swimming pools in Louisiana and people could swim for a charge of $1. Every Father's Day the family gathers and cleans out the pool for the summer swimming season and upcoming crop. (Courtesy Ray Hebert.)

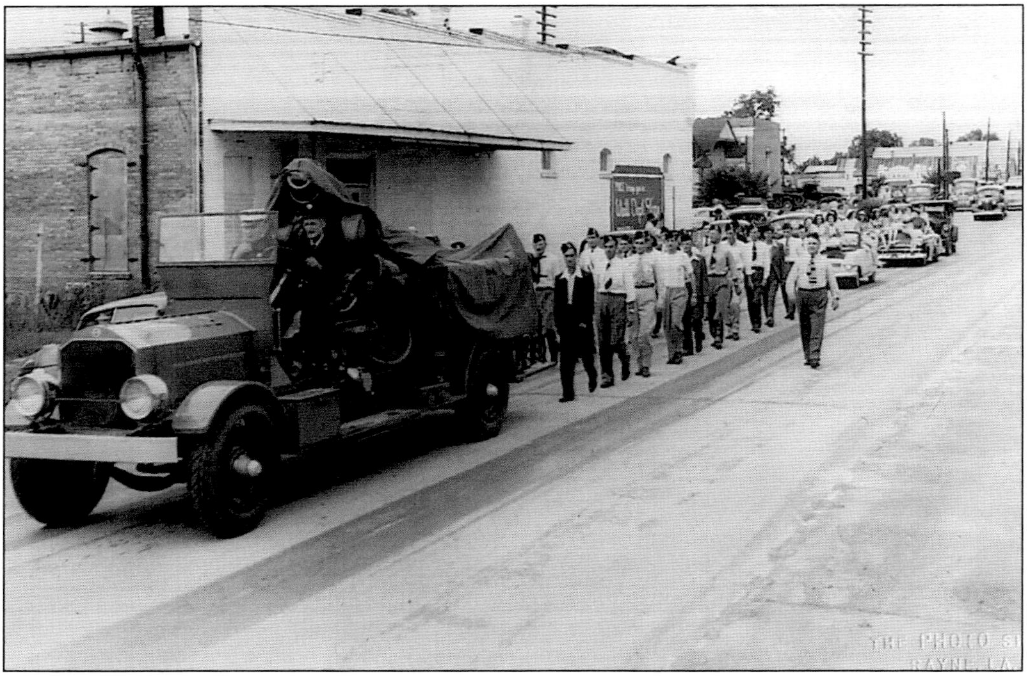

Rayne has a military population that was honored at various patriotic-themed parades throughout the years. Members of the American Legion can be seen marching down the main street in this special remembrance and celebration. (Courtesy Donald Petitjean.)

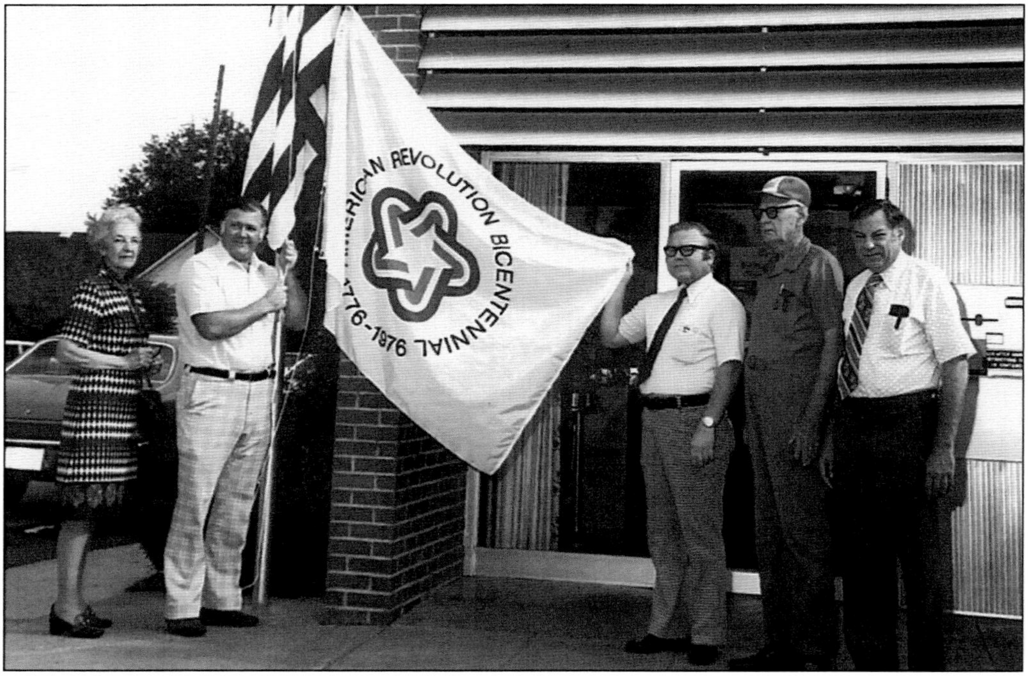

The U.S. Flag and the American bicentennial flag were raised on the new City Hall flagpole. From left to right are Irene Petitjean (Governors Bicentennial Program committee member), Hilary Olinger (Rayne Bicentennial chairman), Joe Richard (Rayne city clerk), Milo Daboval (Rayne historian), and Adley Boyer (mayor of Rayne). (Courtesy Hilary Olinger.)

Miss Rayne, Nicole Fruge, is shown in this promotional photo with a bumper sticker reminding citizens of the Rayne Centennial Celebration being held in 1983. Many activities were planned to get the community involved and included having a recreation of old Rayne businesses and a beard-growing contest for the men. (Courtesy Jo Cart.)

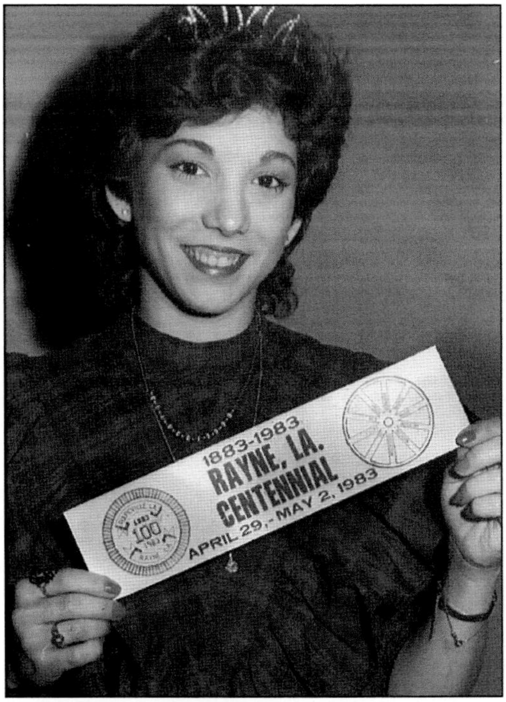

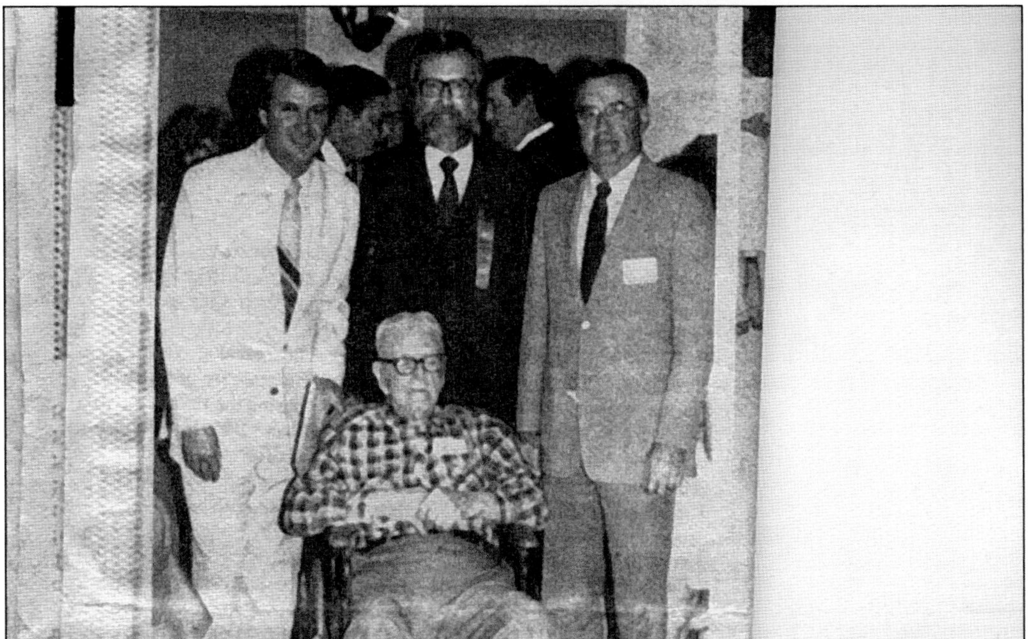

Martin Richard celebrated his 100th birthday the same year Rayne celebrated its centennial. In an interview with Charles S. Stutes, he recalled coming to Rayne in a buggy and there were only four buildings, two of which were saloons. In what Stutes calls one of the most touching moments of the entire centennial, Martin said in French "le temps pas vite"—time sure flies by. He is shown seated with Congressman John Breaux, Rayne mayor Ralph Stutes and Lafayette mayor Dud Lastrapes. (Courtesy Rose Marie Stelly.)

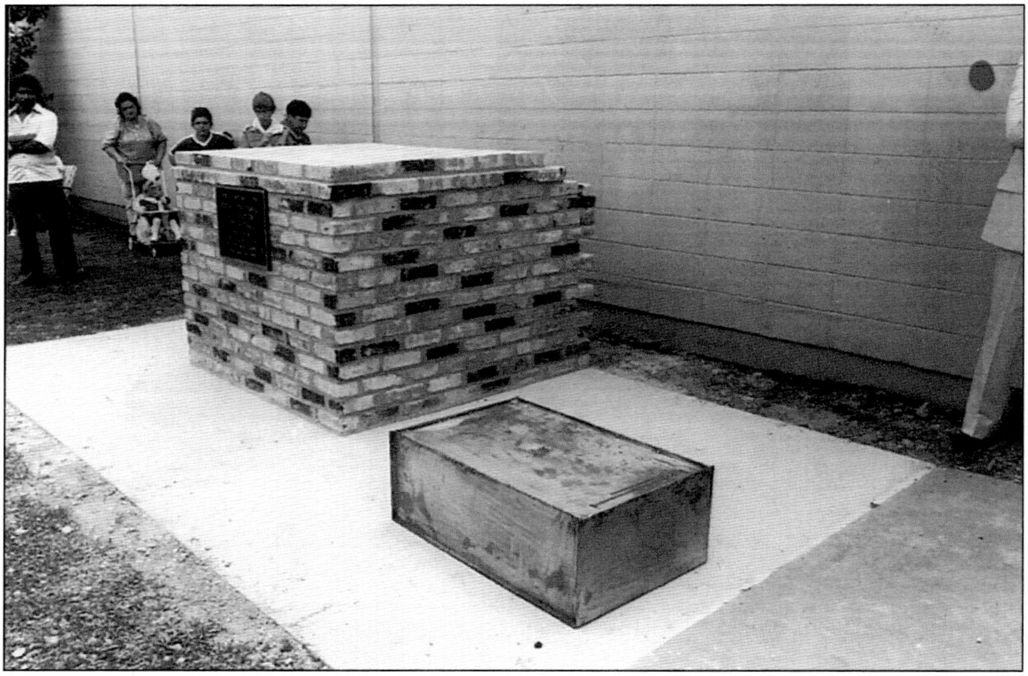

The Centennial Time Capsule was encased in a brick vault in front of the police station. Citizens were asked to donate items for the capsule, which will be opened in 2083 for the Bicentennial. (Courtesy Jo Cart.)

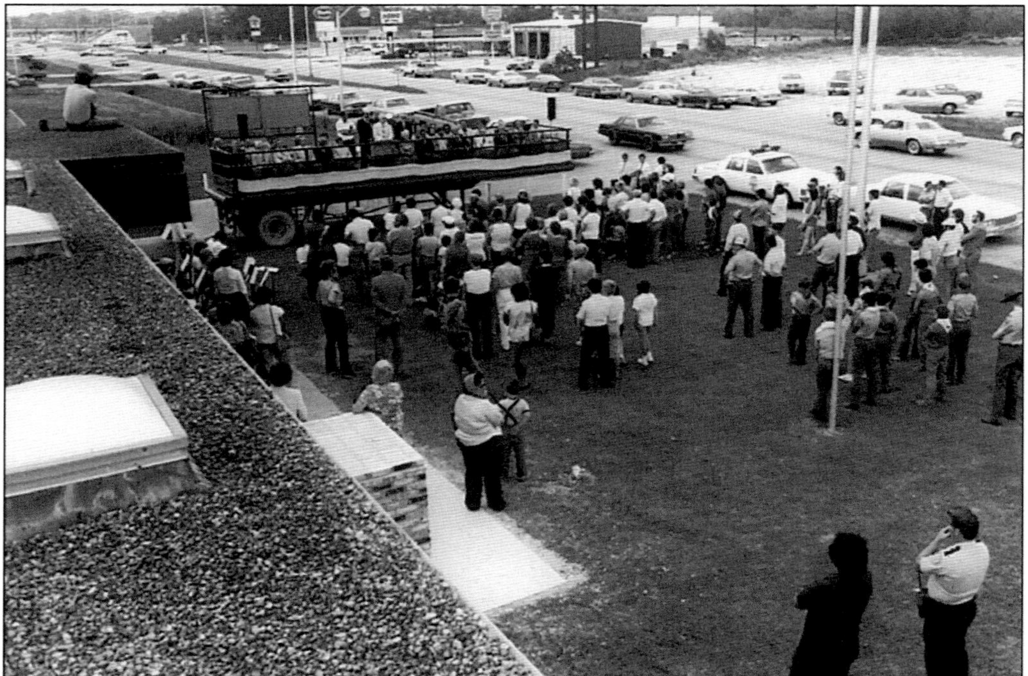

Rayne Centennial speeches and the time capsule presentation took place at the Rayne Police Station, whereupon the capsule was sealed in a brick vault which now stands as the next much-anticipated chapter as Rayne's history unfolds. (Courtesy Jo Cart.)